APPOINTING COMMERCIAL AGENTS IN EUROPE
The Essential Facts

The Essential Facts Series

Bright/The EU: Understanding the Brussels Process
0-471-95608-2 250 pages

Cameron Markby Hewitt/Business Guide to Competition Law
0-471-95704-6 325 Pages

Taylor Joynson Garrett/Doing Business in the UK
0-471-95694-5 200 Pages

Forthcoming titles

Barnett/Avoiding Unfair Dismissal Claims
0-471-96564-2 275 Pages

Landman/Doing Business in the US
0-471-96160-4 300 Pages

Lewis/Professional Error: Identifying, Making and Defending Negligence Claims
0-471-97207-X 300 Pages

APPOINTING COMMERCIAL AGENTS IN EUROPE

The Essential Facts

Edited by
Alex Roney LLB Barrister
London Chamber of Commerce

Compiled by
John Rhodes LLB Solicitor
Pritchard Englefield
and members of Pannone Law Group EEIG

JOHN WILEY & SONS

Chichester • New York • Brisbane • Toronto • Singapore

Published in 1996 by John Wiley & Sons Ltd,
Baffins Lane, Chichester,
West Sussex PO19 1UD, England

National 01243 779777
International (+44) 1243 779777
e-mail (for orders and customer service enquiries): cs-books@wiley.co.uk
Visit our Home Page on http://www.wiley.co.uk
or http://www.wiley.com

Other Wiley Editorial Offices

John Wiley & Sons, Inc., 605 Third Avenue
New York, NY 10158-0012, USA

Jacaranda Wiley Ltd, 33 Park Road, Milton,
Queensland 4064, Australia

John Wiley & Sons (Canada) Ltd, 22 Worcester Road,
Rexdale, Ontario M9W 1L1, Canada

John Wiley & Sons (Asia) Pte Ltd, 2 Clementi Loop #02-01,
Jin Xing Distripark, Singapore 129809

Library of Congress Cataloging-in-Publication Data
Appointing commercial agents in Europe: the essential facts/edited by Alex Roney.
p. cm.
Includes index.
ISBN 0-471-96438-7
1. Commercial agents-Europe. 2. Agency (Law)-Europe.
I. Roney, Alex.
KJC2079.A96 1996
346.4'0299-dc20
[344.0629] 96-28879
CIP

British Library Cataloguing in Publication Data

A catalogue record for this book is available from the British Library

ISBN 0-471-96438-7

Typeset in Times by Poole Typesetting (Wessex) Ltd, Bournemouth, Dorset
Printed and bound in Great Britain by Redwood Books, Trowbridge, Wiltshire
This book is printed on acid-free paper responsibly manufactured from sustainable forestation, for which at least two trees are planted for each one used for paper production.

CONTENTS

LIST OF CONTRIBUTORS

This book was produced in conjunction with Pritchard Englefield and the Pannone Law Group EEIG, using many of their contacts in Europe, and specifically with the help of Olivier Chambord at the London offices in co-ordinating submissions.

Pritchard Englefield is a well-known City of London law firm with 28 partners and approximately 120 staff and with other offices in Frankfurt, Guernsey and Hong Kong. The firm is one of the leading law firms in the areas of Anglo-German, Anglo-Italian and Anglo-French trade and regularly advises clients in continental Europe. The firm advises not only, of course, on English law but on German and Austrian law. Approximately half of the firm's partners and many of the assistants and support staff in London are fluent in German, Italian or French and the firm includes four German and two Italian lawyers and an Austrian-qualified lawyer. Two of the German and one of the Italian lawyers are dually qualified as English Solicitors. Correspondence and meetings are regularly conducted in the language of the client. Particular emphasis is placed on mergers and acquisitions, property, corporate and tax advice including offshore structures and trusts, commercial litigation, banking law, employment law and all aspects of commercial law. The firm has extensive contacts to commercial law firms all over the world.

In 1996 the firm was awarded "Best European Law Firm" (Silver Award) by the magazine "The Lawyer" in conjunction with legal publishers Sweet & Maxwell.

Contact: John Rhodes or Malcolm Keogh

Address: 14 New Street
London EC2M 4TR
Tel.: +44 171–972 9720
Fax: +44 171–972 9722
Wiesenau 51,
60323 Frankfurt/Main
Tel.: +49 69 710 1824
Fax: +49 69 710 3022

Other offices: Guernsey and Hong Kong.

Languages: German, French, Italian, Spanish.

Pannone Law Group EEIG was founded in 1988 and was the first grouping of law firms to adopt the unified structure of a European Economic Interest Grouping (EEIG). It now counts amongst its members thirteen firms, all specialising in business law, many of whom have contributed chapters to this book

In 1995, Pannone Law Group expanded beyond the frontiers of Europe to admit, for the first time, a North American firm, and further expansion is planned in other European and non-European jurisdictions.

Further details about PLG and its members are available from:

The Secretary General
Pannone Law Group EEIG
avenue de Sumatra 41
B-1180 Brussels
BELGIUM
Tel: +32 2 374 88 46
Fax: +32 2 374 90 61.

John Rhodes is one of the German-speaking commercial partners in the City law firm of Pritchard Englefield. John studied at Highgate, Queens' School Rheindahlen (in Germany) and has an Honours degree in law from Exeter University. He was articled to Pritchard Englefield in 1974 and has remained with the firm ever since. His clients are exclusively German, Austrian and Swiss companies and individuals with commercial interests in the UK. John is Chairman of the British-German Jurists' Association. John is a member of the Board of the Pannone Law Group EEIG. He is co-author of a book on the laws affecting European Economic Interest Groupings.

All the chapters in the book were edited by Alex Roney LLB Barrister.

Mrs Roney has been the Legal Counsellor at the London Chamber of Commerce since 1973 when she was one of the first stagiaires after the United Kingdom joined the EC to go to work for the Commission in Brussels.

She is the author of the EC/EU Fact Book, now in its 4th Edition, and has contributed to and edited several other books.

She is an external examiner in law for the South Bank University, and a member of the exclusive Club of Rhodes (only for ex-nominees and recipients of the Woman of Europe award), and is on various "legal" committees.

Enthusiastic about the environment, Alex Roney is Deputy Chairman of the London in Bloom campaign committee which encourages local authorities, businesses and residents to make London a more attractive place in which to live and work.

Introduction and UK

Alex Roney

Austria

Dr Andreas A. Lintl is admitted in Austria and practises in Vienna. He has also been a Consultant with Pritchard Englefield since 1991.

He obtained a doctorate of law at Vienna University in 1983. He specialises in commercial law and employment law.

In 1993 Dr Lintl was part of a team advising the Slovenian government on privatisation issues. He has published various articles both in Austria and in the United Kingdom. Dr Lintl is a "Law Society checked expert witness" for Austrian law (1996).

Belgium

Daniel Tondreau, partner of Tondreau & Daem.

Tondreau & Daem are a member of Pannone Law Group E.E.I.G., the administrative centre of which is situated at their offices.

Tondreau & Daem are very active in all fields of business law, tax law, banking law and transport law in so far as counselling and litigation are concerned and regularly intervene in national and international arbitration.

Tondreau & Daem have a long tradition of collaboration with foreign clients in the field of acquisitions, mergers and joint ventures and can assist their clients in French, Dutch, English and German.

Denmark

Steen Rosenfalck of Abbot King and Troen.

Steen is a Danish lawyer, qualified in 1991, and also holds a Master of Law Degree from the University of London.

He is a member of the Danish Law Society and is admitted to Landsretten (The Danish High Court) and So-og Handelsretten i Kobenhavn (the Maritime and Commercial Court in Copenhagen). He is a registered foreign lawyer and a member of the Law Society for England and Wales.

Within Abbot King & Troen Steen specialises in international law with an emphasis on commercial law, property transactions, tax planning and civil-jurisdiction litigation.

Abbot King & Troen was the first English law firm recognised by the Law Society of England and Wales as a multi-national partnership incorporating English Solicitors and Danish Advocates.

Abbot King and Troen,
Holbrook House,
14 Great Queen Street,
London WC2B 5DG

Tel: 0171 430 1709
Fax: 0171 831 4441

Copenhagen office:
Tel: +45 33 366100
Fax: +45 33 366101

Finland

This chapter was written by Alex Roney with the invaluable help of the Ministry of Justice of Finland, who provided legal texts in English, and Mr Timo Vuori of the Central Chamber of Commerce of Finland who gave invaluable advice, and of Nils-Henrik Wasonius of the law firm Seppala and Wasonius OY of Uudenmaankatu 15 A 9, 00120 Helsinki, who provided useful text.

France

Antoine Lemétais and Christophe Héry, Partner and Associate of the Parisian law firm C. L. & A.

This firm, specialising in business law, has acquired much experience in advising clients and representing them in litigation for the preparation or performance of cross-border contracts, and especially for all agreements relating to distribution of products or services.

The firm C. L. & A. is very active in all fields of business law and, in particular, in corporate and commercial matters, mergers and acquisitions, tax matters, employment law, commercial law, contracts, property and environment, and has great experience in advising foreign clients in France or French clients abroad.

C. L. & A.'s activities are advising clients as well as representing them in litigation or arbitration.

C. L. & A. is a member of Pannone Law Group:
Contact: Antoine Lemétais or Christian Connor
Address: 5 rue Beaujon – 75008 Paris
Telephone: 53 81 53 00 – Telecopier: 53 81 53 30
Languages: French, English, German, Spanish, Italian

Germany

Dr Sybille Steiner, Partner at Pritchard Englefield

Dr. Sybille Steiner is a German lawyer qualified in 1986 and has also been a Solicitor of the Supreme Court of England and Wales since 1993. She became a Doctor of Law in 1989.

Dr. Steiner specialises in international law, with her main interests being in commercial law and the conflict of laws.

Pritchard Englefield is a well-known City of London law firm with 28 partners and approximately 120 staff with other offices in Frankfurt, Guernsey and Hong Kong. The firm is one of the leading law firms in the areas of Anglo-German, Anglo-French and Anglo-Italian trade. In 1996 the firm was awarded "Best European Law Firm" (Silver Award) by the magazine "The Lawyer" in conjunction with legal publishers Sweet & Maxwell.

Greece

Lila Vassilaki LLB (Athens), LLM (Bristol), Kyriakides and Partners.

The author is a Member of the Athens Bar Association and concentrates on corporate law and EC legislation.

Kyriakides and Partners is a well established prestigious firm with wide ranging expertise among its seven partners, five associates and ten professors acting as Counsel.

Kyriakides and Partners
6 Queen Sophia,
10674 Athens,
Greece

Tel (01) 7243 072
Fax (01) 7250 670

Ireland

Tony Burke, assisted by **Wendy Hederman**, of Mason, Hayes & Curran.

Tony Burke qualified as a solicitor in Dublin in 1978 and has been a partner in Mason, Hayes & Curran since 1985, specialising in commercial and European law. He has appeared as an advocate at the Court of First Instance at the European Court of Justice and is a member of the EU Law Committee of the Council of the Irish Law Society.

Wendy Hederman, solicitor in Mason, Hayes & Curran's commercial department since 1993 is a law graduate of Trinity College, Dublin and the recipient of a Masters degree in European law from the Université Libre de Bruxelles. Wendy advises on European-related legal issues, domestic and European competition law, intellectual property and technology matters and the full range of commercial agreements.

Mason, Hayes & Curran is one of Ireland's leading full service law firms. It is commercially focused and provides legal services to Irish and overseas corporations, institutions, businesses and individuals.

Italy

Antonietta Marsaglia
Milan, Piazza S. Pietro in Gessate 2
Tel: 02/55.18.75.69
Fax: 02/55.18.75.70

Antonietta who has an LLB London U.C. 1971, Università Cattolica Milan 1977, has been registered with the Milan Bar since 1980 and is a senior partner of Spreafico Marsaglia, the PLG office in Milan, offering comprehensive advice on Italian law to foreign business operating in Italy and judicial assistance in litigation before the Italian courts.

Luxembourg

Jean Brucher and Mark Sunnen of Brucher & Tabery.

Jean Brucher is senior partner of Brucher & Tabery and was admitted as a lawyer in Luxembourg in 1975. He has degrees from the Universities of Aix en Provence and Paris. His languages are French, English and German.

Mark Sunnen was admitted in Luxembourg in 1994 and has a law degree from the University of Louvain. His languages are French, English and German.

Brucher & Tabery is a law firm specialising in company and commercial law, national and international tax law, bankruptcy and financial law, litigation and intellectual property.

Brucher & Tabery
Rue Pierre d'Aspelt 10
PO Box 619
L–2016 Luxembourg

Tel: (352) 456262
Fax: (352) 459465

Netherlands

Jan Willem Bitter is a partner with Trenité Van Doorne in Rotterdam and also advisor to the Latvian government within the framework of an EC-

PHARE programme on Technical Assistance to the Development of Economic Legislation in Latvia.

Educated at Caen University, he studied law at Leiden University and took a Masters in Dutch Law. From 1978 to 1981 he was a researcher at the European University Institute in Florence where he took a doctorate in 1989 on a thesis entitled "The Treaty-making power in Spain 1967–1984".

He joined Van Doorne & Sjollema as a lawyer in 1983 and became a Partner in the merged firm of Trenité Van Doorne in 1990. His main areas of interest are arbitration, litigation, labour law, contract law and maritime law. In 1992 he undertook a fact finding mission to the Baltic States as a consultant for EC/PHARE on the setting up of financial markets in the region.

Portugal

Jaime Medeiros is a partner of Coelho Ribeiro & Associados, a Portuguese law firm created in 1983 (CR&A).

CR&A has acquired great experience in civil and commercial law, in contract and corporate law, in mergers and acquisitions as well as in the areas of banking and finance law, tax law, international and EC law.

CR&A also has a long tradition of dealing with litigation and arbitration.

This law firm is a member of the Pannone Law Group.

Address: Av. Eng. Duarte Pacheco, 19–3º
1070 Lisbon
PORTUGAL

Tel: +351 1 385 31 82
Fax: +351 1 385 32 02

Spain

Juan Santamaría with the collaboration of **Laura Mora** and **Jesús Martrat**, all of Bufete Pintó Ruiz.

Juan Santamaría is Licensed in Law by the Autonomous University of Barcelona, is a member of the Barcelona Bar Association and of the

International Bar Association and is Professor of Commercial Law at the Instituto Superíor de Derecho y Economía.

Laura Mora is Licensed in Law by the Central University of Barcelona and is a member of the Barcelona Bar Association.

Jesús Martrat is Licensed in Law by the Central University of Barcelona and is a member of the Barcelona Bar Association.

Bufete Pintó Ruiz was established in Barcelona in 1889 and has a very well-known reputation in commercial, foreign investments, international, civil and company law and litigation.

This firm is a member of the Pannone Law Group.

Bufete Pintó Ruiz
Abogados & Econmistas
Beethoven 13, 7 planta
08021 Barcelona

Tel: (9) 3–414 58 85
Fax: (9) 3–414 28 85 & 3–414 11 57

Sweden

Thomas Pousette is an associate of Lindhs Advokatbyrå HB, which he joined in September 1994. He has got an LLM (Juris kandidat) degree from the University of Stockholm and an LLM from King's College London. For three years, 1991–1994, Mr Pousette worked as an assistant judge; the first two at one of Sweden's Courts of First Instance and the third at a Court of Appeal.

Lindhs Advokatbyrå HB, with its 27 lawyers, is one of the larger law firms in Sweden. The firm works in most fields of business law – international as well as Swedish – such as tax law, company law, contract law, property law, securities law; to mention but a few.

Lindhs Advokatbyrå HB is a member of Pannone Law Group EEIG.

Lindhs Advokatbyrå HB
Postbox 7515
Regeringsgatan 42
Stockholm S. 10390
Sweden

Tel: 46 8701 7800
Fax: 46 87 96 82 23

THE MEMBER FIRMS OF THE PANNONE LAW GROUP

ANDORRA

MAS & GRAU
Edifici la Llar
Prat de la Creu 93,1/6
Andorra la Vella

Tel : (+376) 828 4 41
Fax : (+376) 861 3 10
Manuel Mas; Francesc Grau

BELGIUM

TONDREAU & DAEM
avenue de Sumatra 41/
Sumatralaan 41
1180 Bruxelles

Tel : (+32) 2 375 70 76
Fax : (+32) 2 374 30 36
Daniel Tondreau

CANADA

JOLI-COEUR LACASSE
LEMIEUX SIMARD
ST-PIERRE S.E.N.C.
2600 boulevard Laurier
(Tour de la Cité)
Bureau 960
Sainte-Foy (Québec) G1V 4W2

Tel : (+1) 418 654-0550
Fax : (+1) 418 654-0566
François-Xavier Simard Jr

SPAIN

BUFETE PINTÓ RUIZ
Beethoven 13,7º
08021 Barcelona

Tel : (+34) 3 414 5885
Fax : (+34) 3 414 1157
José-Juan Pintó; Joan Vidal

BUFETE HERNÁNDEZ-GIL
Calle Serrano 87
28006 Madrid

Tel : (+34) 1 563 1012
Fax : (+34) 1 563 6065
Antonio Hernández-Gil

FRANCE

GROUPE LEXEL
91 cours Lafayette
69006 Lyon

Tel : (+33) 72 74 53 00
Fax : (+33) 78 52 26 00
Jean-Paul Burnier; Roland de Villers

CL&A – COURNOT
LEMÉTAIS ET ASSOCIÉS
5 rue Beaujon
75008 Paris

Tel : (+33) 1 42 89 17 43
Fax : (+33) 1 45 63 70 73
Christian Connor; Antoine Lemétais

ITALY

SPREAFICO MARSAGLIA
Piazza S. Pietro in
Gessate 2
20122 Milano

Tel : (+39) 2 5518 7569
Fax : (+39) 2 5518 7570
Franco Spreafico; Antonietta Marsaglia

PORTUGAL

COELHO RIBEIRO E ASSOCIADOS
Av. Engº Duarte
Pacheco 19 3º
1070 Lisbōa

Tel : (+351) 1 385 31 82
Fax : (+351) 1 385 32 02
Jaime Medeiros; Maria Clara Lopes

SWITZERLAND

CANONICA, CLOSTRE &
ASSOCIÉS
2 rue Bellot
1206 Genève

Tel : (+41) 22 347 4747
Fax : (+41) 22 346 4027
Dante Canonica; François Canonica

SWEDEN

LINDHS ADVOKATBYRÅ
Box 7315
Regeringsgatan 42
103 90 Stockholm

Tel : (+46) 8 701 78 00
Fax : (+46) 8 20 90 04
Tom Rune; Tommy Ekholm

UNITED KINGDOM

PRITCHARD ENGLEFIELD
14 New Street
London EC2M 4TR

Tel : (+44) 171 972 9720
Fax : (+44) 171 972 9723
Malcolm Keogh; John Rhodes

PANNONE & PARTNERS
123 Deansgate
Manchester M3 2BU

Tel : (+44) 161 832 3000
Fax : (+44) 161 834 2067
Søren Tattam; Michael Jones

PLG SECRETARIAT: BELGIQUE

avenue de Sumatra 41/
Sumatralaan 41
1180 Bruxelles

Tel : (+32) 2 374 88 46
Fax : (+32) 2 374 90 61
Julienne Laveaux

CONTENTS OF CHAPTER 1

Introduction

1. INTRODUCTION

Alex Roney, Legal Counsellor of the London Chamber of Commerce and Industry, United Kingdom

It is vitally important for anyone thinking of entering into an agency agreement, whether as a principal or as an agent, to know what is involved. If you do not, you cannot properly assess your position, and may make costly mistakes. This book is intended to provide an outline of the sort of issues which must be addressed and to give a basic understanding of the legislative provisions relating to commercial agents in the different countries explained in the following chapters.

The book is written in a carefully thought out format, in the form of basic questions that different lawyers were asked to answer in respect of each country. This is to enable the reader to compare the position in say, the United Kingdom and Denmark, or the Netherlands and Belgium. The answers may influence the areas and ways in which a business may decide to develop, although it is recognised that market forces will provide the most powerful incentives.

Sometimes these answers are not given in the same order as in the United Kingdom section, for example. This is because there are varying priorities in the different Member States, which provide an important insight into their thinking, and so the text has not been tortured into the set format. It should perhaps here be noted that both principal and agent are referred to throughout this book as "he".This term is used for convenience and should be taken to include both the female gender and enterprises as appropriate.

The Editor is grateful to the many distinguished lawyers who have contributed to this book, and in particular thanks are due to Pritchard Englefield and the Pannone Law Group who have orchestrated so many of their colleagues and contacts both at home in the United Kingdom and in the rest of Europe to make this book possible.

(1) General preliminary advice for those wishing to set up a commercial agency

It is most important that before an individual, an enterprise, or, indeed any company even thinks of appointing a commercial agent particularly in a different country, they should ensure that their home market business is secure. They should also carry out the appropriate market research to ensure that there is a viable market for their goods (or services) in the place concerned. Then the form of representation should be considered. Would it be more efficient to appoint a distributor, or even open a branch? Presuming, for the purposes of this book, that the appointment of a commercial agent is decided on as being the best way forward for the business concerned, what are the next steps?

- The potential principal should contact the local Chambers of Commerce and other business organisations in the relevant field who may provide appropriate names or lists of possible agents.
- He should seek out contacts from colleagues but should not rely solely on their advice. So many disastrous agency agreements have been concluded on a word of mouth basis.
- Having found a potential agent, a principal should check out the agent's previous performance by visiting him on the agent's home ground and make sure credit checks, and any other available reports are sought **before** appointment.
- Ensure local provisions as to the protection of the agent are complied with and ensure that the agreement is properly drafted with the needs of both parties, either principal or agent, properly taken into account.
- Use as many sources of information as is possible. Relevant data is never wasted. A list of useful sources of information and organisations is set out in Appendix B.
- Parties should then think about their aspirations concerning the agreement, and the precise way in which they would like the agreement to work – this should avoid misunderstandings.
- Each party, and particularly the principal should then seek expert advice to ensure the contract to be presented to the agent meets these requirements, and the legislative requirements for protection of the agent, at the same time protecting the principal's interests wherever possible.

(2) What should be included in a contract with a commercial agent?

Firstly, it is most important that the agency agreement should be clearly set out in writing. There is no U.K. legal requirement that the agreement should be in writing unless one party requests this, but it is sensible to have all the matters dealt with clearly to enable parties to avoid misunderstandings, and costly disputes, and to limit the liability of the principal as far as possible, taking into account the provisions of the regulations. Thus the contract or agreement should cover at least:

- The parties;
- The definition of the type of agent appointed;
- The purpose of the contract;
- The scope and territory concerned;
- Date and duration of the contract;
- The right to periodic review of:
    - objectives, promotional and advertising campaigns;
    - costs related to above and generally;
- Duties of the agent:
    - to represent the principal properly and not, unless authorised make contracts for or on behalf of the principal with third parties;
    - to keep the principal fully informed about the situation in the territory and/or among customers and local requirements;
    - not to pledge the credit of the principal improperly;
    - to seek viable customers only – so as to minimise the risk of bad debts;
    - to agree to treat information received (for example lists etc of customers) as confidential, and not to use this information improperly or to the detriment of the principal;
    - to set out the responsibilities and needs in respect of training for the agent. (It is important that the agent be well versed not only in the function and technicalities of the actual product but also in respect of, for example, a manufacturing principal's enterprise to give accurate information to clients);
    - possibly a clause to ensure the agent does not solicit orders from outside the territory; and
    - agreement by the agent to use his best endeavours to promote the products in his territory;

- Duties of the principal:
  - to supply conditions of sale to agents and clients;
  - to supply promotional material (and to apportion costs as appropriate);
  - to comply with the requirements of local provisions in respect of giving the agent information;
  - to ensure the agent is trained as appropriate;
  - to specify delivery details, processing of orders and quality of goods for orders – and to deal with orders received promptly;
  - prices and terms of payment for goods should be referred to, but generally set out in an annex to be amended from time to time;
  - to set out sales targets, *i.e.* guaranteed minimum targets may be agreed on an annual or longer basis;
- A product liability clause detailing responsibility and insurance provisions;
- A clause indicating there should be no responsibility for non-delivery for reasons of *force majeure* (*i.e.* circumstances beyond the control of the parties);
- A provision relating to the use of sub-agents;
- A termination clause with notice periods for the principal and agent which complies with the applicable provisions;
- A provision allowing for the indemnity of the agent on termination;
- A provision to cover assignment of the agreements;
- A provision to cover insolvency or death of the agent (and if appropriate the principal);
- A clause providing that there should be no alteration of provisions except by written agreement of both parties;
- Any (reasonable) restrictive clauses, for example to stop the agent representing competitors;
- A conciliation/arbitration/alternative dispute resolution clause if required;
- A choice of law clause, *i.e.* to provide which law should govern the agreement;

- Signatures, as appropriate, ensuring those signing have authority to sign on behalf of their organisation; and
- The schedules, which should include details, technical and descriptive, of goods, sales objectives, advertising provisions and other necessary details.

It may be appropriate to also include details in respect of relevant trade marks or other intellectual property rights to ensure they are protected in the territory, and that goods sold do not contravene works existing there and protected already.

It is stressed that the suggested clauses above are listed only for guidance and not written in detail, as it is felt to be most important that each agency agreement is tailor-made and at the least checked by a professional lawyer to ensure it meet the needs and aspirations of the parties, and complies with the applicable law.

(3) After the contract

It is most important that both parties keep a continuing watch on the other, as it is far easier to rectify grievances and problems at an early, rather than a later, stage. It is also wise to ensure that there are periodic performance reviews, whether or not the contract is for a specified period only. Never be embarrassed to ask questions, or clarify situations. With luck, and chiefly good management, an agency agreement can prove very profitable for both parties. Badly handled it can be an expensive mistake.

(4) What are the pitfalls which the principal should watch for when appointing an agent, and how can he avoid them?

An agent can only really be successful if he is promoting the right product in the right market in the right way, so it is important to check out these elements first. It is important to have an agent with some experience. Learning on the job can prove expensive. It is vital to ensure the product does not contravene any national regulations, packaging provisions or intellectual property rights before it is launched. What is done with packaging waste is becoming a hot issue, and should be borne in mind. It is important to assess whether showrooms are necessary and what kind of agent you require, training needs and costs, advertising and other promotional costs, and the pragmatic time scale for financial returns. Ensure you have installed close credit control mechanisms to avoid small payment problems becoming large ones. It is important not to appoint an agent and hope for the best. A "hands-on" policy with help given when appropriate is valued by agents and their customers. Performance should be monitored regularly and information sought and supplied to maximise market potential. Possibly the most important piece of advice, all too often ignored, is not to presume that you can cobble together an adequate agency agreement. By all means set out what you need, but get an expert to check it for you to ensure your interests are protected as best they may be, whether you are a principal or an agent, and that no costly disputes will arise due to lack of clarity of the agreement. Lastly the International Chamber of Commerce have produced a model commercial agency agreement for international trade, and this may be a useful starting place for establishing your particular needs.

As there are some pieces of legislation and conventions which are referred to frequently in this book, under slightly different titles, I have decided that it would be useful to indicate here their full dates and titles for ease of reference for those who wish to study their provisions further:

- EEC Directive 1986/653 of 18 December 1986 on the Co-ordination of the laws of Member States relating to Self-employed Commercial Agents (86/653/EEC).

  The implementing statutes in the different EU Member States for this EC Directive are not listed here, but are referred to in the chapters concerned.

- The Brussels Convention: the EEC Convention of 27 September 1968 on Jurisdiction and the Enforcement of Judgments in Civil and Commercial Matters. The latest amendment to this was in 1989 with the accession of Spain and Portugal.

- The Lugano Convention: the Convention of 16 September 1988 on Jurisdiction and the Enforcement in Civil and Commercial Matters (the Convention of Lugano) signed at Lugano (between the EC Member States and the EFTA Member States).

- The Rome Convention: the Convention of 19 June 1980 on the law applicable to Contractual Obligations (with Protocol and joint declarations).

- The Vienna Convention: the United Nations Convention on Contracts for the International Sale of Goods concluded at Vienna 11 April 1980. It should be noted the UK is not a party to this.
- The Hague Convention of 15 June 1995 on the Law applicable to International Sale of Goods. This was amended by a further convention with the same title on 22 December 1986. It should be noted the UK is not a party to either Convention.
- The New York Convention of 10 June 1958 on the Recognition and Enforcement of Foreign Arbital Awards.

CONTENTS OF CHAPTER 2

United Kingdom

2. UNITED KINGDOM

Alex Roney, Legal Counsellor of the London Chamber of Commerce, United Kingdom

The chapter on the UK is placed first to provide a useful yardstick for readers.
The text of the EC Directive on the co-ordination of the laws of the Member States relating to self employed commercial agents is reproduced as Appendix A.

(1) What is meant by "commercial agent" in the UK?

The term "agent" (particularly in the UK) can have a wide meaning, often with totally different connotations – for example, a stockbroker may be acting as an agent in purchasing shares on behalf of his client but he is not within the scope of this book, as he is not a "commercial agent" as defined in the legislation.

To understand the present position in the UK as to the legislation relating to agency, it is important to understand that until 1 January 1994, when the EC Directive on the Co-ordination of the laws of the Member States relating to Self-employed Commercial Agents (86/653/EEC) ("the 1986 Directive") was brought into effect, there was little UK legislation governing agency relationships – which were governed primarily by the agreement between the parties and the common law which (*inter alia*) presumed fiduciary duties by the agents and the right to reasonable pay, but which included little protection for agents.

Since 1 January 1994, the law has been different, and the new provisions have come as something of a shock to those used to the previous position. The principal/agent relationship is now governed, for whenever it comes within the appropriate definition, by the Commercial Agents (Council Directive) Regulations 1993 (SI 1993/3053) ("the Regulations") which brought the provisions of the 1986 Directive into effect in the UK, and the rights, duties and protections that it imports for the parties. It is beyond the scope of this book to deal with all the different forms of agent, but it is useful to describe some possible relationships, for example where an agent acts:

(a) for a named principal (the most common form);
(b) for an unnamed principal, but where it is known that the agent is acting for a principal; and
(c) for an undisclosed principal where the fact of the agency is not disclosed.

Generally in (a) and (b) the agent is not himself liable on the transaction between the principal and the third party (unless he states this is his intention). In (c) the principal may later disclose his position, and then the third party may elect to accept this or may treat the (disclosed) agent as the principal.

These agents should be distinguished from *del credere* agents who are those who undertake some financial risk, in that they agree to indemnify the principal should the customer introduced by the agent fail to pay the principal for the goods, usually for reasons unconnected with the goods themselves, for example because of the client's insolvency. This book deals only with commercial agents within the Regulations which for these purposes defines a commercial agent as: "A self employed intermediary having continuing authority to negotiate the sale or the purchase of goods on behalf of another person (the 'principal') or to negotiate and conclude the sale or purchase of goods on behalf of and in the name of his principal."

(i) Are agents for services included in the definition?

It depends on whether the agents are for services only, or for goods and services. If for services only they do not come within the definition and the protections it brings. If for goods and services, then the agent may come within the definition with the protections afforded by the Regulations in the UK.

(ii) What is the meaning of self-employed in this context?

This is confusing, because although the definition specifically refers to "self-employed commercial agents" the provisions apply whether or not the agent is self-employed, or whether the agent appointed is in fact a company.

(iii) *Are any persons who act on behalf of another excluded from the scope of the Regulations?*

Yes, the Regulations specifically provide that **not** included in the scope of the regulations are:

- an officer empowered to bind a company or association, for example a director;
- a partner authorised to bind his partners;
- an insolvency practitioner;
- a commercial agent whose activities are unpaid;
- a person who is operating on a commodity exchange or in a commodity market;
- agents for overseas governments and administrations; and
- a person whose activity as an agent is secondary.

It is easy to understand most of these definitions, but some difficulty may arise with regard to secondary activities. It is important to assess carefully the actual situation so as to know whether the agent's activities as an agent are indeed primary, and their other activities secondary, or vice versa. Thus for example a mail order catalogue agent for consumer goods, where customers select goods and place orders through the agent is generally considered as undertaking a secondary activity and so outside the protection provided for.

It is important to know when an agency relationship is covered by the 1993 Regulations, because they introduced mandatory protections for agents. This means that a written agency agreement, quite legal and enforceable prior to 1 January 1994, may suddenly have become a very different instrument, as it automatically includes all the protections of the 1993 Regulations. Equally a new agreement not complying with the provisions will also be "caught" and unwary principals may find they have duties and liabilities they had not bargained for. This might make the difference between ultimate profit and ultimate loss. This book will deal with these rights and duties later (see (7) below).

(2) What is the difference between a commercial agent and a distributor?

Distributors are often loosely and confusingly referred to as distribution agents and are in a very different legal position in the UK to agents. They buy goods from a supplier, and then sell them on to another buyer or consumer. They usually (but not necessarily) hold stocks of the goods concerned, but do not act on behalf of the supplier. Generally, their remuneration comes from the difference between the purchase and sale price. If the representative takes title to the goods, even if he does not have them in his possession at any time, then he is not a commercial agent within the 1993 Regulations. A distributor is frequently referred to as a commission agent (or *commissionaire*) in other European systems.

(3) What about a person acting for a single or limited number of deals?

He may be similar to an agent but he is not a commercial agent within the protection of the 1993 Regulations, as he has no continuing authority to act on behalf of the principal so he is best referred to as an intermediary.

(4) What are the advantages of appointing a distributor?

These will become more clear as the duties and liabilities of appointing a commercial agent are explained – it being understood that distributors do not have the protection of the 1993 Regulations. In purely business terms, however, the use of a distributor should be considered in the context particularly of a new and expanding market. It may well be that a local distributor will know the needs and preferences of the likely customers in his area. He may have access to details about local standards, hygiene or storage requirements, packaging, labelling and waste provisions (*i.e.* whether packaging should be biodegradable or recyclable). He may also take much of the burden of expanding into a new market away from the supplier, in that he may have a ready made network for distribution or he may be able to provide after sales service.

(5) What are the rights and duties of distributors?

These are governed by the distribution agreement made between the parties to the agreement. An agreement will generally cover:

- The parties to the agreement;
- The goods covered with specifications, usually in an annex so that the agreement can be easily extended to new lines of goods;
- The purpose of the agreement;
- The area or customer base to be handled by the distribution agent on an exclusive, non-exclusive or sole basis;
- Duties of the principal to supply on time;
- Provision of technical know-how etc;
- Duties of the distributor, for example stock maintenance etc;
- A provision relating to any relevant trade marks, patents or other intellectual property rights – for example design copyright;
- Delivery and transport details – periods allowed, costs etc;
- Insurance – both in respect of transport, the product itself and product liability;
- Title provision, *i.e.* when title shall pass – possibly with a retention of title until payment clause;
- Publicity and sales campaigns and materials;
- Provisions relating to prices;
- Payment details and credit terms;
- Non-competition clauses;

- Termination provisions;
- Dispute settlement; and
- Choice of law provisions.

(6) How do franchise agreements differ from distribution agreements?

The manufacturer or supplier (or franchisor) has a standard structure and form for contracting business or producing a service with which the franchisee must comply. The EC Council Regulation 4087/88 on competition law and franchise agreements defined a franchise as a package of industrial or intellectual property rights relating to trade marks, trade names, shop signs, utility models, designs, copyrights, know-how or patents to be exploited for the resale of goods or the provision of services to end users. The agreement enables the franchisee to exploit the franchise in a closely regulated way, to market certain goods or services, while undertaking certain obligations to the franchisor. While beyond the scope of this book it is useful to note that the Commission does have a block exemption from the competition provisions for complying franchise agreements (Commission Regulation (EC) 240/96 on the Application of Article 85(3) of the Treaty to Certain Categories of Technology Transfer Agreement).

(7) Having distinguished the different forms of agency, what are the duties of a principal under a commercial agency agreement?

- There is a general mandatory requirement, usually also included in the agreement, that the principal should act dutifully and in good faith;
- Under the 1986 Directive (and Regulations implementing it) a principal must
  - provide his commercial agent with the necessary documentation relating to the goods concerned;
  - obtain for his commercial agent the information necessary for the performance of the agency contract; and

  - in particular notify his commercial agent within a reasonable time once he anticipates that the volume of commercial transactions will be significantly lower than that which the commercial agent would normally have expected;

- A principal shall in addition, inform his commercial agent within a reasonable period of his acceptance or refusal of, or any non-execution by him of, a commercial transaction which the commercial agent has procured for him.

These duties cannot be derogated from or excluded by contract. Particularly the clause concerning notification of a downturn in volume of transactions could cause difficulties for a principal, who is thereby required to watch the agent's market, and notify him of such changes as envisaged. Otherwise he may be in breach of his contract and so liable to pay compensation, even if the agent himself is in a better position to assess the likelihood of a downturn.

(8) Can any of these duties be avoided?

The mandatory provisions listed above cannot be avoided, and particularly the clauses relating to information may prove costly, as principals will have to keep separate records for agents, with in-built checks to ensure that periodically information is given to them so that these clauses are complied with. Equally, the issue of confidentiality arises, as records and their use must also comply with data protection regulations.

A principal may undertake other duties, which may be limited or extended by contract; these include the free supply of samples and sales literature, or assistance with marketing, advertising and promotions in the agent's territory; reimbursement of the agent's expenses reasonably incurred on the instruction of the principal; or, and most importantly, the right to maintain his discretion to accept or refuse to enter into a contract, or to perform a contract or undertake an obligation following from the activities of the agent.

While both the principal and agent have a duty to act in good faith, careful drafting of the clauses relating to the duties of the principal and rights to remuneration of the agent can prevent abuses.

(9) When is commission payable to the agent? What about bad debts? Must a principal pay the agent commission even when he himself has not been paid?

The 1993 Regulations set out in detail provisions relating to the remuneration of the agent. Thus if no provisions are detailed in the agreement, then he will be entitled to the level customary in his area of activities. If there is no such customary allowance, then he will be entitled to a reasonable remuneration taking into account all aspects of the transaction. If he is entitled to be paid by commission, then he will get payment for transactions concluded during his agreement and sometimes thereafter under the regulations (these circumstances are explored later in this chapter). In general, the commission becomes due as soon as or to the extent that one of the following occurs:

- the principal has executed the transactions;
- the principal should, according to his agreement with the third party, have executed the transaction; or
- the third party has executed the transaction.

The commission shall become due at the latest when the third party has executed his part of the transaction or should have done so if the principal had executed his part of the transaction as he should have. The commission shall be paid not later than the last day of the month following the quarter in which it became due; and for the purposes of the Regulations, unless otherwise agreed between the parties, the first quarter period shall run from the date the agency contract takes effect. Any agreement to derogate from the second and third provisions above to the detriment of the commercial agent shall be void. This means that careful drafting of commission clauses is necessary.

The Regulations state that the right to commission can only be extinguished if, and to the extent that, it is established that the contract between the third party and the principal will not be executed; and where that fact is due to a reason for which the principal is not to blame. In addition, the agent has to refund commission paid on transactions which fail, so that the right to commission is extinguished. The agent does not have responsibility for bad debts arising out of transactions promoted by him in good faith, but as stated below, the agent should be put under a duty to try to avoid likely bad debt situations.

(10) What are the duties of a commercial agent towards his principal?

As stated above, there is a primary mandatory duty for both principal and agent to act dutifully and in good faith towards each other, and the agent must:

- look after the interests of his principal;
- make proper efforts to negotiate the transactions he is instructed to take care of;
- communicate to his principal all the necessary information available to him; and
- comply with reasonable instructions given by his principal.

These are mandatory duties, and the parties may not derogate from them.

As may be seen from the suggested areas to be included in the contract above, the agent's duties and activities will generally be set out in more detail, and may be limited in the agreement, for example, to particular goods in a particular territory, or among a specific customer group. The agent's authority to negotiate on behalf of the principal, to hold samples or stock, to maintain business premises and facilities to enable him to operate efficiently, to collate and assess relevant business information in the territory, to assess future market requirements or developments and keep the principal informed to deal with (or not to become involved in) advertising and promotional campaigns, may and indeed should, all be detailed in the agreement.

Equally the agent's activities may be prohibited or limited with regard to pledging the credit of the principal, incurring liabilities for the principal in the designated area, or, he may indeed be prohibited from taking part in disputes between the principal and third parties. He may be prohibited from soliciting, marketing, negotiating or concluding contracts outside his area of operation, and he may have precise instructions about how to deal with moneys paid directly to him as an agent for the principal. He will have to maintain proper records, and enable the principal to inspect them; and try to avoid customers likely to incur bad debts.

(11) Can any of these duties be avoided?

Other than those expressed to be mandatory, the duties of the agent will be governed by contract. Care should be taken to ensure restrictive clauses do not contravene the national or EC competition provisions.

(12) Should a principal include performance quotas for a commercial agent?

Much will depend on the agency concerned, but it is one way in which the principal can monitor the activities of an agent; and if the agent does not reach the target quotas (provided they are reasonable) his agreement may be lawfully terminated by the principal for breach of contract by the agent, who would be likely then to lose his right to compensation on termination of the contract.

(13) Are there any other ways in which a principal can monitor his agent's performance?

Much will depend on the type of business concerned, but regular scrutiny of his records and reports should prevent unpleasant surprises.

(14) To what extent is the principal responsible for the acts of his agent?

It is important to consider the type of agency created.

The principal's liability to third parties is governed not only by the agreement between the principal and the agent, but also by the perception of third parties of the position, influenced by the action of the principal.

(15) Is there any way of minimising this risk of liability for the agent's actions?

The obvious recommendations are to take great care before taking on an agent, monitor their activities closely, possibly require an indemnity in respect of improper action (but this must be carefully drafted), and define parties' rights and duties carefully in the agency agreement.

(16) How can you get rid of an agent for: a) bad performance; b) misrepresentation?

The agreement may be for a fixed term or for an indefinite period, but in any event should be determinable by either party giving a specified period of notice to the other.

It should be noted that if a fixed period agreement continues after that period it is automatically converted into an agency contract for an undefined period under the 1993 Regulations. The statutory minimum periods of notice for indefinite period agency contracts are:

- one month for the first year of contract;
- two months for the second year commenced; and
- three months for the third year commenced and subsequent years.

Mutually agreed periods may be longer, but that to be given by the principal must be at least as long as that to be given by the agent. Unless agreed otherwise, periods of notice should coincide with the end of a calendar month.

(17) When is an indemnity or compensation payable?

As may be seen from the above, the principal may terminate an agency agreement by giving the due notice. However, the 1993 Regulations provide for the agent to be entitled to an indemnity, if:

- the agent has significantly increased business through his efforts to the continuing benefit of the principal; and
- payment of an indemnity is equitable (*i.e.* fair) in the circumstances.

It is provided that the indemnity must not exceed one year's payment, calculated on the basis of the last five year average, or if the agency is shorter, of the period of the agency. However, the agent can take an indemnity and still pursue the principal for damages (which would be likely to take account of any indemnity agreed).

It should be noted that the 1993 Regulations provide the alternative of an entitlement by the agent to compensation, for the damage he suffers as a result of the termination of his relations with his principal, and this takes into account not only loss of commission but also the inability of the agent to amortise the costs and expenses he undertook in respect of his agency on the advice of his principal, and the substantial benefits which the principal gets from termination, which are linked to the agent's activities.

An entitlement to an indemnity or compensation for the agent also arises where the agency contract is terminated by reason of the death of the commercial agent.

If the agency contract does not make any provision for payment of an indemnity instead, the commercial agent, under the Regulations, will be entitled to be compensated, rather than indemnified.

The Regulations also state that the commercial agent loses his entitlement to the indemnity or compensation for damage under the Regulations, if within one year following termination, he has not notified the principal that he intends pursuing his entitlement.

(18) Are there any grounds for excluding payment of an indemnity or compensation?

Yes, but the grounds for excluding payment of indemnity or compensation are limited. They are not payable where:

- the principal has terminated the agency contract because of a default attributable to the commercial agent which would justify immediate termination of the agency contract; or
- the agent has himself terminated the agency contract, unless this termination was justified by either circumstances attributable to the principal or on the grounds of the age, infirmity or illness of the commercial agent in consequence of which he cannot reasonably be required to continue his activities; or
- the commercial agent, with the agreement of his principal, assigns his rights and duties under the agency contract to another person.

This means that a principal may have difficulty in getting rid of an agent for mere bad performance, without payment of an indemnity or compensation, unless he has stipulated reasonable performance quotas, which the agent has not achieved, and so is in breach of his contract. However, if this under-achievement is not such as to justify immediate termination, then he may still be protected by the compensation/indemnity clauses.

(19) When would a party be able to terminate the agency summarily – *i.e.* without due notice?

Either party has the legally recognised right to terminate the agency contract immediately either if there are exceptional circumstances; or because of the failure of one party to carry out all or part of his obligations under the contract.

Thus, if a principal wishes to dismiss an agent for a misrepresentation which goes to the basis of the agreement, then this might be regarded as justifying immediate termination. If not, then the indemnity/compensation provisions could apply under the 1993 Regulations.

Equally, if a principal wished to terminate because the agent suddenly stops working for him, or represents someone else or himself, then his ability to terminate summarily would depend on the contract and there could be a question of degree. If this activity is written in as action justifying immediate termination, then usually the principal could take this course, and avoid compensation/indemnity provisions. If, however, the agent stops working for the principal because he has died, or has become ill or infirm, then the principal will not be absolved from paying him compensation or indemnity even though the agent's condition is not of his making.

(20) What should be remembered when drafting a clause which restricts the activities of the agent: a) during the period of the agency; or b) after termination of an agency?

It is usually possible to prohibit the agent during the period of the agency from acting in such a way as to be competing directly or indirectly with the activity he is carrying out on behalf of the principal. When this prohibition is extended after the end of the agency period, then it becomes a restraint of trade clause.

The 1993 Regulations specify that a restraint of trade clause shall be valid only if and to the extent that:

- it is concluded in writing; and
- it relates to the geographical area or the group of customers and the geographical area entrusted to the commercial agent, and to the kind of goods covered by the agency under the contract.

It is provided that a restraint of trade clause shall be valid for not more than two years after termination of the agency contract. Finally, the Regulations state: "nothing in the regulation shall affect any enactment or rule of law which imposes other restrictions on the validity or enforceability of restraint of trade clauses or which enables a court to reduce the obligations on the parties resulting from such clauses".

In the UK the courts have always treated restraint of trade clauses as enforceable only when they are reasonable, in the public interest, and are designed to protect legitimate interests, so they have been narrowly applied. In the wider European context the question of how agency agreements are affected by Article 85 of the EEC Treaty is a difficult one. The Commission issued what has been termed "an unofficial group clearance" in December 1962 which referred to risk-taking as a decisive criterion. Since then, it has been argued that the extent of integration of an agent into a principal's business must be looked at to determine status as either an agent or an independent trader or a risk-taking trader. Article 85 expressly prohibits agreements between and decisions by undertakings, and concerted practices such as price fixing which aim to prevent, restrict or distort competition unless the provisions are not applicable because the decisions, agreements or practices are aimed at improving the production of goods or their distribution, or at promoting technical or economic progress – at the same time allowing consumers a fair share of the resulting benefits. However, these practices must not enable the elimination of competition in those products or a substantial part of them – or impose unnecessary restrictions on the undertakings concerned.

(21) Should the agency agreement be for long or short fixed terms, renewable or indefinite?

Much will depend on the requirements of the parties, the goods concerned and the market to be developed. Where an agency agreement is for a fixed term, then there is a certain discipline imposed to check its effectiveness periodically. However, if it is allowed to run on, then it is converted into an indefinite term agency agreement, with the previous terms "tagged on" for notice periods, compensation and indemnity calculations etc.

It should be noted that even if a fixed term agreement expires, this may not exclude payment of compensation or indemnity, and the agent may still be entitled to receive commission on future orders. It is important to ensure commission, compensation and indemnity clauses are drafted carefully, preferably by an expert.

(22) What is the effect of termination on the responsibilities of: a) the principal; b) the agent?

Both the principal and the agent have, during the currency of the agreement, the duties set out and explained above and those set out in the particular agreement. Their duties following termination are less clear. It may be that restraint of trade and confidentiality clauses will apply. The principal may be under a duty to pay continuing commission to the agent on relevant transactions concluded during the period covered by the agency agreement, and on commercial transactions concluded after termination of the agency agreement if:

- the transaction is mainly attributable to the agent's efforts during the agency agreement;
- the transaction is entered into within a reasonable period of the termination of his agreement; or
- the customer was introduced by the agent previously for transactions of the same kind.

It is urged that the situation as to payment of commission following termination is complicated, and termination clauses should therefore be carefully drafted.

(23) What about the choice of law if the agent is in: a) another EC/EU country; b) a third (*i.e.* non-EU) country?

It should be noted that while a choice as to the law to be applied to the contract may be made, this may be overridden by national laws, usually on public policy grounds, in this area.

In the UK, the 1993 Regulations specifically govern the relations between commercial agents and their principals in relation to the activities of agents in Great Britain, unless their relations are regulated by the law of another EU Member State. However, if an agent is appointed in the UK to act wholly in a third, *i.e.* non-EU country, then unless specifically included in the agreement, the Regulations will not apply. If an agent is appointed by a third country principal to act wholly in the UK, then the

Regulations will apply, but depending on the courts of the third country concerned, and any conventions which may apply, there may be practical difficulties in enforcing the provisions against a principal.

(24) Can part of a law be chosen, for example, English law except for the provisions relating to commercial agency?

It is immaterial which law is chosen to apply to a commercial agency agreement for an agent operating in the UK as the 1993 Regulations will automatically apply, unless the law of another EU Member State has been chosen. If the agency activity is to be carried out in a third country, it is possible to apply UK law to the contract; and while it might be sensible to specifically exclude the operation of the Regulations, yet this is probably unnecessary where the agreement relates to activities wholly outside the UK, as the Regulations are stated to apply only to principal/agent relations for activities of the agent in Great Britain. As to the remaining countries of the European Economic Area (Norway and Iceland), it is suggested that they would be likely to apply the provisions of the 1986 Directive as being part of the *Acquis Communautaire*.

(25) If a dispute arises between an agent in a) another EU country; b) an EFTA country; or c) a third country, is it possible to provide for litigation to be in the country of the principal, and will the national law of the agent or principal ever be applicable?

Many agency agreements involve parties situated and resident or even domiciled in different States, with resultant jurisdictional difficulties. Within the original 12 members of the EU, the 1968 European Convention on Jurisdiction and the Enforcement of Judgments in Civil and Commercial Matters of 27 September 1968 ("the Brussels Convention") is likely to apply to establish the forum, *i.e.* the place of the court where a matter will be heard. A parallel convention applies in respect of countries formerly or currently belonging to EFTA, namely the Convention of 16 September 1988 on Jurisdiction and the Enforcement of Judgments in Civil and Commercial Matters ("the Lugano Convention"). These conventions are designed to operate in all 15 EU Member States, and specifically state that a person domiciled in one contracting State may be sued in another contracting State, as regards a dispute arising out of the operation of a branch, an agency or other establishment, in the courts for the place in which the branch, agency or other establishment is situated.

It is recommended, therefore, that the agency agreement should indicate that the parties submit to a particular jurisdiction, or the law and place of domicile of the defendant. Given the complexities of choice of laws issues, this is a matter for discussion with legal advisors. As has been stated above, it is possible that national law will be applicable in some respects in any event in respect of the rights of agents on termination.

It should be noted that consumers may consider pursuing the principal through an agent as importer of goods, thereby implying the domicile of the principal in that particular place. It should be noted that a judgment given in one contracting State will be recognised without any other special procedures being required in another contracting State, and so is directly enforceable there. A further analysis of the effects of the Convention is beyond the scope of this book.

(26) Is it advisable to put an arbitration or conciliation and alternative dispute resolution clause in the agreement?

There are differing views as to the merits and demerits of including a conciliation, alternative dispute resolution or arbitration clause in the agency agreement. Preference will depend on the parties and the countries concerned. However, whichever clause is chosen, it should be carefully drafted to avoid delays and confusion, and an extra area of dispute.

(27) What about product liability? Does the agent carry any responsibility and should he be insured?

Liability for defective products has become increasingly important in the last few years as claims have become more significant in volume and size. While generally the principal will carry liability for defects in his products, there are some circumstances in which the agent may be pursued instead of, or even in preference to, the principal, either as he is in the same country as the claimant, or is more readily identifiable than the principal. It is important therefore that this should be considered when drafting the agency agreement and when settling insurance requirements. For example, the agent may find himself with a primary responsibility by reason of being the named importer of the goods, although this is more likely in a distributorship situation.

(28) What about the liability of the principal? Does having an agent in a country constitute carrying on a business in that country?

Under the Brussels Convention the question as to whether or not a person (and this includes a firm) is domiciled in the particular contracting country where the court is dealing with the matter is established firstly, by the internal law of that country. If that party is not domiciled in that State, then they will apply the law of another contracting State to establish whether he is domiciled there. Under the Convention as implemented by the UK Civil Jurisdiction and Judgments Act 1982, an individual is domiciled in the UK if, and only if, he is resident in the UK; and the circumstances of his residence indicate that he has a substantial connection with the UK. As to companies and legal persons or associations, their seat shall be treated as the domicile, and in the UK such a body only has its seat in the UK if it was incorporated or formed under the law of (that part of) the UK, and has its registered office or official address in the UK – or its central management and control is exercised in the UK. For the purposes of Article 53 of the Lugano Convention (Domicile of Corporations or Associations) it would appear sufficient to show that a corporation or association has a seat in a particular place if it has a place of business there, and for consumer contracts a person may be deemed to be domiciled in the UK by virtue of having an operational branch, agency or other establishment in the UK.

It would seem therefore that certainly in respect of consumer contracts, the operation of an agency would be sufficient to bring the principal within the jurisdiction of the Brussels Convention, and its parallel convention, the Lugano Convention . With regard to tax matters, the situation is more complex and beyond the scope of this book.

As to litigation options generally in the UK, an informal procedure is usually available for claims up to £3000; claims of up to £25,000 are heard in the County Court and over £50,000 in the High Court. Where jurisdiction could fall within either court, reference should be made to the current practice rules.

CONTENTS OF CHAPTER 3

Austria

3. AUSTRIA

Rechtsanwalt Dr Andreas A. Lintl, admitted in Vienna, of Pritchard Englefield, London

(1) What is meant by "commercial agent" in Austria?

The law of agency in Austria is regulated by statute in the Commercial Agents Act (*Handelsvertretergesetz, HVertG*) 1993. This Act has replaced the previous Commercial Agents Act 1921. It is worth mentioning that Austria was one of the first countries in which legal protection of commercial agents was introduced by a specific act.

Section 1 Commercial Agents Act 1993 defines the commercial agent as follows:

> Any person who is charged by another (hereinafter referred to as the "principal") with the negotiation or conclusion of contracts, other than contracts concerning immoveables, in the name and for the account of the principal on a continuous basis and who performs this activity independently and as a trade, is deemed to be a commercial agent.

Austrian agency law applies to all categories and forms of agency where goods and services are concerned. It does not, however, apply to insurance contracts or real estate agents who conclude transactions concerning immoveable property which are explicitly exempted from the scope of the commercial agent definition.

(2) What makes a distributor different?

An agent (*Handelsvertreter*) should not be confused with a distributor (*Vertragshändler, Eigenhändler*).

Distributorship agreements (*Eigenhändlerverträge*) lack specific statutory regulation in Austria. Hence the general provisions of the Austrian Commercial Code and the Austrian General Civil Code apply.

A distributor enters into contracts in his own name and for his own account. On the one hand he concludes contracts with his own supplier and on the other hand with his customers.

If distributors are closely tied into the sales structure of their suppliers, Austrian courts have in published precedents held that such distributors should be granted some of the legal protection which is normally only granted to commercial agents. This in particular applies to the claim to compensation upon termination of the agency/distribution agreement.

(3) What are the advantages of appointing a distributor?

The advantages of appointing a distributor arise out of the legal relationship between the supplier and the distributor. As the distributor sells the products in his own name and for his own account, the risk involved in selling on those products to customers lies with the distributor and not with the manufacturer, which would be the case if goods are sold through an agent.

A further advantage can be that the manufacturer is not forced to set up and maintain a large distribution network himself. Hence costs of acquiring or renting business premises, employing staff, keeping goods in stock, etc can be avoided for the manufacturer since such costs are borne by the distributor who acts as an independent enterprise on his own account.

(4) What are the rights and duties of distributors?

The legal relationship between manufacturer and distributor is normally determined by contract in the distribution agreement which they enter into at the outset of their relationship. Usually the distribution agreement includes the following duties on the part of the distributor:

- To protect the interests of the manufacturer with the care of a diligent businessman;
- To continually promote the turnover of the contractual products;
- To look after the business relationship with customers;
- Continually to keep the manufacturer informed about the distributor's operations, market developments and the operations of competitors;

- To advertise the contractual products inside the contractual territory on his own account;
- To comply with the rules of fair competition;
- To inform the manufacturer of any infringement or breaches of the rules of fair competition or infringements of trade mark or patents or other intellectual property rights;
- Not to compete with the manufacturer for the period of the distributorship by manufacturing or dealing with the distribution of competing products (restrictive covenant);
- To acquire the contractual products only from the manufacturer (exclusive purchasing requirement);
- To build up after-sales care services such as a repair service in the contractual territory;
- To acquire the necessary spare parts from the manufacturer; and
- Not to use or make known to third parties any business secrets of the manufacturer, which become known to him during the period of the distributorship, without the consent of the manufacturer.

The rights of the distributor arise out of the relevant duties of the principal (manufacturer) as set out under (5) below.

(5) What are the general rights and duties of principals with distributors

The distributorship agreement usually imposes on the manufacturer the following duties:

- To allocate a specific and clearly ascertainable contractual territory in which he will carry out his duties of distribution and to grant him exclusivity rights for such territory;
- To grant remuneration to the distributor for each sale which the manufacturer concludes directly with a customer in the contractual territory;
- To prepare accounts of such direct sales from time to time at reasonable intervals;

- To deliver the contractual products at good delivery times and in accordance with agreed conditions of sale;
- Not to entrust the distribution rights for the contractual products to any third parties in the contractual territory (restrictive covenant); and
- To keep the distributor continually informed about technical developments of the contractual products and to provide him with all reasonable information which he may require to service the customers effectively.

In addition the distributorship agreement regularly provides general conditions relating to the products and objects, period of distributorship, termination and the consequences of termination.

The rights of the manufacturer arise out of the relevant duties of the distributor as set out under (4) above.

(6) Having decided to appoint a commercial agent, what should you do?

You should contact the Chambers of Commerce or other business organisations in both the United Kingdom and Austria who may provide information on or lists of possible agents.

Once you have found an appropriate commercial agent, seek expert advice in particular to draw up an appropriate agency agreement which can help to reduce possible pitfalls.

(7) What should be included in a contract with a commercial agent?

Agency agreements should at least contain the following provisions:

- Names of the parties;
- The legal position of the agent;
- The territory of the agent;
- List of products;
- Exclusive or non-exclusive agency agreement;
- Commencement of the agreement;

- Termination of the agreement;
- Powers of the commercial agent;
- Pricing;
- Invoicing;
- Rate of commission including conditions for the right to a commission (for example receiving orders, confirming orders or receipt of payment etc);
- Due dates for commission payments;
- Advertising and marketing competition provisions;
- General provisions such as the limitation period for claims arising out of the agency agreement;
- Place of jurisdiction of disputes and method of dispute settlement; and
- Choice of law clause.

(8) What are the duties of the principal?

The duties of the principal are set out in Austrian law in section 6 of the Commercial Agents Act 1993.

The principal has to support the commercial agent in his activities. In particular the principal has to provide the commercial agent with all necessary documents and all information which are relevant for the commercial agent's activities. The principal further has to notify the commercial agent immediately once it becomes foreseeable that the amount of business will decrease substantially in comparison to previous periods. The principal further without delay has to notify the commercial agent when accepting or refusing an order which was made through the commercial agent.

Section 8 of the Commercial Agents Act 1993 provides for the principal's duty to pay commission to the commercial agent.

(9) Can any of these duties be avoided?

Section 7 of the Commercial Agents Act 1993 states that the duties contained in section 6 cannot be amended either to the detriment of the commercial agent or of the principal.

(10) What about bad debts? Must a principal pay the agent his commission even when he has not himself been paid?

According to section 9 paragraph 1 Commercial Agents Act 1993 the claim for commission arises if and in so far as:

- the principal has performed his duties; or
- the principal should have performed his duties; or
- the third party, *i.e.* the customer has performed his duties, *i.e.* he has effected payment.

According to section 9 paragraph 3 no claim for commission arises if and in so far as the duties arising out of the agreement between the principal and the customer are not performed and this is not caused by circumstances for which the principal is responsible.

Section 9 paragraph 3 explicitly states that in cases of bad debts the principal has to prove that he has taken all reasonable steps in order to obtain payment from the customer. This will normally involve instituting debt collection proceedings in the courts unless it is obvious that the customer is insolvent.

The right to remuneration, however, can be freely negotiated. It is usual for remuneration to be paid in the form of commission. However, a different form of remuneration may be agreed, for example a fixed fee, a premium payment for specific services or even a share of the total turnover or profits of the main business which the agent represents. It is also possible to have a combination of commission and another form of remuneration. In the absence of a specific agreement, the rate of commission customarily applied in the respective branch of business at the agent's place of business is deemed to have been agreed upon.

(11) What are the duties of the commercial agent?

Section 5 of the Commercial Agents Act 1993 contains the duties of commercial agents under Austrian law. The commercial agent must use his best endeavours to broker or conclude business on behalf of his principal. He has to safeguard the principal's interests with the duty of care of an orderly business man. Furthermore, the commercial agent has the duty to inform the principal and notify him of each and any contract he has concluded for the principal.

(12) Can any of these duties by avoided?

According to section 27 paragraph 1 of the Commercial Agents Act 1993 the duties contained in paragraph 5 of that section cannot be amended to the detriment of either the principal or the commercial agent.

(13) Should performance quotas for a commercial agent be included?

Prescribing minimum sales to be achieved can be a useful measure to ensure that the agent continues to use his best endeavours to promote successfully sales of the principal's goods where the level of sales required by the principal depends primarily on the agent's effort and endeavours. In addition it makes sense to prescribe minimum turnover quotas to justify terminating the agency contract based on breach of contract by the agent, if the minimum agreed turnover is not met.

(14) Are there any other ways in which the principal can monitor an agent's performance?

On the one hand one can rely on the statutory provisions (section 5 of the Commercial Agents Act 1993) which imposes on the agent a particular duty to keep the principal fully and immediately informed in particular of each transaction which the agent concludes on his behalf. The information which the principal receives in this manner should enable the principal to monitor the sales activities of the agent.

It does, however, make sense to include specific monitoring provisions in the agreement. This would in particular be advisable if the principal has a large number of commercial agents in different territories and moreover in different countries. Such a monitoring clause would enable the principal to obtain the same standard of information in various different countries despite the fact that different legislation might provide for differing standards of duties to provide information.

(15) To what extent is a principal responsible for the acts of his agent?

Generally because the agent is not a party to the contract between the principal and the customer which he may have helped to bring about, the principal takes the primary risk that the customer shall perform his obligations under the contract.

If an agent who is only entrusted with the procurement of business nevertheless concludes the transaction on behalf of the principal, the principal must repudiate the transaction without delay after learning of it or the contract will be deemed to have been accepted by him. Even if not authorised to conclude contracts the commercial agent is considered the principal's representative. Hence offers and orders being made to the commercial agent are deemed to have been made to the principal. Limitations of the commercial agent's authority are only effective against the third party if the latter knew or ought to have known of such limitations.

(16) Is there a way of minimising that risk?

As mentioned above, limitations of the agent's authority are only effective if the third party knew about such limitations. Hence it is advisable for the principal to formally notify all customers of any limitations of the commercial agent's authority that he is imposing.

(17) How can a principal get rid of an agent for: a) bad performance; b) misrepresentation?

Although the Commercial Agents Act 1993 does not explicitly state that there is a duty to work on the part of the commercial agent, such a duty to work for the principal derives from the agent's duty to safeguard the principal's interests. A violation of this duty can be considered a material reason (*wichtiger Grund*) for the premature termination of the agency agreement without notice according to section 22 of the Commercial Agents Act 1993. It is important, however, to point out that in the case of a legal dispute, the principal has to prove that such a material reason for the premature termination of the agreement does indeed exist. In other words, the burden of proof lies with the principal.

As far as misrepresentation is concerned, similar principles apply. Although not specifically listed in the Commercial Agents Act 1993, the generally accepted rules of good faith in commerce in Austria mean that a duty of loyalty on the part of the commercial agent arises in his relationship towards the principal. Any serious breach of such loyalty, including misrepresentation, can constitute a material reason (*wichtiger Grund*) which entitles the principal to terminate the agreement without a notice period. As far as proof is concerned, the above mentioned principles apply to impose the burden of proof on the principal.

(18) Does the principal have any remedy if the agent suddenly stops working for him or represents someone else or himself?

As noted in (17) above, Austrian law imposes both a duty to work and a duty of loyalty on the commercial agent. Hence, should the commercial agent stop work altogether or represent someone else or himself, this could be considered a material reason (*wichtiger Grund*) which would entitle the principal to terminate the agreement. It should also be mentioned that according to section 23 of the Commercial Agents Act 1993 the principal would be entitled to claim damages if the agent's breach of contract was caused by his intentional or negligent act.

(19) What should be remembered when drafting a clause which restricts the activities of an agent: a) during the period of the agency; b) after termination of the agency?

Unless otherwise agreed in the agency agreement an independent commercial agent, unlike an employed agent, is not generally obliged to refrain from competitive activities. It is therefore of the utmost importance to include a written clause in the agreement to the effect that the commercial agent undertakes to refrain from direct or indirect competitive activities.

It must, however, be noted that section 25 of the Commercial Agents Act 1993 states that any agreement which restricts the commercial agents in respect of competitive activities after the termination of the agency agreement is void.

(20) Should the agency agreement be for long or short fixed terms, renewable or indefinite?

It will generally depend on the specific circumstances in the individual case as to whether the agency agreement is entered into for a fixed period of time, renewable, or for an indefinite period of time.

It can be an advantage to enter into an agreement for a pre-agreed period of time to avoid having to adhere to notice periods. A short pre-agreed term can in particular be advisable if the parties do not yet know each other or it is difficult to predict how successful the penetration in a specific market may turn out to be.

It has to be pointed out, however, that compensation payments upon termination of the agreement may also become payable in cases of pre-agreed fixed terms. Under the previous Commercial Agents Act 1921 principals in Austria frequently chose agency agreements for fixed terms to avoid potential compensation claims after the expiry of the agency agreement. This has changed with the introduction of the 1993 Commercial Agents Act and therefore this benefit is no longer available to principals.

(21) What is the effect of termination *i.e.* what are the responsibilities of: a) the principal; and b) the agent?

Section 24 of the Commercial Agents Act 1993 provides for the agent to receive compensation upon termination of the agency agreement:

- if the commercial agent has introduced new customers or he has substantially expanded business with existing customers;
- if it can be expected that the principal will benefit from the customers introduced by the commercial agent even after termination of the agency agreement; and
- if payment of compensation would be reasonable considering all aspects of the case.

If the above conditions are achieved, the commercial agent will be entitled to compensation upon termination of the agreement unless:

- the commercial agent has given notice;
- the negligent behaviour of the commercial agent has given the principal a material reason to give notice; or

- the commercial agent has assigned his rights and obligations to a third party.

The commercial agent has to return all documents and papers relating to the agency such as samples, price lists and conditions of sale, goods and his correspondence with customers to the principal upon termination of the agency agreement.

(22) What about the death or incapacity of the agent through for example illness or retirement of the agent? What are the respective duties then?

In the case of an agent's death, the agency agreement lapses.

In a case of the agent falling ill or becoming otherwise unable to continue his activities, both the principal and the agent are entitled to terminate the agreement without the requirement of a notice period. In both cases, however, the commercial agent or, in case of death the agent's estate, are entitled to claim compensation according to section 24 of the Commercial Agents Act 1993 if the principal continues to benefit from the previous activities of the commercial agent.

(23) What about the choice of law if the agent is in: a) another EU country; b) an EFTA country; c) a third country?

All three alternatives are governed by the Austrian Conflicts of Law Act (*internationales Privatrechtgesetz*) 1979. The parties to an agreement including an agency agreement are generally free to determine the governing law of the contract (section 35 of the Conflicts of Law Act 1979). If no choice of law is made, section 36 states that for contracts under which one party primarily owes money and the other party is obliged to provide a specific performance, the law of the country in which the party owing performance has its regular seat of business is applicable. In an agency agreement the performance of the commercial agent would be considered the characteristic performance of the agreement and hence the law of the country in which the commercial agent is based would be the applicable law to the agreement. If, for example, a principal from the United Kingdom enters into an agency agreement with an Austrian commercial agent in relation to the Austrian market, Austrian law would apply unless a choice of law clause in the agreement provides for the law of another country to apply. Please note that the choice of law is not restricted to English or Austrian law but it could also be the law of a third country, for example Swiss law or German law.

(24) Can part of the law be chosen? For example, English law except for the provisions relating to commercial agency?

As set out in (23) above the parties are generally free to make a choice of law. This enables only parts of the agreement to be governed by such a chosen law. It is important, however, to point out that under section 6 of the Conflicts of Law Act 1979 (*order publique*) a provision under foreign (non-Austrian) law will not be applied by the Austrian courts if such provision would lead to a result which is in conflict with the fundamental values of Austrian law. In such cases Austrian courts would apply Austrian law instead.

Please note, however, that the Austrian Supreme Court has decided that the fact that a foreign legal system does not provide for compensation upon termination of the agency agreement (section 24 of the Commercial Agents Act 1993; section 25 of the Commercial Agents Act 1921) does not violate the fundamental principles of Austrian law. Hence under Austrian law the parties are free to agree on a legal system which does not provide for such compensation claims. Before the EC Council Directive of 18 December 1986 on the Co-ordination of the laws of the Member States Relating to Self-employed Commercial Agents (Dir 86/653/EEC) ("the 1986 Directive") came into effect there used to be common practise in Austria in agreements between United Kingdom principals and Austrian agents to apply English law in order to avoid compensation claims under section 25 of the Commercial Agents Act 1921.

(25) If a dispute arises between an agent in (23) a), b) or c) above, is it possible to provide for litigation to be in the country of the principal and will national law ever be applicable?

Jurisdiction clauses providing for the exclusive jurisdiction of the courts in the country of the principal are possible and valid under Austrian law. Hence it is possible, for example, for an English principal to agree to the exclusive jurisdiction of English courts to decide disputes with an Austrian commercial agent. It is then up to the English courts which legal system they apply. It is, however, advisable for an English principal who wants to avoid the application of Austrian law to include a choice of law clause in the agreement.

(26) Is it advisable to put an arbitration or conciliation and alternative dispute resolution clause in the agreement?

Proceedings in Austria can be lengthy and time-consuming if they concern international disputes. This arises out of the fact that all documents have to be provided in German and in cases involving original documents in a foreign language, for example English, certified translations into German have to be provided. Another frequent reason for delays in proceedings is the fact that some witnesses have to be heard outside Austria. This is done by courts abroad who are requested to provide judicial assistance through diplomatic channels.

In order to avoid such difficulties, many international agreements, including agency agreements, include arbitration clauses which provide for any dispute to be settled by arbitration. Arbitration proceedings in Austria can be done in English. The Austrian Federal Chamber of Commerce (*Bundeswirtschaftskammer*) provides an arbitration tribunal which is frequently used in Austria.

(27) Is there a small claims procedure which could apply to the settlement of disputes between principals and agents of up to a certain figure?

There is no major procedural difference under Austrian law depending on the amounts in dispute. Whilst for claims up to ATS 100,000 (approximately £6,000) the local district courts have jurisdiction, disputes in excess of ATS 100,000 are decided by state courts (*Landesgerichte*). The procedure in both courts, however, is fairly similar in cases where claims are being disputed by the defendants.

(28) What about product liability? Does the agent carry any responsibility and should he be insured?

A commercial agent does not become a party to the contract himself but simply brokers agreements between the principal and a third party. Hence no contractual claims based on product liability can be made.

The Austrian Product Liability Act 1988 which imposes strict liability refers to liability of the manufacturer and of the domestic Austrian enterprise which has brought into circulation the product in Austria. In normal cases, *i.e.* if the commercial agent brokers a contract between a non-Austrian manufacturer and a domestic Austrian wholesaler or retailer who then sells on the product to an end-user, the commercial agent will not be affected by potential product liability claims. It would, however, be possible to imagine that the commercial agent could face a product liability claim if no other Austrian business or enterprise were involved in the chain between the non-Austrian manufacturer and the Austrian customer. In such cases it would be arguable that the Austrian commercial agent has brought into circulation the product in Austria.

It could therefore be a good idea to include the commercial agent in a third party or product liability insurance if only to defend potential claims against the commercial agent.

(29) What about the liability of the principal? Does having an agent in a country constitute carrying on a business in that country?

Austrian procedural law provides for the possibility of instituting proceedings against a non-Austrian party with no place of business or registered office in Austria only if such party has assets in Austria. This is the so-called venue of assets (*Vermögensgerichtsstand*) Rule, according to section 99 of the Austrian Jurisdictional Act 1895 (*Juristiktionsnorm*). This means that if for example a United Kingdom manufacturer has claims arising out of invoices issued to Austrian customers, such claims would be considered assets and could satisfy the requirement for establishing the jurisdiction of the courts in Austria. This would also enable the commercial agent to proceed against the principal in Austria unless there was a jurisdiction clause in the agency agreement excluding the jurisdiction of Austrian courts.

(30) What are the pitfalls which the principal should watch for in Austria and how can he avoid them?

First of all, a principal entering into an agency agreement with a commercial agent in Austria should be aware of the fact that Austria has a long-standing legal tradition providing for the protection of commercial agents. As mentioned in (1) above, Austria was one of the first countries to introduce a Commercial Agents Act in 1921.

Although a lot of provisions contained in the Commercial Agents Act 1993 are compulsory provisions, *i.e.* they cannot be amended or excluded by the parties, there is some scope for improving and safeguarding the principal's position by drafting an appropriate agency agreement. As far as jurisdiction clauses which intend to eliminate the jurisdiction of Austrian courts are concerned, non-Austrian defendants have frequently found themselves in a position whereby courts in Austria have accepted their jurisdiction despite the fact that jurisdiction clauses were included in agreements due to the fact that the jurisdiction clauses did not contain the word "exclusive". Hence a jurisdiction clause providing for the jurisdiction of English courts for example and at the same time trying to exclude the jurisdiction of Austrian courts would have to refer to the **exclusive** jurisdiction of the courts of England.

CONTENTS OF CHAPTER 4

Belgium

4. BELGIUM

Tondreau & Daem, Brussels

(1) Introduction

The purpose of this chapter is to explain the general characteristics of the status of an independent commercial agent under Belgian law, bearing in mind that this is not the only category of commercial intermediary.

This chapter sets out to distinguish between independent commercial agents and other types of traders involved in dealing with exported goods; briefly describes the difference between a contract of agency and an exclusive sales distributorship; and seeks to give practical advice throughout.

(2) Definition of forms of agency and other representational agreements

Many expressions are used, mostly erroneously, to designate commercial intermediaries such as a commercial agent, a commercial traveller/business agent, a travelling salesman, a reseller, a distributor, an owner of a franchise, a concessionary, a wholesaler, an importing salesman, a broker, etc.

The countries in which common law applies do not seem to make as strong a distinction among commercial intermediaries as do countries in western continental Europe, where civil law applies.

In Belgium, the broad types of commercial intermediaries are clearly distinguished. They are as follows:

- the independent commercial agent;
- the distributor;
- the salaried business agent/commercial traveller;
- the commission agent;
- the broker; and
- the owner of a franchise;

The common law system developed a unitarian conception of agency, which covers any relationship established by an authority given by one person to another person, the latter agreeing to act on the former's account.

Thus an agency contract in common law may concern not only strictly defined commercial agents, but also intermediaries of any kind such as salaried people who have been entrusted with powers of representation, for example brokers, buyers/commission agents and even certain distributors.

Under Belgian law the term "agent" is much more restrictively used. However, an exhaustive legal and commercial comparison of the different sorts of commercial intermediaries is beyond the scope of this chapter, but they are listed briefly below, to assist the foreign producer or principal to decide on the structure of the sale or of the export business which he wishes to organise.

Thus, a producer can decide to sell his goods on the international market in different ways.

- If he does not wish to have any selling or distribution organisation abroad, he can sell his products by:
  - direct sale;
  - use of an occasional intermediary such as a broker or commission agent;
  - by selling directly to wholesalers of his choice;
- If he already has his own organisation – or is willing to establish one – the manufacturer can operate in two different ways, *i.e.* by:
  - selling directly
    - by means of a salaried commercial representative whose task is similar to that of an independent commercial agent except in relation to the control exercised over him by the company upon which he is dependent;
    - by means of the creation of a branch or subsidiary company, in which case the exporting manufacturer entirely controls his sales establishment which is structurally integrated into his network.

      This solution involves investment, fixed costs and management expenses which are relatively high, which may be justified, for example, when the company wishes to achieve a substantial volume of business in a precisely-defined market; or

- selling indirectly via a commercial agent, a distributor or a franchisee.

These last three types of intermediary, *i.e.* selling via a commercial agent, a distributor or a franchisee, will reflect the concern of the company to set up a controlled, yet autonomous sales or distribution organisation in order to establish long-lasting relationships with commercial partners who fit into a pre-established network of sales and distribution in a functional and economic way.

In each case, a carefully-drawn contract will enable the manufacturer to organise and control the activity of the local commercial intermediary on whom it is possible to impose certain conditions relating to the sale of the products.

The manufacturer should select his type of commercial intermediary only after his need in respect of the Belgian market has been fully determined, and preferably advice should be sought from a lawyer, on the legal and commercial differences between the alternative arrangements open to the manufacturing exporters.

If the manufacturer finally decides to appoint an independent commercial agent, he can obtain help in terms of finding a suitable agent either from banks and Chambers of Commerce or from organisations such as the "*Belgische Federatie van Handelsvertegenwoordigers*" for the Flemish part of Belgium, or "*La Société Générale des Représentants Commerciaux*" for the Walloon part of the country.

It is particularly important to note the differences between an independent commercial agent and an exclusive sales distributor under Belgian law because the former is protected by a new law of 3 April 1995 in force since 12 June 1995, whereas the latter is protected by a law from 27 July 1961 as amended by a law from 13 April 1971.

(3) What are the differences between an independent commercial agent and an exclusive sales distributor?

The differences between these two entities are of (i) legal; (ii) commercial; (iii) legislative; and (iv) judicial character.

(i) Legal differences

(a) The contract of commercial agency

By virtue of the Belgian law of 13 April 1995 (article 1) which implements the EC Council Directive of 18 December 1986 on the Co-ordination of the laws of the Member States relating to Self-employed Commercial Agents (86/653/EEC) ("the 1986 Directive"), the contract of commercial agency is defined as a contract by which one of the parties, the commercial agent, is assigned on a permanent basis and against payment, by the other party, the principal, to negotiate and to conclude transactions on behalf of and for the account of, the principal, by whom he is not controlled.

In general terms:

- The commercial agent represents one or more exporters on a permanent basis, in a town, a region or a country, by means of his own organisation.
- The commercial agent also acts in the name and on behalf of the manufacturer or exporter, who is his principal.
- The agent devotes his efforts entirely towards concluding contracts between the exporter, *i.e.* his principal, and the final clients. The contracts, once concluded, merely bind the exporter and the client. This explains the custom of the manufacturer or exporter, *i.e.* the principal, to invoice in his own name and to arrange delivery to the client.

(b) The exclusive sales distribution contract

The distribution contract (whether or not exclusive) is a contract whereby the manufacturer or exporter agrees, for a fixed period, to supply certain products to its local distributor, who undertakes to resell them in his own name and on his own account in the market which has been granted to him and on terms arrived at by mutual agreement.

The essential difference as against the independent commercial agent lies in the fact that the distributor acts in his own name and for his own account so that he purchases the products from the exporter and resells them to the final clients to whom he delivers them and invoices them, thus making his profit. He is, therefore, quite simply a dealer and not an agent as such.

(ii) Commercial differences

An exporter or manufacturer may find it more advantageous to appoint a distributor rather than a commercial agent for the following reasons:

- The distributor alone is responsible for the holding of stock, for purchasing and reselling the products, so the exporter should be certain of his good financial standing or obtain guarantees to support the payment of deliveries made to him.
- The distributor is responsible for obtaining payment for products sold. These tasks are normally the responsibility of the manufacturer or exporter in the case of an agency contract.
- The distributor, if he wishes to play an active role, should maintain adequate stocks to enable him to satisfy his customer's requirements without delay; frequently he organises an after-sale or technical support service.

Nevertheless, the exporter may consider that there are disadvantages in using a distribution contract instead of an agency contract, in that the manufacturer more often than not:

- has no contact with the customers of a distributor, as the distributor deals himself with the sales process, invoicing, delivery and payment; and
- generally cannot impose his own pricing policy upon his local or national distributor, whereas when he is dealing with a commercial agent, he can easily exercise such control over contacts with the clients, invoicing, etc, since the majority of these functions are carried out exclusively by the principal.

(iii) What is the applicable legislation?

(a) For the commercial agent

The legal status of the commercial agent is newly regulated by the Belgian law of 13 April 1995, in force since 12 June 1995 which substantially changes the relationship between the principal and the commercial agent.

As stated at (3)(1)(a) above this law introduces the 1986 Directive into Belgian legislation so it is recommended that parties already bound by a commercial agency contract should compare the contract with the new legal provisions and adapt the provisions of their contract accordingly.

In particular, the Act regulates the period of notice, compensation on termination and non-competition clauses. These subjects will be dealt with more fully later in this chapter.

(b) An exclusive sales distributor

On the other hand, the exclusive sales distributor is protected by very precise and tightly-worded Belgian legislation (the law of 27 July 1961 amended by the law of 13 April 1971). The question of termination of contract is dealt with in a very detailed way, affording protection to the financial interests of the distributor. In the event of unilateral termination by the manufacturer of an open-ended distribution contract by the manufacturer, the law can impose (a) a reasonable period of notice; or (b) the payment of compensation in lieu of notice; as well as (c) additional damages of such a sum as may be equitable, taking into account (1) redundancy payments which may have to be made to personnel; (2) the costs of advertising which may have been incurred for the marketing of the manufacturer's products; and (3) other relevant matters.

Even in the case of termination of a fixed term distribution contract, the termination requires notice by registered letter of at least three months and not more than six months prior to the contractual termination date.

Finally, a fixed term distribution contract which is renewed twice automatically becomes an open-ended contract. It must be added that the provisions of the law of 1961 are obligatory and cannot be excluded by contract.

(iv) Jurisdiction of the courts in the event of a dispute

The new law of 13 April 1995 provides that every activity – even outside of Belgium –63 of a commercial agent, who has his principal place of business in Belgium, falls within the Belgian legislation and has to be brought before Belgian courts.

The law specifies that the courts cannot derogate from the application of international treaties. Here the Brussels Convention of 27 September 1968 on Jurisdiction and the Enforcement of Judgments in Civil and Commercial Matters and the Treaty of Rome of 19 June 1980 have to be borne in mind, which can both lead to the application of the law of another country rather than Belgian legislation.

(4) The contract of commercial agency

The contract of agency need not be in any particular form.

However, a certain number of elements of the contract of commercial agency should be drawn up in a written contract, in order to be valid:

- the non-competition clause;
- the *del credere* clause; and
- the clause relative to the duration of the contract.

The new law of 13 April 1995 also provides that each party has the right to ask for a written and signed contract of commercial agency, notwithstanding any contrary provision.

(i) The language of the contract

The foreign exporter should not lose sight of the fact that there are two main languages used in Belgium, namely French and Dutch.

It is important, therefore, that the commercial agent chosen should be completely bilingual to operate throughout Belgium. The choice of the language in which the contract will be drawn up is left entirely to the parties.

(ii) Contractual objects

In order to avoid friction or conflicts, a written contract must necessarily define (a) the general or specific functions of the agent and his powers; as well as (b) the territory for which he is responsible over which (c) he will be required by the exporter to seek sales of the whole or part of the exporter's products.

(a) What are the functions and powers of the agent?

The agent's main functions are searching for customers, negotiating with customers to encourage them to place orders with the exporter whom he represents, and if he has such powers under the agency agreement, to conclude contracts.

Certain agency contracts can also detail specific functions, such as:

- customs clearance;
- checking unloading of goods; and
- the setting up and commissioning of certain machines.

In the context of carrying out his functions, it is useful to define carefully whether or not the agent is granted specific powers to represent the exporter:

- When no power of representation is granted, the agent merely searches for customers, provides information about the products, prices, etc. When the customer wishes to place an order, the agent merely forwards the order to the manufacturer, who is free to refuse or to accept the order.
- When power of representation is granted, the agent can himself conclude sales in the name of, and on behalf of, the manufacturer, and he is entitled to negotiate, with the result that he creates a direct legal relationship between the manufacturer and the final customer.

The latter alternative gives rise to a degree of risk in that, in effect, the manufacturer can make no prior assessment as to the creditworthiness of the customer or the size of the order. Furthermore, he might find himself unable to deliver by reason of a shortage of production or temporary absence of stock.

The exporter is, therefore, well advised to define carefully the extent of the representational powers given to his commercial agent.

An agency contract will normally require compliance by the agent with general conditions of sale and prices fixed in the manufacturer's price lists. The parties should, however, always bear in mind that the commercial agent must act in the capacity of an independent agent.

In order to avoid any possible prejudicial confusion as to the status of the agent, it is preferable to enter into an agency contract with a limited company rather than an individual. If this is not possible and there is no choice but to appoint a private individual as an agent, it is essential to take great care in respect of the content of the contractual obligations which may otherwise show too great a dependence upon the exporter. It is desirable, for example, to avoid imposing upon an individual agent the obligation to follow instructions or to submit detailed and regular accounts, as either of these elements would suggest that the independence of the agent is greatly reduced.

(b) *Territory*

The agent shall carry out his functions in a contractually defined territory, and the parties should take care to make the extent of the territory appropriate, given the commercial and financial capacity of the agent.

(c) *Products*

The parties should define the products to which the contract relates, as it is not always in the interests of the exporter to entrust to one agent representation rights for the entire range of products manufactured and being sold at the time the contract is signed or products which he may manufacture or sell later. The manufacturer may limit the agency agreement to certain categories of articles, services, objects or products. Generally, the products for which the agent is responsible are set out in a schedule to the contract. This enables changes to be made to the list easily as the need arises.

(iii) *What are the agent's duties?*

The law provides that an agent is obliged to carry out his functions in good faith and with loyalty.

In particular, the agent must:

- use his best efforts to negotiate and conclude sales;
- communicate all relevant information to the principal; and
- comply with the time frame set out by the principal.

The information that the agent has to communicate to the principal concerns not only his own activities (the contract can provide that the agent has to communicate regular reports, as long as this obligation does not affect the agent's independence), but also other information enabling the commercial development of the products or the protection of rights, namely intellectual rights, or interests of the principal.

Other obligations – not mentioned by the law – imposed on the agent, ensue from the principle of good faith and loyalty.

The agent is obliged to treat as confidential any information coming to his knowledge during the contract of agency.

Likewise, the agent must refrain during the contract from competing with the principal either on his own account or on the account of another principal.

The function of the agent consists of negotiating and sometimes concluding contracts on behalf of, and on the account of, the principal, and the agent has to carry out his functions in good faith. The agent collaborates with the principal to seek the development of his business, meaning that the agent has to be active, which implies that he should actively search for customers.

Thus the search for customers, and the active search for orders are as inherent to the function of the agent as much as to the function of the salaried business agent.

Apart from these general principles, it is suggested that specific clauses, set out below, may usefully be included in an agency contract.

(iv) Should minimum quotas be set?

The object of a minimum orders clause is to encourage the agent by setting him minimum sales objectives which he must attain. This seems to be almost essential where the agent has territorial exclusivity. It is, however, important to be realistic in fixing the level of minimum orders, which should ideally be based upon market research or upon comparison of figures obtained from other agents selling the same products in other territories of a similar nature.

Minimum orders may be defined either in terms of quantity or value. They should not be fixed for too long a period but should include provisions to revise periodically the levels set, without necessarily requiring the agreement of both parties. They may, for example, be automatically amended on the basis of average increases in other sectors, which may be chosen in the contract as references.

A whole range of sanctions may be provided in the event that the prescribed minimum orders are not placed. The most fundamental sanction would be the termination of the contract where the contract is open-ended, or its non-renewal if it is a contract for a fixed term. Without going so far as termination, it is possible to provide for lesser sanctions such as the withdrawal of exclusivity if it has been granted, or alternatively a reduction of the agent's territory.

(v) What are the provisions relating to del credere *agency agreements?*

This type of clause is subject to five conditions:

- such a clause whereby the commercial agent guarantees payment to the exporter for the sold products by the final customer must be set out in the contract to be valid;
- the clause only concerns contracts that the agent personally negotiates or concludes. This excludes contracts concluded directly by the principal.
  Moreover, a *del credere* clause loses its validity if the principal changes the conditions of payment or delivery without the agreement of the agent;
- unless the contract specifically provides otherwise, this clause merely guarantees the creditworthiness of the customer;
- the agent cannot guarantee a higher sum than the agreed commission, unless his guarantee concerns a specific contract, or contracts that the agent concludes on behalf of the principal. This is because when the agent concludes a contract himself, the principal does not get the opportunity to assess the creditworthiness of the customer before the sale is concluded; and
- if there is a clear disproportion between the risk taken by the commercial agent and the agreed commission, the judge can reduce the guaranteed sum to the amount of the commission.

In the event of a dispute, the judge takes into account all the circumstances, in particular the manner in which the agent has taken care of the principal's interests.

A *del credere* clause is useful in cases where the agent has been granted full representation powers whereby he can conclude a sale without first referring it to the principal.

(vi) Appointment of sub-agents

The law allows the agent to appoint sub-agents, paid by him and for whom the agent is responsible, but it should be noted that an agency contract can validly exclude or limit the appointment of sub-agents.

The law of 3 April 1995 (*Loi relative on Contat D'Agence commerciale*) applies to the relationship between the agent and the sub-agents. However, the sub-agents cannot claim directly against the principal, but must proceed with any claim against the primary agent (*i.e.* their principal).

There is, however, a limitation which arises from the character of an agency contract, and this prohibits the main agent from appointing one or more sub-agents to carry out all his duties in his place. Substitution of the agent in this way would quite simply be equivalent to an assignment of the contract.

(vii) *What is the position with regard to stockholding and after-sales service?*

The exporter may wish to retain a stock of products or spare parts with the agent, but he must take care to ensure that in this case the agent does not become the owner of the stock or spare parts for a number of reasons:

- If the stock belongs to the agent, this could suggest that, in reality, he is an exclusive sales distributor;
- if the stock belongs to the agent, should the agent become bankrupt, the stock would form part of his assets and would be sold at a forced sales price for the benefit of his creditors.

It is important that the contract should set out the obligations of the agent concerning insurance, theft, inventories, invoicing, additional remuneration for stock management, etc.

Simple after-sales service can easily be set up for so-called consumer products where faults appear upon delivery or first use, whereby the agent can, with the prior agreement of the manufacturer, quite simply replace the faulty product from the stock held by him. A properly drawn agency agreement provides for either an additional commission in such circumstances or whatever other method of compensation for the agent the parties consider appropriate,

(viii) *What is the position relating to non-competition clauses during the term of the contract?*

The principle of good faith prohibits the agent from distributing products of the same nature and that compete with the products which are subject to the contract, without the consent of the principal.

It should be noted that the law only regulates the non-competition clause after the termination of the contract and does not prohibit such a clause for the duration of the contract.

A non-competition clause does not need to be set out in any particular form to be effective, but it should be remembered that in the absence of any clause providing to the contrary, the agent can act as an agent for one or more exporters or carry out the functions of agent both for third parties and on his own account at the same time.

(ix) What are the advantages of appointing a non-exclusive agent?

Where the products are complementary and don't compete with each other, they can be targeted at the same customer base, and sales techniques often require the same commercial and technical competence. In this case, the range of the agent's products is greater, and sales of one product can generate sales of others. Also, as far as the agent is concerned, it avoids the situation whereby he is dependent upon a single exporter, and he can spread his operating costs more efficiently.

(x) What are the disadvantages of appointing a non-exclusive agent?

It may be necessary and in the interest of the parties, and particularly of the exporter, to include a non-competition clause in cases where the agent represents or intends to represent competing products. This contract should define "competing products" as well as competing activities which may be developed by the agent either directly or indirectly – for example, through the acquisition by the agent of shares in another company.

So far as sanctions are concerned, it is reasonable to make a provision for fixed damages to be paid in the event of breach by the agent of a non-competition clause during the existence of the contract.

(xi) What are the duties of the principal?

The law provides that the principal must act in good faith and with loyalty towards the agent.

The following examples illustrate this general obligation.

The principal must:

- make available to the commercial agent all necessary documentation dealing with the products concerned;

- obtain for the agent all necessary information to enable him to carry out the agency contract and inform him when the principal realises that the manufacturing volume may be less than the agent could reasonably expect; and
- inform the agent within a reasonable time of the manufacturer's acceptance or refusal or failure to fulfil an order which the agent has passed to him.

The parties should be careful to define precisely whether the principal retains ownership of sales material placed at the disposal of the agent, and whether the agent is required to return it at the end of the contract.

(xii) What about the payment of the agent?

The principal has an obligation to pay the agent, (a) expenses; and (b) commission.

(a) Expenses

The contract of a commercial agent is similar to a general mandate which requires the reimbursement of expenses incurred by the beneficiary of the mandate in the carrying out of his functions. In order to avoid any confusion, it is therefore recommended that the principal clearly defines in the contract that the agent will himself be responsible for all his own expenses except for exceptional expenses, which should be specified. These could include, for example, taking part in an exhibition, travelling abroad at the request of the principal, etc.

(b) Commission

General principles
The law distinguishes three situations. The payment of the agent can consist either of (a) commission; (b) a fixed amount; or (c) a combination of both.

When the payment is entirely or partially fixed, the law only provides that the fixed part is due monthly, in the absence of any clause to the contrary.

The law also provides that every element of payment which varies with the number or value of the concluded contracts is considered to be commission. For example, when a bonus is granted because a certain level of output has been reached or because a certain number of contracts have been concluded, this is considered to be commission.

The commission can also be a fixed amount per contract concluded by the agent.

Commission rate

The rate of commission must be fixed by the parties. The contract may provide for fixed rates according to the category of customers, to the nature of the products or services or to the role played by the agent in concluding the contract.

The law provides that if the contract does not provide for a fixed rate and if no element of the contract enables a conclusion as to the implicit will of the parties as to the intended rate of commission, the usual rate for similar contracts of the economic sector of the place where the agent has his business is applicable. If there is no such usual rate, the agent should get an equitable rate.

Thus it should be remembered that when the commission rate is not fixed, it is the place where the agency contract is executed that will be the determining factor.

How is the commission calculated?

When the agency contract does not specify this the commission is calculated on the base price of net or gross sales invoiced to the client; that is, before deduction of the transport, packaging and insurance costs, but after deduction of taxes, customs and other taxes.

Concerning discounts and reductions it is logical to deduct these from the base price when the agent has decided to grant them to the customer.

However, when it is the principal who granted the discounts and reductions, they cannot be deducted from the base price for calculation of the commission.

When does the agent's right to commission arise?

The law distinguishes between the case where the commission is due for a contract concluded during the period of the agency and the case where the commission is due for a contract concluded after the termination of the agency.

For the contracts concluded during the agency, the agent has the right to receive a commission when the contract is concluded, following his intervention. This does not necessarily imply that the agent has negotiated and concluded the contract himself. It is enough if the intervention of the agent was effective.

The agent also has a right to commission when it is agreed that the agent acts as sole agent on a specified territory or for a specified group of people, and when the contract is concluded with a customer within the agreed territory or part of the agreed group.

Moreover, the agent has a right to a commission when the contract is concluded with a third party and when the agent has previously concluded similar contracts with the customers of this third party.

The parties can also agree on a commission varying with the direct or indirect intervention of the agent in the conclusion of a contract.

For a contract concluded after the termination of the agency contract the agent has a right to a commission if the order of the customer has been passed with the principal or with the agent before the termination of the agency.

The agent also has a right to receive a commission if a contract is concluded due to his efforts and if it is concluded within six months after the termination of the agency

When does the agent become entitled to payment of the commission?
The law provides for several possibilities:

- on the execution of the order by the principal; or
- on payment for the order by the customer to the principal,

the commission has to be paid at the latest on the last day of the month following the quarter during which the commission became payable.

Does the agent have the right to verify the amount of commission due to him?
The law provides that the agent is entitled to receive from the principal a detailed statement of commission, at the latest the last day of the month following the quarter during which the commission became payable.

The law also provides that the principal must supply the agent with all necessary information; the agent can even examine the accounts of the principal to check the amount of due commission.

When is the agent's right to commission lost?
The law provides that in the following cases the parties can agree that the right to a commission is extinguished:

- When it is established that the third party has not paid for his order, unless this is due to the principal's default.

- When the execution of the order or contract has become impossible and this is not due to the principal.
- When the execution of the contract cannot be reasonably be expected of the principal, especially if the third party has an important reason justifying the non-execution by the principal.

In each of these cases, the commission paid to the agent must be refunded to the principal. The parties cannot provide otherwise in the agency contract.

(xiii) How may an agency contract be terminated?

(a) By giving notice

There is a legal obligation to give notice of termination, unless there is an important shortfall or exceptional circumstances. The law also fixes the period of notice, compensation on termination and regulates the non-competition clause.

The obligation to give notice
When a contract is open-ended or for an indeterminate duration, either party can terminate at any time by giving due notice to the other. This a very important modification brought into Belgium by the law of 3 April 1995.

The period of notice
The period of notice is one month during the first year of the contract. After the first year, the period of notice is extended by one month per additional year started. The period of notice cannot exceed six months. These periods of notice are minimum periods.

Thus the parties cannot agree on shorter periods, but can agree on longer periods of notice in which case the period of notice to be respected by the principal cannot be shorter than the period to be respected by the agent.

The form of notice
The law provides that the notice of termination must be by way of a written document to the other party indicating the beginning and the duration of the notice.

The notification can also be sent by registered mail. The notice will then enter into effect on the third day following the date of sending. In addition, the notice can be delivered by a process-server.

The law provides that in the absence of specific agreement to the contrary, the notice should expire on the last day of any given month.

What is the effect of breach of the obligation to give notice?
The party terminating the agency contract without notice must pay compensation for termination to the other party. This compensation must be equal to the current payment at that period, corresponding either to the period of notice or to the part of that period still running.

When the payment of the agent consists partly or completely of commission, the calculation of the current remuneration is based on the monthly average of commission during the last 12 months preceding the date of termination of the contract.

(b) For breach of contract and in exceptional circumstances

Each party can terminate the contract without notice or – if it is a contract with fixed duration – before the end of the term when exceptional circumstances make any professional collaboration between the agent and the principal impossible or because of an important breach by the other party of his obligations.

An important breach is a circumstance which for a valid reason makes the continuation of the legal relationship between the parties impossible, even during the period of notice.

Examples of important breaches by agent or principal which would enable immediate termination are where:

- the agent accepts a bribe;
- there is a breach of the provisions of the contract prohibiting the agent to conclude contracts for his own account or to represent competing companies;
- the principal appoints a second agent, where the contract provides for exclusivity; or
- there is the death, bankruptcy or incapacity of one of the parties. The fact that the products are not manufactured any more, or the principal loses the distribution rights to the products are also valid circumstances for this purpose.

If one of the parties terminates the contract invoking an exceptional circumstance or an important breach of the agreement and the court to which the other party refers the matter does not consider the character of the invoked circumstance to be sufficiently exceptional or grave, the party who terminated the contract will have to pay damages equal to the current payment, corresponding to the duration of the notice which should have been given.

Thus the termination for important breaches of contract or for exceptional circumstances can always be submitted to the sovereign evaluation of the court.

Furthermore, the law imposes a double time limit of seven days:

- the right to terminate without notice or before the fixed term expires for exceptional circumstances or serious breach may be lost if the person with the right to terminate does not do so within seven days of his having knowledge of the relevant circumstance or breach; and
- the exceptional circumstance or the serious breach which justifies termination without notice must be notified to the other party by notice of a process-server or by registered mail within the seven days after the termination.

(xiv) *What about the provisions relating to compensation on termination?*

The legal provisions concerning compensation upon termination cannot be modified to the detriment of the agent before the end of the contract. The parties are, of course, free to agree on provisions that are more favourable to the agent.

However, after the end of the contract the parties are entirely free to agree on a higher or lower compensation than that provided for in the law.

(a) When does the right to compensation upon termination arise?

The law provides that the agent has a right to compensation upon termination if he has supplied the principal with new customers or if he has considerably developed business with the existing customers, as far as the activity of the agent brings substantial advantages to the principal.

If the contract provides for a non-competition clause, the principal is supposed, in absence of proof to the contrary, to receive substantial advantages.

The amount of the compensation is fixed with reference to the importance of the business development achieved and the supply of new customers.

In the absence of an agreement between the parties, it is the judge who will decide the proper sum.

The law only provides for a maximum amount: the compensation cannot be higher than the amount of the annual payment, calculated on the average of the five last years or, if the duration of the contract is less than five years, on the average of the preceding years.

(b) When can the right to compensation on termination be excluded?

The law provides for three cases where the compensation is not due:

- when the principal terminates the contract due to a serious breach by the agent;
- when the agent terminates the contract, except when it is due to the serious breach by the principal or if the termination is due to illness, infirmity or illness of the agent which does not allow him to continue his activities; or
- when the agent or his heirs, with the agreement of the principal, transfers his activity to a third party.

Thus, in short, the agent has no right to compensation when the termination of the contract is due to his fault or when he transfers his activity. In the latter case, the compensation is supposed to be included in the transfer price.

(c) Can the agent lose his right to compensation?

The agent loses his right to compensation if he has not notified the principal, within one year after the termination of the contract, that he intends to seek such payment.

(d) What about complementary damages?

The law provides that the agent can obtain complementary damages if the compensation on termination does not cover entirely the detriment suffered but of course, the alleged damage must then be proven.

(xv) What limitations are there on an effective non-competition clause after termination of the contract?

A post-termination non-competition clause is only valid when:

- it is in writing;
- it concerns the type of business the agent was in charge of during the contract;
- it concerns the territory or the group of persons the agent has been charged with; and
- it does not continue for more than six months after the termination of the contract.

The law also provides that the non-competition clause will have no effect when the contract is terminated by the principal in the absence of a serious shortfall of the agent or by the agent because of a serious breach by the principal.

Although the non-competition clause creates a presumption in favour of the agent that he has brought new customers, the principal can bring evidence as to the contrary.

The agency contract can also provide for a fixed indemnity in case of violation of the non-competition clause. This indemnity cannot exceed an amount equal to the total annual payment, calculated on the average of the last five years. If the principal wants a higher indemnification, he will have to prove his alleged damage.

Finally, it must be noted that it is in the best interest of the parties to insert a post termination non-competition clause in the contract if the agent represents, or intends to represent in the future, competing products or if he intends to develop competing activities.

Notice

This chapter summarises the main aspects relating to agency contracts in Belgium, but cannot replace the services of an adviser in any particular case. Legislation and caselaw is constantly subject to change.

CONTENTS OF CHAPTER 5

Denmark

5. DENMARK

Steen Rosenfalck, Abbot King & Troen, London

(1) Introduction

The term "agent" has been interpreted widely and does not have a specific legal definition. The term generally covers both commercial agents (*handelsagenter*), factors (*varemæglere*), commission agents (*kommissionærer*), commercial salesmen (*handelsrejsende*) and other representatives (*repræsentanter*). This chapter deals only with commercial agents as defined below.

In a legal context agency agreements should be distinguished from distribution agreements and other commission agreements.

Denmark has incorporated the Council Directive of 18 December 1986 on the Co-ordination of the laws of the Member States relating to Self-employed Commercial Agents (86/653/EEC) ("the 1986 Directive") into Danish law by the Commercial Agents and Salesmen's Act 1990 (*Lov om Handelsagenter og Handelsrejsende* ("HAGL")). The provisions came into force on 3 May 1990.

The rules in the HAGL include mandatory duties which cannot be derogated from or excluded by contract or agreement to the detriment of either the principal or the agent.

The HAGL also contains non-mandatory rules which are used to interpret and supplement contracts which do not fully cover all the aspects of the legal relationship between the parties. These rules are also used where the parties have not entered into a written contract.

(2) How is a "commercial agent" defined in Denmark?

Section 2 of HAGL defines a commercial agent as follows:

> A self-employed intermediary having continuing authority to negotiate the sale or purchase of goods on behalf of another person, (the principal), by soliciting orders to the principal or by concluding agreements in the principal's name in this respect.

Other statutes of relevance to agency agreements include the Agreement and Contract Act 1986 (*Aftaleloven* (AFTL)) and the Commissions Act 1986 (*Kommisionsloven* (KMSL)). These Acts refer to the scope of the power of attorney and to commission agreements, however it is outside the scope of this book to deal in depth with these aspects.

On the basis of the 1986 Directive, the organisation ORGALIME, has produced a model form of an agency contract ("the Model") which in general relates to the sale of goods, and not services. It will be possible to amend the Model to cover services as well. The Model has so far been translated into Danish, English, French and German, and it is a useful starting point for drafting a contract of this type between parties residing in different countries and jurisdictions. ORGALIME has also produced a model form of a distribution contract. The contracts can be obtained from Danish Industries Employers Federation "DIEF", Nørre Voldgade 34, DK – 1358 København K.

(3) What is the difference between a commercial agent and a distributor?

The basic distinction between a distributor and a commercial agent is that the distributor acts for himself in his own interest, whereas the commercial agent acts in the principal's interest and on the principal's behalf.

A distributor trades in his own name and for his own account. He buys the goods from a supplier and then sells them on to another buyer – preferably – for a profit. His working consideration is represented by the difference between the purchase and the sale price. The Danish term normally used is "*forhandler*" or "*eneforhandler*" (sole distributor). The agent's remuneration is usually a commission from the principal based on the invoiced prices of goods sold.

(4) What are the advantages of appointing a distributor?

The distributor acts on his own behalf and does not have the authority to conclude contracts and agreements on behalf of the principal. This fact results in the legal relationship between a supplier and a distributor being simpler; it is basically limited to the parties' contractual performance under the distribution agreement. Generally the problems relating to third parties as to the scope of the agent's authority to bind the principal is of a more limited nature.

Further, the distributor is not caught by the terms of the 1986 Directive and HAGL. From this it follows that the distributor is not protected by the mandatory rules in the Directive and the Statute.

(5) What are the obligations of principals and distributors?

It is highly recommended that a written distribution contract is made between the parties to the agreement. In the contract the obligations of the parties are normally set out and these include:

(i) General provisions

- The identity of the contracting parties to the agreement.
- The products to be supplied under the agreement.
- The territory to be covered by the agreement.
- The contract period.
- The termination provisions.
- The marketing provisions.
- The provisions relating to prices, discounts and delivery terms.
- The choice of law provisions.
- The governing jurisdiction.
- The question of exclusivity.

(ii) The supplier's obligations

- The duty to supply goods.
- A duty not to supply other distributors in the territory if the distribution agreement is an exclusive distribution agreement.
- A duty to supply the distributor with necessary information and documentation.

(iii) The distributor's obligations

- A duty to solicit business upon agreed terms.
- Minimum target quotas.
- Provisions restraining the distributor from marketing other competing products.
- A duty to supply after sale service; including repair and maintenance.
- Secrecy provisions.
- Restraint of trade clause.

(6) What should be included in a contract with a commercial agent?

In accordance with the 1986 Directive and HAGL, the Model is rather comprehensive and contains the following relevant provisions:

- The parties to the contract.
- The object of the contract.
- Definition of the products.
- Definition of the territory.
- Description of agent's functions.
- Performance provisions relating to minimum quotas.
- Provisions relating to advertising and promotional exhibitions.
- Provisions relating to the agent's responsibility for bad debts.
- Provisions relating to complaints from customers.
- Information provisions.
- Agent's undertaking not to compete.
- Secrecy provision.
- Rules relating to sub-agents and sub-distributors.
- Provision in respect of other territories.

- Provisions relating to unfair competition and infringement of intellectual property rights.
- Provisions relating to stock.
- Provisions relating to after sales services and repairs.
- Provisions relating to the extent of the agent's exclusive rights.
- Provisions in relation to the principal's provision of information to the agent.
- Provisions in relation to technical assistance.
- Description of the protection of the agent's exclusive rights.
- Description of commission.
- Description of commission related to orders not accepted and on contracts terminated.
- Description of calculation of commission.
- Description of payment calculation and loss of right to commission.
- Provision relating to the contract period.
- Provision relating to early termination.
- Provisions relating to return of documents and stock.
- Provision in relation to unfinished business.
- Rules on indemnity and compensation.
- Choice of law provision.
- Jurisdiction agreement.

(7) What are the mandatory duties of a principal?

According to the 1986 Directive and section 5 of HAGL the mandatory duties of the principal are that the principal should:

- act loyally and honestly;
- supply the agent with the necessary documentation relating to the goods concerned;

- provide the agent with the information necessary for the performance of the agency contract; and
- notify the agent within a reasonable time of acceptance or refusal of offers, which have been sent from the agent, and of the non-completion of contracts concluded by the agent.

The principal shall within a reasonable time inform the agent if the principal anticipates that the commercial business relating to the agency contract will be significantly lower than the agent would normally have expected.

It should be noted that these rules are mandatory and cannot be derogated from to the detriment of the agent.

(8) What are the mandatory duties of a commercial agent?

In section 4 of HAGL there is a primary duty for the agent to act loyally and honestly; and the agent must:

- make reasonable endeavours to negotiate offers and, if authorised, to conclude agreements in relation to the business covered by the agency agreement;
- notify the principal about offers or agreed contracts and to communicate all necessary information; and
- comply with reasonable instructions given by the principal.

These are mandatory duties, and the parties cannot derogate from them.

(9) Should you include performance quotas for commercial agents?

It will depend on the agent and the agency in question, but this is a primary means of monitoring the performance of the agent. Inclusion of a performance quota is a commercial decision but it will often be in the interests of both the principal and the agent that the contract contains a description of minimum sales, the extent of customer visits, advertising and marketing, so that both parties can monitor the performance.

(10) To what extent is the principal responsible for the acts of the agent?

The relationships with third parties are dealt with in sections 16–21 of HAGL.

The philosophy behind the rules is generally that the agent is authorised only to initiate and arrange for the contact between potential buyers and sellers. According to section 16 paragraph 1, the agent does not have a general power of attorney to bind the principal without the latter's authority.

Chapter II of AFTL also deals with the extent of the principal's relationship to third parties and the responsibility related thereto, and in general relates to different forms of power of attorney, to the agent's power to bind the principal and to the agent's liability towards third parties and the principal.

(11) Is there any way of minimising that risk?

It is important that the agent's functions are clearly described in the agency agreement, so that the parties' obligations are clearly defined. Complex legal situations are likely to arise when the agent enters into agreements with third parties without the necessary authority from the principal. Therefore the agent should be obliged to contract only in his capacity as an agent so as to avoid any liability both for an undisclosed principal and in relation to the agent himself.

A description of the agent's functions is found in article 1A of the Model:

> He has continuing authority to negotiate the sale of the goods indicated under Chapter I on behalf of the Manufacturer (principal).
>
> He shall transmit to the Manufacturer (principal) any offers or orders received by him. He has no authority to make contracts on behalf of, or in any way to bind, the Manufacturer (principal). He shall bring to the notice of the customer the terms and conditions of sale (including delivery periods and payment) prescribed by the Manufacturer (principal). The Manufacturer (principal) shall be free to reject any offers or orders transmitted to him by the Agent.

In addition, it is important to monitor the agent's performance once the principal has entered into an agreement with the agent.

(12) How can you terminate an agreement?

An agreement can be made for either a fixed period or an undetermined period. In the latter case there is a mandatory period of notice in section 22 of HAGL. In the first year of contract, the notice is one month. The period is extended by one month for every year of the contract with a maximum of six months' notice, unless otherwise agreed.

It is possible to agree that the agent – but not the principal – can give three months' notice, even if the contract has been in existence for more than three years. It is not possible to agree a shorter notice period.

The periods of notice should coincide with the end of a calendar month, unless otherwise agreed.

(13) Do you have any remedy if the agent suddenly stops working for you or represents someone else or himself?

It should be noted that an agent is under a primary duty to act loyally and honestly. In the above scenario it is most likely that the agent would be in breach of his duty and thus of the contract.

To counteract this situation the agency contract should contain provisions in relation to non-competition and/or misrepresentation. This will give the principal a clearer and more defined remedy.

If the agent is in breach of the provisions of the agency agreement, it is possible to terminate the agreement immediately where there is a fundamental breach of the contract.

If the breach by the agent itself is not fundamental, it is possible to give the agent a warning. If the agent overlooks this and continues to be in breach or repeats the breach, this may constitute a fundamental breach of the contract enabling immediate termination. These provisions also apply to the duties of the principal; for example, the principal's provision of information to the agent.

(14) What do you have to remember when drafting a clause which restricts the activities of an agent?

It is often advisable to include an undertaking not to compete during the period of the agency among the agent's obligations. The provision can be drafted in various ways, relating to the products and the territory covered.

The period after termination of the agency is often regulated by a restraint of trade clause which is often incorporated in the undertaking not to compete.

Restrictive covenants are covered by section 30 of HAGL. Under this section there are formal requirements for the clause to be valid and there are also limitations as to the scope of the restrictive covenant. Thus, the clause must be concluded in writing, and it must relate to either a geographical area or the customer base and the geographical area covered by the agency agreement; and it must concern the products covered by the agency agreement.

Furthermore, the period of the non-competition clause is limited to two years after termination of the agreement under article 20 of the 1986 Directive and section 30 of HAGL.

In general, the Danish courts will treat restraint of trade clauses as enforceable, but the validity is also subject to section 38(1) of AFTL under which the court can censor or disregard a clause wholly or partly if the court finds the clause inequitable or unreasonable.

It is useful to note that the ORGALIME Model contains an undertaking not to compete.

(15) Should the agency be for long or short fixed terms, renewable or indefinite?

This decision should be based on the situation of the parties, and the goods and markets involved. This is a commercial decision.

Section 22 of HAGL relates to indefinite term agency agreements and section 23 relates to agreements for a fixed term. The rules set out the mandatory periods of notice as discussed above.

(16) What are the responsibilities of the principal and the agent when an agreement is terminated?

Generally, a specific answer to this question would depend on what is agreed to in the agency contract.

In Danish law there is a basic distinction between an ordinary termination of an agreement due to the expiry of the agreement, or because notice has been given to terminate the contract in accordance with the provisions set out in the contract (*opsigelse*), and an extraordinary termination due to a fundamental breach of contract (*ophævelse*). It is outside the scope of this book to deal with this in detail. In general terms if one party is in a fundamental breach of the contract, the other party would be entitled to claim compensation to cover his losses, and this loss will often include an indemnity under the contract.

During the notice period and after the termination of the agreement the parties will still be under a general obligation to act loyally and honestly towards each other. This also follows from the provisions in the Marketing Act 1994 (*Lov om Markedsføring*); especially under section 1.

Under Danish law the inclusion of an indemnity clause in the agency contract is optional, but, if it is included, it may not then by agreement be excluded during the currency of the agreement. It may, however, be excluded after the termination of the agreement by both parties. If the contract does not include provisions in relation to an indemnity, the relationship between the parties will be covered by sections 25–29 of HAFL.

As to the *principal's responsibilities*, there will often be provisions relating to payment of an indemnity or compensation to the agent.

The rules governing the agent's entitlement to compensation are found in sections 25–29 of HAGL.

Under section 25 of HAGL the agent may be entitled to an indemnity if the agent has solicited new customers or significantly increased the business in relation to the existing customer base, and if the payment of an indemnity is equitable under the circumstances.

According to section 26 the indemnity cannot exceed one year's payment on the basis of the average over the last five years or, if the agency is shorter, of the period of the agency.

However, it should be noted that according to section 27 an indemnity is not payable:

- when the principal has terminated the contract due to the agent's fundamental breach of the contract;
- where the agent himself has terminated the contract, unless this was justified either by circumstances attributable to the principal, or on the grounds of the age or incapacity of the agent in consequence of which he cannot reasonably be required to continue his activities; or
- where the agent, with the agreement of his principal, assigns his rights and duties under the agency agreement to another person.

The rules relating to indemnity cannot be contracted out of in the original agreement to the detriment of the agent. Thus, payment of an indemnity is mandatory unless excluded by sections 27–28 of HAGL. According to the last provision, the agent can claim the indemnity within one year after termination of the contract.

The alternative to an indemnity is entitlement to compensation for damages (*cf.* section 6 of HAGL). The scope of compensation is wider than for an indemnity, and the onus of proof is on the claimant to quantify the level of damages and to show a causal connection between the loss and the termination of the agreement. It is possible for an agent to claim compensation in addition to an indemnity in case of the principal's breach of the contract. The indemnity will then be included in the compensation as a part of the agent's losses.

As to the agent's responsibilities under section 6 of HAGL the principal will be entitled to compensation if the agent has neglected his duties under the agreement.

The agent will often have agreed to a clause restraining his trade activities in relation to non-competition with the principal. As mentioned above, the maximum period of the restrictive covenant is two years.

Furthermore, the agent will be under an obligation to return documents, stocks, spare parts and other material, including price-lists to the principal.

(17) What about the insolvency, incapacity or death of the agent?

The HAGL does not deal with the situation where the agent becomes insolvent. This is covered by Chapter 7 of the Insolvency Act 1986 (*Konkursloven*). It is outside the scope of this book to deal with these rules in detail, but in general the effect of the insolvency of both the principal and the agent is to terminate the agreement.

As to the incapacity or death of the agent, this is also not covered by HAGL. In general it should be noted that the agent's entitlement to an indemnity and compensation in these situations will be assigned to the estate of the agent.

Against this background it is recommended that the agency agreement contains provisions in this regard so as to terminate the agent's agreement automatically in the event of the insolvency, death or incapacity of the agent.

(18) What about the choice of jurisdiction and applicable law if the agent is in another country?

In international transactions there are two essential issues which initially need to be addressed. The first question would be the question of jurisdiction; whether a court is competent to enter a binding judgment. The court needs to address the question of its competence before it can consider the merits of the dispute. The second question to be resolved is that of the choice of applicable law.

In order to avoid difficulties and costs arising from a dispute about jurisdiction, the parties should consider entering into a jurisdiction clause which is an agreement as to where proceedings are to be brought in the event of a dispute. The EEC Convention on Jurisdiction and the Enforcement of Judgments in Civil and Commercial Matters ("the Brussels Convention"), and complementary Lugano Convention govern jurisdiction clauses between parties domiciled in the EU Member States.

The principal requirements in order for a clause to be enforceable are that the parties have agreed the jurisdiction clause, and that the agreement is evidenced in writing. Due to the complexities of both choice of law and jurisdiction clauses, this is a matter for discussion with legal advisers and not the subject of further scrutiny in this chapter.

If the parties have not agreed a jurisdiction clause, the general rule is that the action is brought where the defendant is domiciled. There are exceptions to this rule.

The choice of applicable law is often central to international contracts and litigation, and can determine whether a litigant is ultimately successful. For example, there are often different concepts in countries about what constitutes "offer" and "acceptance", and thus whether a binding contract has been concluded.

The choice of law and its effect is not a straightforward issue. Parties can choose one law for the entire contract or they can allocate different choices of law to different parts of the contract. The chosen law does not necessarily need to be the law of either party. In addition the parties' choice of law can be overridden for reason of public policy (*ordre public*) by the Danish courts.

Choice of law is a separate issue from jurisdiction. If the defendant and the witnesses are located in one jurisdiction then that would probably be the most suitable forum (location) for the action. It may be that a national court would then apply the law of another State if that law has the closest connection with the contract or if that law has been chosen by the parties; for example an English court may apply Danish law to resolve a dispute brought before an English court. In these circumstances it is prudent to ensure that professional advisers with an understanding of the different national legal systems draft the jurisdiction and choice of law clauses.

The EU Member States finalised a convention on the law applicable to Contractual Obligations on 19 June 1980 ("the Rome Convention"). The Convention took effect in April 1991 after having been ratified by seven Member States; including Denmark and the United Kingdom.

The basic distinction drawn by the Rome Convention is that where there is an agreement (article 3), as to the choice of governing law the parties' choice is generally followed if the provisions are reasonably clear. If the parties have not made any choice of law, article 4(1) states that the contract is subject to the law of that country with which it has its closest connection. In article 4(2) it is assumed that this will be with the country where the party who is to perform the characteristic obligation of the contract has his domicile or place of business.

The Rome Convention complements a few more limited conflict treaties in effect in some EU Member States; most notably the Hague Convention of 15 June 1955 on the Law Applicable to International Sale of Goods ("the Hague Convention") and the 1980 Vienna Convention on Contracts for the International Sale of Goods ("the CISG"). Both Conventions have been adopted by Denmark but not by the United Kingdom. The Hague Convention has since been updated by a 1986 Hague Convention. The latter has still not come into operation.

The CISG may well be regarded as the most relevant treaty on the choice of substantive law applicable to international contracts because it has been ratified by a substantial number of States.

In Denmark section 1(2) of HAGL states that the rules in sections 22 and 25–27, which deal with the mandatory period of notice, and the payment of indemnity to the agent, cannot be changed to the detriment of the agent in the case where the foreign law does not contain matching mandatory rules. In other words the rules in sections 22 and 25–27 of HAGL are internationally mandatory.

(19) Is it advisable to put an arbitration or conciliation and alternative dispute resolution clause in the agreement?

As stated above, the parties can refer disputes to arbitration and the advisability of this depends on the circumstances of the parties. It is possible to refer any disagreement to alternative dispute resolution (ADR). In

Denmark ADR is covered by the Arbitrations Act 1973 (*Lov om Voldgift*). There are differing views as to the effectiveness of ADR and we refer to Chapter 2 of this book.

(20) Should the agent be insured?

As to product liability, the situation is similar to that set out with regard to the United Kingdom.

In general, the agent has a duty to take care of the goods belonging to the principal in the agent's possession (*cf.* section 7 of HAGL). If the agent neglects his duties the principal may be entitled to damages under section 6 of HAGL.

Normally the agent insures the goods against fire and theft. An agency agreement should contain provisions making clear the parties' respective insurance obligations.

(21) What about the liability of the principal? Does having an agent in a country constitute carrying on a business in that country?

In general this will depend on the internal law of that country. The Danish position is determined in accordance with article 5(5) of the Brussels Convention, which states that a person domiciled in one contracting State may, in another contracting State, be sued as regards disputes arising out of the operations of a branch, agency or other establishment, in the courts for the place in which the branch, agency or other establishment is situated.

Instructing an agent in Denmark may constitute a branch of the principal with the subsequent repercussion that the principal may be deemed present in Denmark and therefore subject to the jurisdiction of the Danish court (*filial*).

The European Court of Justice has decided that the term "operations" must be given an independent definition so that each contracting State may interpret the term individually.

The central issue is whether the activities in the other country are of a relatively permanent character which includes the authority to execute contracts on behalf of the principal. If this is the case, then the principal will be carrying on business in that country. However, the rules are complex, and it is outside the scope of this chapter to deal with these in detail, but it should be noted that if the agent does not have a power of attorney to bind the principal and sign contracts in the name of the principal, then the principal will not generally be regarded as having a place of business in Denmark.

(22) What about bad debts? Must a principal pay the agent his commission, even when he has not been paid himself?

The provisions relating to the agent's entitlement to commission are covered by sections 8–15 of HAGL, which are mandatory.

The starting point is that the agent is responsible for negotiating sale and purchase agreements of relevant products with reliable third parties.

Under section 14 the agent's right to commission is lost if it is established that the contract between the principal and the third party will not be executed, and that fact is due to a reason for which the principal is not to blame.

Any commission which the agent has already received in this respect shall be repaid if the right to it is lost. Thus the agent carries the risk for the execution of the agreement and will lose his rights to commission when the agreement subsequently cannot be fulfilled due to a third party's insolvency or inability to pay.

CONTENTS OF CHAPTER 6

Finland

6. FINLAND

Alex Roney, Legal Counsellor of the London Chamber of Commerce and Industry

(1) Introduction

Finland joined the European Community on 1 January 1995 but had been preparing for some time for the harmonisation of its legislation so as to comply with EC provisions. Although I am not a Finnish lawyer, I have had the valuable assistance in drafting this chapter of the equivalent of the Department of Trade and Industry in Finland, of Mr Timo Vuori who is the Legal Counsellor at the Central Chamber of Commerce of Finland in Helsinki, and indeed Nils-Henrik Wasonius of Seppala and Wasionius Oy-Helsinki, who is a Finnish lawyer. My grateful thanks to them all.

(2) Preliminary considerations when appointing a commercial agent or representative

In Finland trade in goods and services is divided into:

- "regulated trade", which concerns trade involving specified health or safety hazards or financial risks, including manufacture and sale of medical substances and dangerous chemicals, besides banking, insurance and mining activities; and
- "free trade", which generally covers everything else which is not regulated.

The National Board of Patents and Registration keeps a trade register and those carrying on a free trade are normally required to register there, although permission to trade as such is not normally required.

For regulated trade areas, notification of intention to trade must be given to, and a trading permit obtained from, the relevant authorities.

Business people establishing a company in Finland do not need any extra permits, provided they are natural persons, resident in the EU/EEA. If a trade name is used, then it must be registered. There are various provisions relating to the setting up of companies, branches, representation, or partnerships, but other than to draw attention to them, they are beyond the scope of this book. However, it may be useful to note that restaurant and catering services used to be, but are no longer, included in the regulated areas, which means that a special business licence is no longer needed when a restaurant is being established in Finland, although the restaurant premises must be approved by the local public health authorities. Similarly, a special licence to establish a travel agency is also no longer required, but entrepreneurs who wish to act as travel agents in Finland must instead notify the Finnish Consumer Office.

(3) What is the law in Finland which governs commercial agency?

The law in Finland which now governs commercial agency is the Act on Commercial Representatives and Salesmen (8 May 1992/417) ("1992 Act"). The title in Finnish is "*Laki kauppaedustajista ja myyntimiehista*", and in Swedish is "*Lag Om handelsrepresentanter och forsaljare*". This Act entered into force on 1 November 1992, for new agency or "representation" contracts within its scope; but relevant agreements which were entered into before that date have only been governed by this Act since 1 January 1994. Before that date such contracts were governed by the previous provisions such as the Act on Commercial Representatives (30 May 1975) unless otherwise agreed. Thus the Finnish legislation has been harmonised with the EC Directive on the co-ordination of the laws of the Member States relating to Self-employed Commercial Agents of 18 December 1986 (86/653/EEC) (OJ 1986 L 382/17) for some time.

(4) What forms of commercial agency exist in Finland?

Under the 1992 Act there are three different kinds of commercial agency in Finland:

- commercial representatives;
- salesmen as independent entrepreneurs;
- salesmen as employees.

Section 1 of the 1992 Act defines the term "commercial agent" as including both commercial representatives and also salesmen as independent entrepreneurs; and so governs the relationships between a principal and commercial representatives, or a principal and salesmen as independent entrepreneurs.

Salesmen as employees are mainly governed by the Employment Contracts Act (30 May 1970/320), although some provisions of the 1992 Act on representatives and salesmen also govern salesmen as employees.

(5) What is the definition of "commercial" agent in Finland?

A commercial agent is defined in section 1 of the 1992 Act as a trader who has undertaken in an agency agreement concluded with another person, the principal, to promote, on a continuing basis, on his behalf the sale or purchase of goods by procuring offers for the principal or concluding sales or purchase contracts in his name.

(6) What is the definition of a "salesman"?

A salesman is also defined in the 1992 Act, but as an employee who under a contract concluded with the employer, has undertaken to promote the sale of goods in the manner referred to in section 1 on behalf of the employer by travelling from place to place or by visiting clients at the place where the business of the employer is located. A salesman does not carry the goods to be sold with him in Finland.

(7) What is the difference between a distributor and a commercial agent in Finland?

The differences are similar to those listed in respect of English law, and the same considerations apply when deciding whether to appoint a distributor or a commercial agent in Finland as in England.

(8) How does a franchise agreement differ from a distribution agreement?

Here too, the situation is similar to that referred to in respect of United Kingdom legislation.

(9) Must an agency agreement be in writing to be valid?

No, the agency contract may be oral or written, but it is advisable to have a written contract.

Section 3 of the 1992 Act provides that an agency agreement and amendments thereto must be in writing if either of the parties so requests; and terms of an agreement which seek to limit these rights of the parties are invalid. However, although commercial agents are generally not subject to any special registration requirements, it is best to check for any special requirements for foreign enterprises.

(10) What should be included in a commercial agency agreement in Finland?

All the matters referred to below "listed rights and duties" should be included in the contract, to ensure that both parties understand their rights, duties, authority and liabilities. It is urged that the general advice given at the beginning of this book is also relevant to commercial agency agreements in Finland.

It should be noted that parties may not choose a foreign law in order to avoid the mandatory provisions of Finnish commercial agency legislation.

(11) What are the rights and duties of an agent under an agency agreement?

Under section 5 of the 1992 Act the agent has a duty to:

- look after his principal's interests with proper care;
- act dutifully and honestly towards him;
- follow the principal's reasonable instructions to him;
- inform the principal on matters which may be of significance so far as concern his agency functions;
- inform the principal without undue delay of:
  - offers requiring the principal's approval; and
  - contracts concluded in the principal's name.

These duties may not be derogated from and terms of an agreement which seek to do so are invalid.

It should be remembered that the agent is also automatically obliged to investigate the solvency of customers in Finland, and to notify the principal of any matters which might be of significance in respect of his agency activities.

(12) Does an agent have the right to act for more than one principal?

Yes, and he may do so, provided that this does not conflict with his principal duties under the agency contract under section 5 of the 1992 Act listed in (11) above. Whether in fact there is or would be a conflict must be decided on a case-by-case basis.

(13) What about confidentiality?

The agent must not, either during the period of validity of the agreement, nor after its expiry, use for his own benefit or disclose to others business or trade secrets of the principal which have been entrusted to him, or which have otherwise come to his knowledge, if by doing so he would be acting contrary to good commercial practice (section 7 of the 1992 Act).

(14) What about agents with extra duties?

An agent may be made responsible for collecting payment for some or all goods. If so he must keep such goods separate, and is entitled to special (albeit reasonable) remuneration for doing this, unless his commission is intended to include this duty. If his duty goes further, and he is responsible to the principal for compliance by the third party with the contract, including collection of payment and bad debts, there is a *del credere* agency; and the commitment which may be for one or all contracts must be in writing; and the agent has a right to special reasonable commission to remunerate him for taking on this extra liability.

(15) What about the duties of the principal towards the agent?

The principal has a duty to:

- act dutifully and honestly towards his commercial agent;
- provide the agent with the necessary information and materials such as samples, brochures, price lists and models to enable him to perform his duties;
- notify him of matters which may be of significance to the agent with regard to his agency function;
- inform the agent of the acceptance/rejection of offers transmitted through the agent;
- inform the agent of contracts made on his behalf by the agent, even if the agent had no right to conclude such contracts;
- inform the agent of non-fulfilment, or non-performance of a contract negotiated or concluded by the agent; and
- inform the agent if it becomes apparent to the principal that the agent's activities are likely to be on a smaller scale than that envisaged.

Any terms in an agreement which seek to derogate from these primary duties are invalid.

(16) When does the agent have a right to commission?

Under section 10 of the 1992 Act, the agent is entitled to commission on contracts concluded during the validity of the agency agreement if the contract was:

- effected with his assistance; or
- concluded with a third party for whom the commercial agent previously obtained customers for similar contracts; or
- concluded in a certain area, or from among a certain circle of customers which has been allocated to the commercial agent.

Under section 11 the agent is entitled to commission on contracts concluded after the termination of an agency agreement if they would have come within section 10, but the third party's offer reached the principal after termination of the agency contract, or the conclusion of the contract was within a reasonable time of termination and had been concluded largely as a result of the agent's efforts.

If a new agent has taken over the previous agent's area, he will not necessarily be entitled to commission on such contracts, although it might in some circumstances be fair to divide the commission between the two agents.

(17) When does the agent become entitled to be paid his commission?

He becomes entitled to commission when:

- the principal has met his payment obligation under a contract concluded between him and a third party; or
- the principal should have met the above payment obligation; or
- the third party has met his payment obligation under the above contract.

Commission due is payable within one calendar month of the end of the calendar month in which the agent acquires the right to commission.

A contract term providing that the commission shall be paid to the commercial agent later than within one month of the end of the calendar quarter during which the right to commission arose, is not binding on the commercial agent.

If the right to commission is forfeited after payment, either wholly or in part, then it must be paid back to the principal if the principal so requests. If, for example, the principal agrees with the third party without the agent's consent, to change or cancel the contract, then, if for this reason the third party does not fully or partly complete the contract, the agent's right to commission may not be affected, and he may retain his right to full commission.

(18) How is the amount of commission calculated?

This should be set out in the agreement. If it is not, then it will be at the rate that is normal in the agent's place of business for similar equivalent activities. If there is no comparable equivalent, then he will be entitled to reasonable commission taking into account all the circumstances.

It should be noted that the commission is calculated on the purchase price paid by the buyer and in calculating this carriage, packaging, discounts and other costs or duties are not deducted, unless it has been agreed with the buyer that these must be separately specified in the invoice. Reasonable special remuneration is payable to *del credere* agents (see (14) above) who undertake extra liabilities. Costs incurred in connection with the agent's duties are usually included in the commission, but special costs may be paid in some circumstances.

(19) Is the agent entitled to a written statement of commission due from the principal?

Yes. Generally he is entitled to receive this monthly. However the parties may agree that statements be made quarterly, within one month from the end of the quarter in which the right to commission arose. The agent may also check the statement against relevant extracts of the principal's accounts which must be made available to him. If the principal refuses to give the agent this information, or he has reasonable grounds to think it is not correct, then an auditor approved by a Chamber of Commerce ("an HTM Auditor"), or the Central Chamber of Commerce ("a KHT Auditor") may be appointed by the agent. The auditor is empowered to check the principal's accounts to the extent necessary to establish the amount of commission to which the agent is entitled. Any contractual stipulation seeking to restrict the agent's rights in this regard is invalid.

The agent has a right of lien over, and so may retain documents, samples, models or goods belonging to the principal in his possession because of his agency duties if the collection of his commission is at risk, until the principal has paid him, or given him security for the amounts due. Equally when the agent has a duty to collect payments for the principal, he should keep these funds separately.

(20) What about bad debts or cancellation of the contract?

Under section 13 of the 1992 Act, if a principal without the agent's consent cancels or alters the terms of a relevant contract, so that the third party's payment obligation is ceased wholly or in part, this does not affect the agent's right to commission. However, if a relevant contract lapses without being fulfilled, and this is not due to the fault of the principal, or by an agreement with him as above, then the agent may lose his commission. If there is part performance only of the contract in these circumstances, then the agent may be entitled to proportionate commission. Thus although the agent cannot waive his rights under this section in advance, he can sometimes totally or partly lose his right to commission.

(21) What about special compensation?

This may be payable to cover costs of necessary activities by the agent to ensure or enable the proper execution of the agency or representation agreement, but is not normally paid for ordinary general costs which the commercial agent would normally incur.

(22) What are the provisions relating to termination of agency contracts?

Section 22 of the 1992 Act states that:

- a fixed term contract terminates on expiry of the fixed term;
- if the fixed term contract states that it shall only terminate if notice is given before the end of the fixed term, and no such notice is given, then the agreement continues until further notice. Equally if a fixed term contract is ended, and the parties continue without any explicit agreement, then the agreement continues to be treated as valid;
- an agency which is in force and continuing may be terminated by giving notice to terminate at the end of the notice period; and the statutory minimum periods for notice are one month for contracts up to one year.

  Thereafter the notice is extended by one month for each commenced year of contract (section 23), up to a maximum of six months. It should be noted that parties can agree to a three month notice period even for agreements which have been in force over three years. Longer notice periods may be agreed by the parties, but the period provided for when the principal terminates must not be shorter than that required to be given by the agent. If it is, then that is not binding on the agent.

  It is important to note that the notice period is calculated from the end of the calendar month in which it was given to the other party. Any agreement in advance of termination that the termination period shall be shorter than the statutory periods, is not binding on the parties (section 23);

- bankruptcy of the parties: if either party goes bankrupt, the agency agreement is deemed to have expired at the date of lodgement of the petition in bankruptcy with the court;
- immediate termination for good reason under section 25. Even when the commercial agency agreement is for a fixed term and with specified notice periods, either party may terminate it immediately for good reasons. Examples are negligence of the other party or some behaviour or action the result of which is that the first party cannot in fairness be required to continue the agreement. The section sets out the circumstances in which the first party (the party terminating) acquires an acceptable reason for cancellation:
    - if the other party fundamentally misled him when the agreement was concluded;
    - if the other party refused a request for the agreement to be in writing (under provisions of section 3 of the 1992 Act);
    - when the other party is guilty of an action which seriously harms the interests of the first party, or otherwise caused a loss of trust of the first party; or
    - when the other party has failed to meet the obligations under the agency contract in a material respect, *i.e.*, has failed in an essential matter to carry out his duties under the agency agreement.

However it should be noted that the right to terminate can be lost, and shall lapse if it is not used without undue delay after:

- learning of any of these grounds for cancellation; or
- — if the actions constituting the grounds are continuing – after they stop.

It should be noted that where the agency contract lapses owing to the death or bankruptcy of the commercial agent, any compensation due is payable to the deceased's estate, or bankrupt's estate, which may still claim damages for breach of the agreement by the principal if this is appropriate in the circumstances.

Thus either party to a commercial agency agreement can cancel an agreement early, but if he does not have any proper grounds as set out in section 25 explained above, then he is obliged to compensate the other party for their resulting loss. However in these circumstances an agent cannot renounce his right to compensation before the agency agreement is terminated.

(23) When is compensation payable?

Either a principal or a commercial agent who has acted in breach of an agency agreement, or has deliberately or negligently failed to meet the obligations laid down in the 1992 Act or his duties under the agency agreement so as to come within section 25; or the acts complained of have arisen through his bankruptcy, shall be liable to compensate the other party for any loss thereby occasioned. However, an agent or principal intending to claim compensation must without undue delay after learning of the grounds for action, inform the other party of his intention, and if he does not do so, he loses his right to compensation, unless the other party has acted dishonestly, or has through gross negligence caused the intending claimant substantial loss.

Thus either party can terminate early, even if he does not have a due cause described in section 25, but he shall have to compensate the other party for any damage occasioned by his doing so. However, it must be remembered that a waiver by the commercial agent or representative of his right to compensation before the agency agreement is terminated is not binding on the agent.

(24) What is the basis of the indemnity payable on termination?

Payment of an indemnity should be distinguished from payment of compensation. Under section 28 of the 1992 Act, the agent is entitled to an indemnity on termination of a representation contract if and to the extent that:

- he has increased the sales significantly, or has obtained new customers to the considerable benefit of the principal on or after termination; and
- the indemnity is reasonable taking into account all the surrounding circumstances and the commission lost to the agent.

It should be noted that clauses which seek to limit the right to compensation under section 28 before the expiry of the agency agreement are invalid. The indemnity should be no more than the remuneration of the agent for one year, calculated on the basis of his average remuneration over the preceding five years, for agreements subsisting five years or longer, or over the period of the agency (if less than five years). Payment of an indemnity does not prevent a commercial agent, or his estate, from claiming damages for breach of the agency agreement by the principal, but will be taken into account in settling claims.

(25) When is the commercial agent unable to claim an indemnity?

The agent is not entitled to claim an indemnity if:

- the principal has given notice to terminate, or has cancelled the agreement on the grounds of negligence or improper behaviour of the commercial agent; or
- the commercial agent has given notice to terminate or cancel the commercial agency agreement; or
- the commercial agent has assigned his rights and obligations under the commercial agency agreement to another person with the consent of the principal.

The exceptions to this are where the agent has terminated by giving notice, but this is for reasonable cause, for example due to the acts of the principal, or his own failing health. In these circumstances the agent may be entitled to an indemnity, but he will forfeit his right to it if he does not inform the principal within a year of the termination of the representation contract of his intention to claim.

(26) What about the principal's rights on premature termination of the agency agreement?

The agent, or his estate, or trustees in bankruptcy are then obliged to take such steps as are necessary to protect the principal or his estate from loss, provided that this does not cause him significant cost or disadvantage (section 30 of the 1992 Act).

(27) What restrictions can be imposed on the agent's activities following termination?

The agent may be restricted following termination but such clauses must be in writing, limited to the area or range of customers assigned to the agent, and concern goods similar to those the subject of the agency agreement.

If a restriction is for longer than two years, then the clause is not binding on the agent after the first two years.

(28) What about the principal's liability for unauthorised contracts concluded by the agent?

Section 32 of the 1992 Act specifically states that the agent can only conclude contracts on behalf of the principal if he is authorised to do so. However, if the agent has been supplied with forms with the principal's name printed on them, which are completed by the agent, then the resulting contracts are presumed to be authorised, and so binding on the principal.

Equally, if the principal, after learning of an unauthorised contract does not expressly and without delay notify the third party of his intention not to honour it, then he shall be bound by it. The same applies to offers received by the agent, *i.e.* if the principal does not wish to accept such an offer, he must inform the offeror without undue delay after learning of it; and if he fails to do so, he is regarded as having accepted the offer. The section specifically states that this shall not apply if the offeror and the commercial agent have previously agreed otherwise.

(29) What about the collection of payments or alteration of payment terms?

As stated at (14) above, the commercial agent does not generally have authority to collect payment, so even if he does have the authority to make contracts on behalf of the principal, he may not change the terms of those contracts, or credit periods set out, or give price reductions. However, if he does do something in excess of his competence or authorisation, then the principal must, as for unauthorised contracts, notify the third party without delay of his intentions not to accept it, and if he does not, he will be bound by the agent's actions.

(30) What about liability for defective products?

Under section 38 of the 1992 Act commercial agents may receive on behalf of the principal notices concerning the contract, defects in relevant goods, or delay in their delivery, but they may not make any decisions relating to such notices which are binding on the principal without specific authorisation.

In Finland primary liability for defective products lies with the manufacturer or the distributor in Finland of the goods concerned. Generally an agent is not liable for damage caused by the products he sells on behalf of his principal, and a commercial agent is only responsible for defects if he has an extended role under the agency contract, and is the named importer of the product. In Finland, the law relating to product liability in general is governed by the Act on Product Liability (*Tuotevastuulaki* 17 August 1990/694) ("1990 Act") which imposes liability on manufacturers or producers of a product causing damage within the scope of the Act. Under section 5 of the 1990 Act, an importer may be made liable for damage caused by a defective product that he has, in the course of his business, put into circulation in Finland. To explain further, if an agent could be said to be acting as importer of the product, by holding goods in his own warehouse, for example, then he could be held liable, and so would be wise to carry product liability insurance, besides covering this aspect of his liability in his contract with his principal.

(31) What is the scope of the 1990 Finnish Law on Product Liability?

The term "product" for this purpose does not extend to buildings, but does include the component parts of products. The 1990 Act concerns compensation for damage caused by the product in terms of personal injuries, or damage to property which at the time of the damage was primarily in private use.

(32) What is excluded from the scope of the 1990 Act?

Other than buildings, pharmaceuticals are the most notable exception, these being governed by specialist legislation. However the operation of the Act is also excluded where the damage:

- is caused to the product itself; and
- can attract compensation under separate legislation, for example the Road Accident or Employees Accident Insurance Acts.

Compensation under the 1990 Act is based on the premise that the goods, at the time they were put into circulation, did not provide the safety which could reasonably be expected, taking into account all the surrounding circumstances, such as likely use, or instructions provided.

It should be noted that contracts seeking to exclude future liability for defective products are void, and compensation granted may be in addition to other rights in respect of damages.

Further details concerning product liability are beyond the scope of this book.

(33) What about jurisdiction and arbitration clauses?

Finland has signed the Convention of 16 September 1988 on the Jurisdiction and Enforcement of Judgements in Civil and Commercial matters ("the Lugano Convention") which is the sister convention to the Brussels Convention 1968.

It is a matter for the parties to decide whether they should include a clause which refers disputes arising under the agency agreement to arbitration.

CONTENTS OF CHAPTER 7

France

7. FRANCE

Antoine Lemétais and Christophe Héry, Chaney Connor Lemétais & Associés, Paris

(1) What are the different forms of representation available for an enterprise in France?

Distribution of goods and/or services can be achieved by various means. There are (1) non-independent intermediaries; (2) independent intermediaries (commission agents and commercial agents); and (3) distributors.

The purpose of this chapter is to explain the provisions relating to one particular type of independent intermediary: the commercial agent.

However, as to non-independent intermediaries, the company or enterprise may appoint (i) a special employee (such as an "*attaché commercial*") whose activity is to promote only the goods and services of the company or enterprise; or (ii) a salaried business agent ("*voyageur représentant placier*"/VRP) whose activity is mainly to find new clients located within a specific territory.

As regards independent intermediaries, a company may use various types. Thus, a company may appoint a broker ("*Courtier*" or "*Apporteur d'affaires*"), a commission agent ("*Commissionnaire*") or a commercial agent ("*agent commercial*").

The appointment of a broker is the simplest way to conduct business, since the broker has only to put two or more persons or companies into contact. He is a go-between. His activity is not closely regulated except in some specific areas such as financial investments, advertising or cereals. Due to the recent 1991 restrictive regulations on commercial agency (see (2) below), this kind of representation may be used increasingly in the future.

The commission agent's status initially seems quite similar to that of a commercial agent. The commission agent acts for a principal. However, the main difference is that the commission agent appears *vis-à-vis* third parties as an independent enterprise, while it is clearly indicated in the contract executed between the commission agent and his principal that the commission agent acts in his own name but on behalf of his principal. This kind of commission agency contract is not within the scope of the new French regulation on commercial agency since it is an undisclosed agency agreement, and so is also excluded from the scope of the 1986 EEC Directive (see (2) below).

The commercial agent acts in the name of and on behalf of his principal.

As regards independent distributors, a company may set up exclusive or non-exclusive distributorship or franchise networks. A distributor is an independent dealer who buys goods (or services under a franchise contract) from a supplier and resells them on his own account.

The distributorship agreement should in particular contain terms and conditions concerning:

- the purchase prices (price list, condition and form of modification of such list);
- the terms of payment (means of payment, currency, place of effective payment, penalty for delays);
- the duration of the contract (definite term contract or indefinite term contract, consequences of non-renewal and/or termination of the contract);
- the non-competition clause (the distributor usually agrees not to distribute competing products);
- advertising and use of the supplier's trade marks;
- warranties of the products (for default and for hidden flaws);
- territorial exclusivity; and
- minimum quotas (quantities and sanctions of failure to meet such minimum quantities).

In case of cancellation or failure to renew the distributorship agreement, neither party is entitled to ask for an indemnity from the other party unless otherwise provided for in the contract. However, the courts tend to allow damages for a distributor when the cancellation or the failure to renew by a supplier is considered to be wrongful or related to actions which may be considered to be unfair competition acts.

The main advantage for a foreign company (supplier) in appointing an independent distributor is that it does not then bear the financial and commercial risks of conducting business abroad.

(2) What is the regulation applying to commercial agency in France?

The commercial agency relationship is governed by the 28 June 1991 law which replaces the 23 December 1958 Decree on commercial agents ("the 1958 Decree"). The law dated 28 June 1991 ("the 1991 Law") implements the EEC Directive relating to the co-ordination of the laws of Members States concerning Self-employed Commercial Agents dated 18 December 1986 (86/653/EEC) ("the 1986 Directive") in France.

However, in spite of the fact that the 1991 Law did not substantially modify the rules in force since 1958, the French regulation relating to commercial agents appears nowadays unclear due to discrepancies between the wording and the aim of the 1991 Law and the 1986 Directive.

Indeed, between 28 June 1991 and 31 December 1993, two different statutory provisions co-existed: the 1958 Decree was still applicable to agency agreements in force at the date upon which the 1991 Law was brought into force, while the 1991 Law dealt with all new agency agreements executed on or after 28 June 1991. However, since 1 January 1994, the 1991 Law has governed all commercial agency agreements, irrespective of the date of the agreement.

A further cause of current uncertainty arises from the fact that the wording of the 1991 Law is not the exact implementation of the 1986 Directive and has therefore generated controversial commentaries and analysis as to its interpretation and effect.

Moreover, lack of caselaw relating to the 1991 Law further hinders foreign (and local) enterprises in their attempts to appraise precisely the risks and possible consequences and costs of appointing a commercial agent in France.

(3) What is a "commercial agent" in France?

The 1991 Law, as well as the 1958 Decree, defines a commercial agent as an independent representative whose habitual activity is to negotiate and, possibly, conclude contracts in the name of and on behalf of, manufacturers, producers, traders, or, should the case occur, other commercial agents.

Under the 1991 Law, the commercial agent may negotiate and conclude contracts of sale and/or purchase of goods or services while the 1986 Directive only refers to sale and purchase of goods. In any case, a commercial agent operating with regard to services is entitled to the protection of the 1991 Law.

Agents dealing in insurance, travel organisation, real estate and advertising are not regarded as commercial agents. Moreover, a commercial agent should act as a professional and not in a simple or limited number of deals.

The 1991 Law states that a commercial agent can be an individual or a company. Both must be registered with a special register ("*Registre Spécial des Agents Commerciaux*"). It should be noted that neither an Economic Interest Grouping ("EIG"), nor a European Economic Interest Grouping ("EEIG") can be registered in this way and so cannot act as a commercial agent in France.

(4) The registration of the commercial agent

Before starting his agency activity in France, any commercial agent whatever his nationality, should be registered with the special register held by the Registry of the Commercial Court ("*Tribunal de Commerce*") of the jurisdiction where the commercial agent is to be principally established.

A commercial agent not acting in France does not have to comply with this duty, but is still entitled to the benefit of the provisions of the 1991 Law in cases where French law is applicable due to a choice of law clause.

Despite a controversial debate between authors, it is generally agreed that the absence of registration of the commercial agent established and conducting a business in France does not deprive him of the benefit of the provisions of the 1991 Law. Hence, the absence of registration of a commercial agent established or incorporated in a foreign country but having business in France does not deprive him of the benefit of the provisions of the 1991 Law.

(5) What should be included in a contract with a commercial agent?

Notwithstanding the fact that there is no legal requirement for an agency contract to be in writing, it is better for the agency agreement to be in writing. Furthermore, one party cannot refuse to establish such an agency agreement in written form at the request of the other party. It should be added that the lack of written form does not exclude the application of the provisions of the 1991 Law as it is provided for in the 1986 Directive.

In all cases, it is strongly urged that precise details should be set out of all the duties and rights of each party. This is particularly important when both parties, or one of them, wants to derogate from one or more non-mandatory provisions.

The main clauses which should be included in an agency agreement are:

- the purpose of the contract;
- the definition of the territory;
- the granting of exclusivity or the absence of such exclusivity;
- the date of coming into force of the agreement;
- the duration of the contract and its termination (fixed term or indefinite period, notice period, consequences of termination);
- the duties of the principal (payment of commission, good faith);
- the duties of the agent (reporting, good faith);
- the co-operation between parties (provision of sample materials and literature, information);
- the control by the principal of the activities of the commercial agent (reports etc);
- the powers of the commercial agent towards third parties;
- the commission due to the agent (computation, payment, currency, means of payment etc);
- the right to assign the whole or part of the agreement or to empower a sub-agent;
- the definition and the limitation of a non-competition clause during the performance of the contract and after its termination;
- the applicable law; and
- the designation of the court (State Court or Arbitration Court) having exclusive jurisdiction over the parties.

(6) What are the duties of the principal?

The 1991 Law provides that the principal must perform the contract in good faith and put the agent in a position to perform the contract effectively. In this respect, the principal must provide the agent with any relevant documentation, price lists, surveys, samples, etc.

This duty of loyalty and faithfulness also requires the principal to inform the agent, within a reasonable period, of his refusal or non-performance or performance with delay of any transaction that the agent has initiated for him.

Due to the specific nature of the ground (good faith) of these duties they cannot be modified or excluded by contract.

The principal is under a duty to pay to the agent the commission agreed according the conditions mentioned in (8) below.

(7) To what extent is the principal responsible for the acts of his agent?

The French Civil code (Article 1998) provides that the principal is liable towards third parties for any act of his commercial agent bearing in mind that these acts must be performed within the scope and limitation stated in the agency agreement.

Thus, the commercial agent is not personally liable for the acts made in the name, and on behalf of, the principal within his agency agreement.

However, the principal may be held liable towards third parties even for acts or commitments exceeding the defined scope or limitations of the agency agreement. Indeed, this liability is recognised where there has been a fair reliance by the third parties on what is, or appears to be, within the scope of the agreement concerned.

Thus, it is highly recommended that enterprises dealing with a French commercial agent, or with a commercial agent under a contract submitted to French law, should set out precisely the powers and the scope of activities of the commercial agent. Moreover, the principal may impose on the commercial agent a specific clause ("*clause pénale*") stating that in case of actions brought by third parties, the principal will have a right to claim damages (which cover penalty and liquidated damages) against the agent, should these actions be based on faults of the commercial agent.

(8) When is the agent entitled to commission?

The agent is normally entitled to a commission. The payment of the commission is the main duty of the principal.

This commission is based on all commercial transactions concluded during the performance of the commercial agency (and after its termination), which result from the commercial agent's activities. Notwithstanding the fact that most of the time the commission varies directly with the number and the value of the transactions, the parties may agree that the agent will receive a lump sum (for any and all transactions or only specific ones). The parties may also mix the two systems according to one or more criteria (amount or type of the transaction, type or place of location of the client, etc)

The 1991 Law sets out mandatory rules relating to the acquisition and the payment of the commission:

- The commission accrues as soon as the principal executes, or should have executed, the transaction or at least as soon as the third party has performed the transaction or should have performed it (had the principal not been at fault).
- The commission must be paid to the commercial agent no later than the last day of the month following the quarter during which the said commission accrued.
- The agent loses his right to a commission when it becomes clear that the contract between the principal and the third party will not be performed, unless the non-performance results from the act or omission of, or is otherwise the fault of, the principal. Then, in the case of non-performance, the principal may be entitled to claim for reimbursement of any corresponding commission which may already have been paid to the commercial agent.

The principle of good faith and co-operation between parties imposes on the principal a duty of communication of any accounting evidence ("*documents comptables*") to the commercial agent in order to enable him to check the amount of the commission to be paid. This duty cannot be excluded by contract.

In principle, the commission to be paid to the commercial agent covers both his remuneration relating to his activities under the agency agreement and to the expenses incurred in connection with that agreement. However, the parties may agree upon a separate reimbursement of the expenses.

Finally, the principal may compensate the commercial agent for specific services such as:

- *del credere* duty (see (9) below); and
- consignee duty (*contractus aestimatorius*) (see (9) below).

(9) What are the duties of a commercial agent towards his principal?

As mentioned in (8) above, the commercial agent must perform his duties in good faith.

He must therefore comply with the terms of the agreement and the written or oral instructions given by the principal. Moreover the commercial agent has to use his best efforts to negotiate, promote, communicate and, when necessary, conclude any transactions with third parties.

As a representative (article 1993 of the French Civil Code; 1986 Directive) the commercial agent must report on his activity. This duty of information is not, obviously, a weekly duty (as is the one imposed on the salaried business agent ("VRP")) but is a regular and constant duty of information.

In addition, the principle of good faith set out in the 1991 Law imposes on the commercial agent a duty of transmission to the principal of any information which may be useful for the latter to enable him to perform the agency agreement.

As far as specific and optional duties are concerned, the principal may also impose the following clauses:

- The principal may prohibit the commercial agent from representing other principals or only principals supplying competing products or services.
- The commercial agent may be also appointed as a *del credere* ("*clause de ducroire*") agent. In this case, the commercial agent guarantees that ultimately the sums owed by the customer to the principal will be correctly paid. In case of the absence of full payment from the customer, the agent must indemnify the principal totally or partly as appropriate.
- The commercial agent may also be appointed by the principal as a consignee ("*clause de consignation*"). According to this consignment clause, the principal empowers the commercial agent to hold in custody, control, and deliver directly the products of the principal to the customers. In that case, the commercial agent is entitled to specific remuneration calculated on the basis of the value or the tonnage of the goods he holds in custody.
- The parties may also agree upon a minimum quota clause according to which the principal imposes a target on the commercial agent. It is important that such a clause should be carefully drafted.

It should be noted that the non-performance of the minimum quotas by the commercial agent is not *per se* a ground for the principal to terminate the contract without compensation. Indeed, under French caselaw, the principal has to prove that the non-performance is based upon a serious fault of the commercial agent in order to avoid compensation to the commercial agent.

In any case, a minimum quotas clause allows the principal to control directly the activity of the commercial agent. Therefore it is highly recommended to insert such a clause.

(10) How and when can a fixed term agreement be terminated?

The conditions of termination of a fixed term agreement depend on the wording of the relevant clause, so it is important that it is properly drafted:

- The agreement may terminate automatically on the date or at the end of the period mentioned in the agreement for a fixed term. The parties would then have to conclude a new agreement in order to extend its term.
- The agreement may also state that the contract will be automatically renewed at the end of the fixed period unless one of the parties has notified to the other its decision to terminate that agreement at the agreed and foreseen date.
- However, one of the parties may terminate the contract prior to the normal expiration of the term of that contract. In this case, the other party is entitled to claim damages unless, in case of termination by the commercial agent, the commercial agent can prove that such termination is due to age, invalidity or illness.

The 1991 Law provides that a fixed term contract which is renewed is automatically transformed into an indefinite period agreement. However this conclusion is also highly questionable since the terms and the aim of the legal provision applicable are not precise:

- Thus, most commentators suggest that the provision infers that any and all fixed term agreements which are renewed, whatever the conditions of such renewal (*i.e.* in writing and executing a new one or merely by being allowed to run on), become indefinite period agreements.
- However it should be noted that there is an alternative interpretation of this specific clause in the 1991 Law: *i.e.*, that it is only applicable to fixed term contracts the provisions of which state that the contract

should normally and automatically come to an end on an agreed date, but where the contract is in fact extended by the parties without formal decision or specific provisions.

(11) How and when can a party terminate an indefinite period agreement?

Both parties may terminate an indefinite period agency contract at any time. However, the parties must respect the following periods of notice. These notice periods vary according to the length of the agreement:

- one month for termination during the first year of contract;
- two months for termination during the second year of contract; and
- three months for termination occurring after the second year of contract.

The parties may mutually agree upon different notice periods provided that these are not longer for the commercial agent than those imposed by the 1991 Law.

Should the termination be accompanied by acts which constitute unfair competition (for example running down) specific damages can be allotted to the other party (*i.e.* victim of these acts).

(12) What are the financial consequences of the termination of an agency agreement?

Under the 1958 Decree, a commercial agent was only entitled to claim for compensation where there was termination of an indefinite period agreement or anticipatory termination of a fixed term contract. There is no doubt that where there was normal termination on the agreed date of a fixed term agreement, no compensation was payable to the commercial agent, even though the fixed term agreement had been renewed several times.

Under the 1991 Law, the position is uncertain. Indeed article 12 of the 1991 Law provides that in case of "cessation" of the agency relationship with the principal, the agent is entitled to have an indemnity in consideration of the loss he has incurred. The question is then as to whether or not these provisions, which are quite unclear from a legal point of view, should be broadly or narrowly interpreted.

In general article 12 of the 1991 Law is construed as establishing a right to compensation for any type of agency agreement, whatever the cause of the termination (fixed term or termination of an indefinite period agreement). However, other authors suggest that there are grounds to say that through a comparative study of article 12 of the 1991 Law and article 17 of the 1986 Directive (both relating to indemnities), that article 12 of the 1991 Law does not cover termination by natural lapse of time of an agency agreement executed for a fixed period of time.

Since French caselaw is likely to clarify this question in the near future, it is advisable to ask for specialist advice when drafting an agency agreement.

In principle, the indemnity will not exceed the reasonable loss incurred by the agent. Usually, under French caselaw, courts assess such an indemnity as being equivalent to three years of commission calculated on the average of the last four or five years.

Finally, and in all cases, the agent is entitled to an indemnity when the contract is terminated by reason of the death of the agent.

It is strongly recommended that specific legal advice be sought on this question from a lawyer who has specialised in French law when drafting the relevant clauses.

(13) Which courts may have jurisdiction over the parties?

Under the EEC Convention of 27 September 1968 on Jurisdiction and Enforcement of Judgments in Civil and Commercial Matters, modified in 1978 and in 1989 ("the Brussels Convention"), the parties may determine in the contract the court to which any litigation relating to the agency contract will be submitted. It is strongly urged that the country, the town and the type of court having exclusive jurisdiction over the parties be set out in the contract in order to comply with the provisions of article 17 of the Brussels Convention.

Should the parties omit to choose a court, the one having jurisdiction will be determined by reference to the provisions of the Brussels Convention. It is outside the scope of this chapter to detail the provisions of the whole system set out in the Brussels Convention, but it is important to bear in mind that:

- In all cases, proceedings may be introduced by the claimant before the court of the country where the defendant is established.

- Besides the solution mentioned above, a claim brought before a court for a breach of contract will lead to the application of article 5.1 of the Brussels Convention. In this case, it should be stressed that the court which has jurisdiction is not the court of the place of performance of the contract, nor the court where the party offering the characteristic performance *(i.e.* the seller for a sale contract, the bank for a loan contract, the agent for a commercial agency contract, the distributor for a distributorship contract) is established. Indeed, the court having jurisdiction (except where there are two or more defendants) is the court of the place of performance of the right (cause for action) which is the basis of the claim by the claimant *(i.e.* the place where the commission must be legally paid; the place where the non-competition clause should be effective or the place where the accounting evidences should be supplied). In all cases, the determination of the place of performance of such rights will be made by reference to the proper law of the contract and not automatically by reference to the substantive law of the country of the court seised.
- Under French law and under the Brussels Convention, there is no *forum non conveniens* rule as may apply in England when courts deal with cases outside the scope of the Brussels Convention. In those cases, English courts, having *per se* jurisdiction over a case, may however decide, on a balance of convenience, that a foreign court is more suitable and then decline its own jurisdiction.

While the Brussels Convention covers France, United Kingdom, Ireland, Benelux, Germany, Italy, Greece, Portugal, Spain and Denmark, the Convention of 16 September 1988 on Jurisdiction and the Enforcement of Judgments in Civil and Commercial Matters ("the Lugano Convention") which is its "sister convention", regulates litigation occurring between parties established in Switzerland, Austria, Sweden, Finland, Norway and Iceland and also all litigation occurring between parties established within the latter countries and within some countries of the former European Economic Community such as France, United Kingdom, Italy and the Netherlands.

(14) Which law may the parties choose?

Under French international private law, the parties to an international agency agreement may choose the proper law of the contract. Both the Convention of 19 June 1980 on the law applicable to Contractual

Obligations ("the 1980 Rome Convention") and the 1978 Hague Convention on the law applicable to intermediary contracts recognise that the parties have the right to do this.

First of all the parties may choose the law applicable to the contract in a specific clause of an agency agreement. Most of the time, such law is the law of the place where either the principal or the commercial agent is established or conducts his business. However, the law of a third country may be chosen provided that such a choice is not fraudulent *(i.e.* made with the intention of avoiding the provisions applicable under the law which would normally govern the contract).

In cases where the parties do not, either through express or implied terms, choose the applicable law, French courts, provided that they are duly seised and they have jurisdiction under the provisions of the Brussels Convention, will determine the applicable law by reference to the 1978 Hague Convention, which has been in force in France since 1 May 1992. The rules contained in that Convention lead, in principle, to the designation of the law of the country where the commercial agent is established at the date of execution of the agency agreement. It is our opinion that the 1980 Rome Convention is not applicable since the 1978 Hague Convention states more specific solutions to commercial agency agreements than the 1980 Rome Convention which applies to all types of contracts.

(15) Can the law that would normally be applicable to the agency agreement be set aside?

Despite the choice of law clause or the designation by a court of the proper law of the contract, other laws may interfere with the law that will normally be applicable to the agency agreement and may set aside some provisions of the agreement or of the proper law.

Thus there are some specific provisions or statutes which are described as international mandatory or compulsory rules ("*lois de police*" or "*lois d'application immédiate*"). These laws could be the law(s) of one or several countries with which the agency agreement has a close connection, whatever its type: place of performance, of execution, of payment or of an establishment of either of the parties.

Most of the time, mandatory rules of the country where the commercial agent is established may prevail over the proper law of the contract.

In France, the 1991 Law imposes some international mandatory provisions on the parties to an international agency agreement such as, for example, the provision granting to the commercial agent the right to an indemnity at the end of an agency contract.

It should be noted that there are no clear provisions or decisions with regard to the definition of what are "international mandatory rules" and "internal mandatory rules", the latter not interfering with a foreign law chosen as the proper law of the contract. The border between these two types of rules will be determined by French caselaw, so legal advice should always be taken.

(16) Does the agent carry any responsibility for product liability?

As a general principle, the commercial agent cannot be held liable for defective products.

However, the commercial agent could be sued, along with the principal, when he acts as a consignee and then imports and delivers the goods of the principal to customers. However, he is not solely liable since the real importer and supplier of the products is the principal. This liability cannot be excluded so the principal should normally fully indemnify the agent in respect of any such claim. In all cases, this question cannot be deleted from the provisions of a commercial agency agreement (article: co-operation between parties). Thus, the principal should normally indemnify and hold free the agent against such claims.

CONTENTS OF CHAPTER 8

Germany

8. GERMANY

Pritchard Englefield, German Law Department, London

(1) What is meant by "commercial agent" in Germany? Does it include agents for services?

The law of agency in Germany is regulated by statute in sections 84 to 92c of the "*Handelsgesetzbuch*" (Commercial Law Code) ("HGB"). These regulations lay down special rules over and above the general rules of the HGB and BGB (*Bürgerliches Gesetzbuch*, the General Civil Code). The definition of the commercial agent is contained in section 84 of HGB. According to that section a commercial agent is someone who as a self-employed businessman/trader is continually entrusted with the task of arranging business for, or concluding business in the name of, a principal. Determining factors for the activity of a commercial agent are:

- The arranging or conclusion of contracts;
- For or on behalf of a principal;
- The independence as a trader; and
- The continuing appointment for such transactions.

Arranging transactions means that the agent paves the way for, and then encourages the conclusion of, business between the principal and a third party, by acting in the interests of his principal given the willingness of the third party to conclude a contract.

In addition to arranging an agent may conclude contracts in the name of, and for the account of, the principal. In this event the agent appears as an authorised representative of his principal and concludes the relevant transaction with the third party himself. Agents with such power to conclude business are called conclusion agents, "*Abschlußvertreter*".

A commercial agent normally receives commission for his activities which is calculated on the basis of the amount of turnover achieved for his principal. An agent is viewed commercially as a continual provider of business for his principal and as such is an independent trader and businessman as defined in German commercial law. Legally speaking he differs from a wholesaler or retailer in that he is incorporated into the distribution system of another business; his position is also different to the position of a pure broker in that the relationship is a continuing one. The agent as opposed to an employee, however, retains his independence. In the absence of such independence, he will be an employed salesman with the additional provisions regarding commissions applying.

In commercial practice the agent appears in a large number of differing guises. The giant distribution company with marketing power, on which the manufacturer relies, such as a particular importer, can be an agent just as much as a legally independent, but commercially dependent, commercial agent, or a part-time agent whose main activity is different or someone who represents only one company where the relationship is much closer to that of an employee (and where some provisions relating to employees apply).

The basic protection given by German commercial agency law applies uniformly to all categories and forms of agency, whether goods or services are concerned. That includes insurance agents; to which, however, some special rules apply.

(2) What makes a distributor different?

An agent ("*Handelsvertreter*") should not be confused with a distributor ("*Vertragshändler*").

The agent is only concerned with the arranging or conclusion of transactions for his principal with third parties; there is only a contractual relationship between the principal and the third party; the agent himself does not become a contracting party.

Herein lies the essential difference to the role of the distributor. The distributor buys and sells goods in his own name and sells them on to third parties for his own account; he operates a commercial business using his own firm or company. Two transactions arise: firstly the contract between the main business (usually the manufacturer) and the distributor and secondly the contract between the distributor and the third party. Unlike the position of the agent, the distributor becomes a contracting party with the third party, and he is described as an "*Eigenhändler*" (a dealer operating for himself). The *Eigenhändler* does not act on behalf, and in the name, of the principal.

A further difference between a distributor and an agent is that a distributor normally, unlike the agent, has a stock of the manufacturer's goods and his own substantial stockroom and business premises. The distributor is normally tied by some (periodic) contract to a manufacturer or dealer. This agreement will oblige him to protect the interests of his contracting party as well as promoting the distribution and sales of the contractual products through his business efforts. His remuneration is normally the margin between his sale price and the price at which he purchases the goods from the manufacturer or dealer, which is often at a discount off list-price.

(3) What are the advantages of appointing a distributor?

The advantages and disadvantages of appointing a distributor to distribute goods arise out of the legal position between the main business and the distributor. As the distributor sells the contractual products in his own name and for his own account, the risks involved in selling on those goods either to another dealer or to the end consumer lie with the distributor and not with the manufacturer, which is the case where goods are sold through an agent. A further advantage can be that the manufacturer is not forced to set up and maintain a large distribution network and business relationships with a multiplicity of contacts or end consumers. He can limit himself to concentrating on delivering to a restricted number of distributors, who must themselves take over the risks involved in selling on their own account. The manufacturer thereby avoids the costs of storing his goods, as the distributor normally has his own warehouse in which to store the contractual products until the sale to the third party has been concluded.

(4) What are the rights and duties of distributors? What are the general rights and duties of principals with distributors?

The legal relationship between manufacturer and distributor is normally determined by the contract of distributorship which they enter into at the outset of their relationship. Normally the distributor undertakes in accordance with the distributorship contract to:

- Protect the interests of the manufacturer with the care of a diligent businessman;
- Continually promote the sale of the contractual products;

- Look after the business relationships with customers;
- Continually inform the manufacturer about his operations, market developments and the operations of competitors;
- Advertise the contractual products inside the contractual territory on his own account;
- Comply with the rules of fair competition;
- Inform the manufacturer of any infringements or breaches of the rules of fair competition or infringements of trade mark or patents or other property rights;
- Not compete with the manufacturer for the period of the distributorship by manufacturing or dealing with the distribution of competing products (restrictive covenant);
- Acquire the contractual products only from the manufacturer (exclusive purchasing requirement);
- Build up after-sales care services such as a repair service in the contractual territory;
- Acquire the necessary spare parts from the manufacturer; and
- Not to use, or make known to third parties, any business secrets of the manufacturer, which became known to him during the period of the distributorship, without the consent of the manufacturer.

The distributorship agreement usually imposes on the manufacturer the following duties:

- To allocate a specific and clearly ascertainable contractual territory in which he will carry out his duties of distribution and to grant him exclusivity rights for such territory;
- To grant dealers' discount to the distributorship in respect of the contractual products;
- To grant remuneration to the distributor for each sale which the manufacturer concludes directly with a customer in the contractual territory;
- To prepare accounts of such direct sales from time to time at reasonable intervals;
- To deliver the contractual products at agreed delivery times and in accordance with agreed conditions of sale;

- Not to entrust the distribution rights for the contractual products to any third parties in the contractual territory (restrictive covenant); and
- To keep the distributor continually informed about technical developments of the contractual products and to provide him with all reasonable information which he may require to service the customers effectively.

In addition a distributor agreement regularly includes general conditions relating to the products and objects, period of distributorship, termination and the consequences of termination.

It should be noted that in some circumstances, in addition to the conditions mutually agreed in the distributorship, some clauses of the HGB which apply to commercial agency contracts may be applicable to the distributorship agreement. Examples of this are the principles laid down in paragraph 86 of HGB concerning the duty to protect the interests of the manufacturer and the restrictive covenant against competition as well as the rules of paragraph 89b of HGB which deal with compensation on termination. The conditions required in order for the agency law to apply to a distributorship relationship are, however, contentious under German law and depend on the facts and circumstances of each individual case and are beyond the scope of this chapter.

(5) Having decided to appoint a commercial agent, what should you do?

The general advice given in the introduction of this book applies equally in Germany.

(6) What should be included in a contract with a commercial agent?

It is, of course, vital to conclude an agency agreement in writing. Under German law no particular form is prescribed for agency agreements. Nevertheless the following points to the necessity of a written document: firstly paragraph 85 of HGB states that both the principal and the agent have the right to have the content of their arrangement committed to written form in a document and that this must be signed by both contracting parties. In addition questions such as the assumption of liability for the performance of third party's obligations through the agent (*del credere* liability, paragraph 86b of HGB) or agreement to any restrictive covenant against competition which applies after the period of the agency must be in writing. Finally written form enables the parties to be precise in defining their respective rights and obligations and thereby avoid misunderstandings which could lead to future litigation.

Basically an agency agreement should contain the following details or terms:

- the contracting parties;
- the determination/definition of the contractual territory and/or class of clients;
- definition of the products;
- the tasks imposed on the agent;
- the powers of the agent;
- the duties and obligations of the principal or manufacturer;
- the duties and obligations of the agent;
- the liability of the agent towards the obligations of customers for the transactions he concludes on behalf of the principal and (where agreed) a *del credere* liability and commission;
- the rate of commission (including provisions as to how commission arises, when it is due and payable, how it is calculated and the amount);
- the consequences of an agent's inability to perform his tasks as a result of disability such as illness or holiday;
- the duration/period of the agency;
- provisions for termination, notice and expiry of any fixed term;
- competition provisions;
- general provisions such as the limitation period for claims arising out of the agency relationship;
- the place of jurisdiction for disputes; and
- a choice of law clause.

(7) What are the duties of a principal?

The duties of the principal are laid down in German law in sections 86a and 87 of HGB.

- The principal must make available to the agent all necessary documents and items such as samples, drawings, lists of customers, lists of prices, conditions of sale etc.
- Furthermore the principal must give the agent necessary information concerning the acceptance, rejection or inability to perform any transaction which the agent has put to his principal.
- Arising out of these duties of the principal in section 86a of HGB German law construes a general duty of the principal to support and be considerate of the requirements of the agent corresponding to the duty on the part of the agent to protect his principal's interests.
- Under section 87 of HGB the principal has a duty to pay commission to the agent.

(8) Can any of these duties be avoided?

The duties of support and provision of information contained in section 86a of HGB cannot be avoided by contrary contractual arrangement. However, the right to remuneration can be freely negotiated. It is usual for remuneration to be in the form of commission, but a different form of remuneration may be agreed, for example a fixed fee, a premium payment for specific services or a share of the total turnover or even a share of profits of the main business which the agent represents. It is also possible to have a combination of commission and another form of remuneration.

Section 92a of HGB envisages a possible future regulation to provide, in certain circumstances, a compulsory minimum remuneration for an agent who represents only one firm. No such regulation is presently planned or in force.

(9) What are the duties of a commercial agent?

The main duties of a commercial agent are described in section 86(1) of HGB. Under that section, the agent must use his best endeavours to arrange or conclude business on behalf of his principal (the duty to use best endeavours). As this is a fundamental duty, it is insufficient if the agent only carries out this duty from time to time, although he is not obliged to transact as much business as he could by using strenuous effort. However, after a running-in period, the principal can expect certain sales success. Thus, the agent must make reasonable efforts to carry out his agency functions.

On the other hand, another fundamental duty of the agent is to protect the principal's interests whilst carrying out his sales function (duty to protect interests). This duty is so absolutely fundamental for the agency contract that it covers not only the attempts by the agent to arrange and conclude business, but also the entire business activity of the agent. The agent must do everything which could possibly assist the interests of his principal and desist from doing anything which could harm those interests. So, for example, the agent must ascertain details of creditworthiness and general status of each potential customer within the scope of his sales activity and notify his principal of the results of those enquiries. The agent does not, however, have to take any liabilities in respect of the payments due from customers, unless that has been specifically agreed (*del credere* liability).

A number of other obligations on the part of the agent have developed out of the obligation to protect the principal's interest, some of which have been implied, and others laid down by law. These include:

- the duty to inform the principal of the arranging or conclusion of transactions;
- the duty of care of an ordinary businessman (section 86(2) and (3) of HGB);
- the duty of confidentiality;
- the covenant on use of business and trade secrets (section 90 of HGB); and
- the restrictive covenant against competition. The covenant states that the agent shall not act for another business which may compete with his principal, nor deal with products which may compete with those of his principal.

  It must be noted that during the contractual period of the agency, the covenant against competition does not need any special agreement, but follows automatically from the general duty to protect the interests of the principal. But for the period after termination of the agency agreement, a covenant against competition needs to be specifically agreed in writing in order to be valid (see (17) below).

(10) Can any of these duties be avoided?

The duty to use best endeavours, to arrange or conclude business, to protect the principal's interests and the duty to provide information, are mandatory. In other words they can neither be expanded nor limited. If on the other hand the above-mentioned duties are made more specific, then this is considered valid. In all other respects the legal relationship and the duties between the parties are open to be agreed by the parties.

(11) Should you include performance quotas for a commercial agent?

Prescribing minimum sales to be achieved can be a useful measure to ensure that the agent continues to use his best endeavours to promote successfully sales of the principal's goods, where the level of sales required by the principal depends primarily on the agent's effort and endeavours. In addition it makes sense to prescribe minimum turnover quotas to justify terminating the agency contract based on breach of contract on the part of the agent if the minimum turnover requirement, which has been contractually agreed, is not met. However, minimum quotas have to be reasonable to be enforceable.

(12) Are there any other ways in which a principal can monitor performance of the agent?

On the one hand, one can rely on the statutory provisions which impose on the agent a particular duty to keep the principal fully and immediately informed in particular of each transaction which the agent has arranged or concluded on his behalf. The information which the principal receives in this manner should enable him to monitor the sales activities of the agent.

If the principal wishes to impose stricter duties on the part of the agent to ascertain creditworthiness and status of particular customers, then there should be imposed specifically in the agency agreement an obligation that the agent is liable for the performance of obligations arising out of any particular contracts, at least in the amount of the commission which the agent would receive (*del credere* liability). Under German law the agent then, however, has a claim to the payment of *del credere* commission (section 86b(1) sentence 1 of HGB) in addition to his ordinary rate of commission.

(13) To what extent is a principal responsible for the acts of his agent?

If an agent who is only entrusted with the procurement of business concludes the transaction on behalf of the principal, the principal must advise the third party that he wants to repudiate the contract without delay after learning of it or the contract will be deemed to have been accepted. Even if not authorised to conclude contracts the commercial agent is considered the principal's representative. The same applies if an agent, despite in principle having power to conclude contracts, concludes a transaction which he is not entitled to do. Limitations of a commercial agent's authority are only effective against a third party if the latter knew about it.

(14) Is there any way of minimising that risk?

As mentioned above, limitations of the agent's authority are only effective if the third party knew about them. Hence it is advisable for the principal to formally notify all customers of any limitations of the agent's authority.

(15) How can an agency agreement be terminated?

An agency agreement can be terminated by:

- Expiry of the fixed period;
- Death of the agent (section 376 of BGB) or in the case of a legal entity or other type of body its dissolution or bankruptcy of the principal (section 23(2) of Bankruptcy Law (*KO/Konkursordnung*)); and
- The giving of notice (sections 89 and 89a of HGB).

The German law of agency differentiates between:

- ordinary termination of an agency relationship (under section 89 of HGB); and
- extraordinary termination (under section 89a of HGB).

(i) Ordinary termination by expiry of term or by giving due notice

With ordinary termination one must further differentiate between agency agreements of indefinite duration and those for a fixed term.

The period of notice for agency agreements of indefinite duration depends on the length of the agency relationship as at the time of intended termination. In the first year it is one month; in the second year two months; in the third, fourth and fifth years it is three months and thereafter six months. Whatever the duration of the contract, notice must always be given to the end of a calendar month. These minimum periods of notice can be lengthened by agreement between the parties but not shortened. They may not be shorter for the principal than for the agent. Notice must be given to the agent; no particular form is prescribed. It is, however, advisable for reasons of proof to provide in the agency agreement for the notice to be given in writing. It is neither necessary to give grounds for termination nor that there necessarily be any grounds, as long as the proper notice period is given. Termination is therefore possible in the case of poor performance by the agent of his duties as well as misrepresentation.

An agency agreement is concluded for a fixed term if its duration is determined either by stating a particular expiry date, a particular period or notice period or the duration is defined by the character or purpose of the agency such as representation during a particular season (*e.g.* in the clothing industry). The fixed term agreement normally ends when the fixed term expires; in other words on the contractually agreed calendar date. If the parties wish to extend such a fixed term agency contract, then under German law the agreement is deemed to have been extended for an unlimited period. The legal nature of the agency agreement is changed: out of the fixed term contract arises a contract of indefinite duration. This contract, originally for a fixed term but then of indefinite duration, is terminable on the same conditions as a contract which had been entered into for an indefinite period from the outset. The length of notice period is, however, not calculated from the time of extension; the relevant time is the commencement of the very beginning of the agency period (section 89(3) of HGB).

(ii) For extraordinary or summary termination

The extraordinary notice provisions contained in section 89a of HGB apply both to fixed term and indefinite duration agency agreements.

According to this section, the agency agreement can be terminated by either party summarily (in other words without prior notice) if there is an "important reason" ("*aus wichtigem Grund*") for doing so. An important reason exists if the person giving notice cannot reasonably be expected to continue the agency relationship. When this will apply cannot be answered generally but will depend on the particular facts in each case. However examples are fundamental breaches of contract by the agent such as:

- gross and selfish disregard of the interests of the principal;
- unjustified refusal to perform agency services;
- substantial breaches of duty leading to falling turnover;
- substantial breaches of trust such as gross insults against the principal or similar behaviour which diminish the authority or reputation of the principal in the eyes of customers;
- further repeated failure to notify the principal of the conclusion of contracts or other information which would be important to the principal;
- in particular breach of a contractually agreed restrictive covenant against competition; and
- impossibility of performance of important duties on the part of the agent such as, for example, the bankruptcy of the agent or the agent's composition with creditors or closure of his business.

One must particularly bear in mind when considering extraordinary termination the following:

- the onus of proving an important reason lies under German law with the person seeking to terminate; and
- some warning must be given before giving extraordinary notice, if the reason for the notice is a deterioration of the carrying out of the duties by the agent (contrasting with the duties of trust where this is not necessary). Without such warning German law considers that no important reason exists so that summary termination is invalid. Under certain circumstances it can, however, then be regarded as ordinary termination and become valid to expire on the first available ordinary date. The agency agreement can be terminated summarily without a warning in cases of very serious breaches.

(16) Do you have any remedy if the agent suddenly stops working for you or represents someone else or himself?

The final and unjustified end of agency activity on behalf of the principal amounts to an important reason pursuant to section 89a of HGB just as much as the breach of a restrictive covenant, for example the carrying out by the agent of agency services on behalf of a competitor to the principal. Both of these justify the principal terminating the agency agreement without notice. In addition extraordinary termination can give rise to a damages claim by the principal against the agent, if the termination results from the fault of the agent.

(17) What do you have to remember when drafting a clause which restricts the activities of an agent: a) during the period of the agency; b) after termination of the agency?

When drafting such a restrictive covenant one must differentiate between the time during the continuance of the agency and the period thereafter. The legal basis, requirement of form and validity are quite different in these two cases.

- During the continuance of the agency contract the restrictive covenant is based on the general provisions relating to protection of interests contained in section 86 of HGB. No specific agreement is necessary. This covenant can be extended by agreement, as long as the interests of the agent which require protection and the criteria and limits laid down by both German and European cartel and competition law are observed. This is discussed further below.
- As far as a restrictive covenant after termination of the agency relationship is concerned, following Germany's implementation of the EEC Council Directive on the co-ordination of the laws of the Member States relating to Self-employed Commercial Agents dated 18 December 1986 (86/653/EEC) a specific competition agreement is required. The pre-conditions for such an agreement are contained in section 90a of HGB. The most important provisions, which cannot be varied to the detriment of the agent, are the following:

- The time of making the restriction: section 90a only applies to agreements on restrictive covenants made before termination of the agency agreement;
- Required form: such an agreement entered into after or at the time of the original making of the agency agreement must be in writing and a document signed by the principal must be handed to the agent who must confirm the contents of the agreement;
- Maximum duration: a maximum of two years following termination of the agency agreement;
- Extent of the covenant: the agreement on competition must be restricted to the contractual territory contained in the agency agreement, the agent's customers and the contractual products which the agent has endeavoured to sell for his principal; and
- Duty by the principal to compensate: the principal is obliged to make a payment of reasonable compensation to the agent for the period of restriction on competition. The level of such compensation is determined by the disadvantages suffered by the agent as a result of the limitations. A breach of the covenant against competition will lead to a claim for damages against the agent and under certain circumstances can lead to summary termination of the agency relationship.

(18) Should the agency be for long or short fixed terms, renewable or indefinite?

The question whether an agency relationship should be for a fixed or indefinite term cannot be answered generally but must be determined from case to case. The particular needs of the contracting parties, in particular those of the principal, must be taken into account. The question is actually of no great importance as the differences between both types of agreement are not vast. One main advantage of the fixed term over the indefinite duration agreement is that the parties can review the effectiveness and success of their contractual relationship at the end of the fixed term with a view to discussing renewal without having to adhere to notice periods. A fixed term agreement might therefore be chosen if the parties do not yet know each other or where it is difficult to predict whether a product will be successful on the market. On the other hand an agency agreement with indefinite duration is also capable of being determined providing that the above-mentioned time-limits for notice are adhered to and can therefore also be reviewed by the parties at that stage.

(19) What is the effect of termination, *i.e.* what are the responsibilities and liabilities of: a) the principal; b) the agent?

- The termination of the agency agreement has no effect on the claim by the agent for commission in respect of business which has still to be concluded. Under certain conditions he can be entitled to commission on later business which he may have prepared (section 87(3) of HGB). Furthermore the agent may have a compensation claim under section 89b of HGB against his principal. This is consideration for services which the ordinary payment of commission during the agency relationship has not fully compensated or covered, such as creating a customer base which the agent has built up for his principal and from which the principal will continue to benefit after termination of the agency. The claim for compensation is excluded in certain cases, for example where the principal terminated for an important reason.
- The agent is obliged after termination of the agency relationship to return all documents and papers relating to the agency such as samples, price lists, conditions of sale, goods and his correspondence with customers to the principal.

(20) What about the death or incapacity of the agent through, for example, illness or assignment of the agency, or retirement of the agent? What are the respective duties then?

In the case of the agent's death or — if we are talking about a legal entity as agent, then dissolution of that entity — the agency relationship comes to an end.

Furthermore the impossibility of the agent performing fundamental contractual duties, even if this is not his fault, can create a reason for extraordinary and summary termination of the agency relationship by the principal in accordance with section 89a of HGB. Circumstances which justify impossibility of performing fundamental contractual duties are, for example, the opening of bankruptcy proceedings over the assets of the agency, the opening of composition proceedings, the cessation of business or assignment by the agent, and permanent invalidity or incapability of the agent (even if not his fault) with the consequence of permanent inability to work.

Termination of the agency agreement by either party due to age or ill health does not preclude the agent's compensation claim.

(21) What are the provisions in Germany concerning the choice of law?

Irrespective of whether the agent carries out his duties within a Member State of the EU, EFTA or in a third country, the question of the applicable law in the agency agreement is determined in principle according to German rules of private international law. Under these rules, in principle, the parties are free to choose the applicable law and can therefore freely determine which law governs their agency relationship. It is disputed whether the parties can choose a foreign law neither of them has any connection with and if and what German rules might nevertheless apply. In so far as the parties do not make an express choice of law, the agency agreement will be subject to the law of the country with which the agency has the closest connection. As it is the agent who carries out the characteristic services in the agency relationship, it is normally the country in which the agent carries on business which determines the applicable law.

If German law applies to the agency contract, then the compulsory provisions of German agency law must be regarded. It is different, if the agent does not carry out his activities within the EU or EFTA. The parties are then free to exclude the compulsory provisions of German agency law; for example they can agree that the agent is not entitled to compensation after termination of the contract.

(22) If a dispute arises between an agent and a principal in different countries, is it possible to provide for litigation to be in the country of the principal and will national law ever be applicable?

Where the agent and the principal are in different countries, it is advisable to have a clause in the agency agreement stating an agreed place of jurisdiction for disputes to be heard. This is advisable to avoid a lengthy dispute concerning the jurisdiction of a particular court and to enable a speedy resolution of any dispute. In so far as both contracting parties carry on their business in a Member State which is a party to the EEC Convention on Jurisdiction and the Enforcement of Judgments in Civil and Commercial Matters dated 27 September 1968 ("the Brussels Convention") (and this includes most EU States such as the United Kingdom and Germany), then such an agreement as to place of jurisdiction will be recognised in both countries if it is in accordance with article 17 of the Brussels Convention. In addition, in such a case it will be possible to utilise the provisions of that Convention to enforce judgments.

If no agreement on jurisdiction has been made the general rules will apply; this means the rules of the Brussels Convention as to jurisdiction if the parties carry on their business in a State which is a party to the Convention.

The court that has jurisdiction to hear the matter will decide which law applies according to its private international law rules. It is advisable to include a choice of law clause in the agreement.

(23) Is it advisable to put an arbitration or conciliation and alternative dispute resolution clause in the agreement?

Whether or not it is sensible to insert an arbitration or conciliation or alternative dispute resolution clause in the agency agreement depends on the wishes and requirements of the parties. It might well be sensible to insert an arbitration clause as arbitrations are normally carried out more quickly than ordinary litigation. In so far as the applicability of foreign law is concerned, one must check carefully whether the relevant foreign law recognises the agreement to an arbitration or conciliation or alternative dispute resolution clause.

(24) What about product liability? Does the agent carry any responsibility and should he be insured?

The question of product liability basically depends on the relationship of the contracting parties; in other words between the principal and the third party. As mentioned in (2) above, the commercial agent does not become a contracting party. The principal is therefore solely responsible in principle for quality, safety and absence of defects in the products which he manufactures. Since 1989 this has been regulated under German law in the Product Liability Law. According to section 1(1) of the Product Liability Law the manufacturer of a product is basically obliged to compensate for loss or damage sustained by someone who suffers loss or damage resulting from a defect of that product including where death or personal injury result or whereby something is damaged. If, however, in certain cases the agent could be regarded as having brought a product into circulation in Germany, liability might arise.

In very rare cases the agent can be personally liable to the third party in certain strictly limited circumstances where fault can be shown at the time of making the contract, such as where the third party places an extraordinary degree of trust in the agent's specialist technical skills. It is not sufficient to render the agent personally liable to point to his direct personal commercial self-interests, such as his continuing interest in obtaining commission in the event of a conclusion of a contract.

(25) What about the liability of the principal? Does having an agent in a country constitute carrying on a business in that country?

One of the questions arising in this context is whether a principal can be sued in a country where he has no other representation apart from his agent. The Brussels Convention states that a person or legal entity can be sued in another contracting State if the dispute concerns the business of a branch, agency or representation. The European Court of Justice has, however, decided that the fact that a business may be represented by an agent in another EU Member State does not of itself lead to it being able to be sued in the country where its agent carries on business.

The German procedure provision that a non-German defendant can be sued in Germany if he has assets there is specifically excluded under the Brussels Convention (article 3), *i.e.* does not apply where the parties concerned belong to a Member State to the Convention.

Secondly, it has to be carefully considered under which circumstances an agent would create a permanent establishment for his principal as far as the principal's tax liability is concerned.

(26) What about bad debts? Must a principal pay the agent his commission even when he has not himself been paid?

As stated in (1) above, the normal remuneration of an agent is his commission. It is a payment for success. In principle the agent has a claim to commission as soon as, and to the extent that, his principal or the third party has performed the contract which he has introduced (section 87a of HGB). The parties can agree that the agent will only receive the commission when the third party has fulfilled his obligations under his contract with the principal, *i.e.* when the third party has paid. In that case the agent has a right to demand an advance on the commission as soon as the principal has fulfilled his obligations under the contract.

The claim for commission of the agent ceases to exist if it is clear that the third party will not perform the transaction which the agent has introduced; in other words, not carry out the obligations required in the contract. In this event commission payments which may already have been paid must be repaid. The mere assumption or probability that the third party might not perform his contractual obligations towards the principal does not suffice to extinguish the commission claim. In fact the principal must basically enforce his rights if necessary by proceedings to prove objectively that his customer is unable to perform the contract. There is an exception, namely if it is unreasonable to expect the principal to take proceedings against the third party, if for example it is clear that the third party is unable to honour his financial commitments for a lengthy period (such as recently declared bankruptcy). In practice any repayment of commission already received by the agent is dealt with by way of set-off against new commission claims by the agent.

The agent is still entitled to commission if the principal does not perform the contract fully or in part as had been agreed, such as where the goods are delivered late or are defective or he refuses to perform the contract. Commission is, however, not payable where the principal is not liable for such failure to perform the contract. The principal, for example, is responsible for difficulties in his own factory or as a result of cash-flow or other financial difficulties of his own, fault by sub-contractors or his suppliers, incorrect calculations, rescission of the contract by the customer because of late or improper delivery on the part of the principal etc. The principal does, however, not have to be responsible for circumstances which do not fall within his sphere of risk and where he cannot exert any influence over them. This includes, for example, interference by higher authority such as embargoes affecting material, transport, export or import imposed by the State, which were not foreseeable and which are imposed after the contract with the third party has been entered into; and natural catastrophes.

(27) How do competition provisions affect agency agreements?

Restraint of competition in agency agreements has always to be checked against provisions of German and European competition law.

The relevant German law is the *Gesetz gegen Wettbewerbs-beschränkungen* ("GWB") (anti-trust law). It can, however, be said that in principle no competition provisions are violated if the restrictive covenants preventing competition are kept within the parameter of the rules and provisions of the Commercial Code relating to commercial agents.

The prohibition against fixing prices and conditions set out in section 15 of GWB are not applicable to an agent as proper, as the principal bears alone the risks involved in the business which the agent introduces. The agent does not become a contracting party and there is therefore no second agreement as required by section 15 of GWB.

The Commission Announcement of 24 December 1962 provides a block exemption for agency agreements from the operation of article 85(1) of the Treaty of Rome. Article 85 was not to apply to (real) commercial agents who were not independent traders. The European Court of Justice applies varying criteria; looking in part at the integration of the agent into the business of his principal and in part at the bearing of the risk of the agent as though he were an independent trader.

The Commission is currently drafting a new announcement which is to replace the 1962 announcement. The Commission is said to be taking over assuming the "integration theory" (*Eingliederungs-theorie*) of the European Court of Justice. The final version is not yet to hand.

A detailed analysis of both German and European competition law would go beyond the scope of this book.

CONTENTS OF CHAPTER 9

Greece

9. GREECE

Lila Vassilaki LL.B (Athens), LL.M (Bristol),
Kyriakides and Partners, Athens

(1) What is meant by "commercial agent" in Greece?

Presidential Decree (P.D.) 219/91 regarding "Commercial Agents", as subsequently amended by P.D.s 88/94 and 312/95 ("P.D.s"), was promulgated in compliance with EEC Council Directive of 18 December 1986 on the co-ordination of the laws of the Member States relating to Self-employed Commercial Agents (866/653/EEC) ("the Directive").

According to article 1, paragraph 2 of P.D. 219/91: "For the implementation of this P.D., commercial agent shall mean an independent intermediary who has continuing authority to negotiate the sale or the purchase of goods on behalf of another person (the principal), or to negotiate and conclude such transactions on behalf of and in the name of that principal in consideration of a certain remuneration" (articles 2 and 5 of P.D. 219/91). This definition reflects articles 1, 2 and 6 of the Directive.

According to the above definition a commercial agent can:

- organise freely his commercial activity without the intervention of the principal;
- maintain his own business place; and
- have sub-agents in his registered offices or in other cities within the geographical territory in which he exercises his business activity.

The ambit of the P.D.s covers only independent commercial agents, namely, those who have immediate contact with the principal by whom they are remunerated by way of commission.

As P.D. 219/91 is applicable to commercial agency agreements executed from 30 May 1991 onwards and to agreements concluded before 30 May 1991 but which will not have been terminated by 1 January 1994, it is obvious that there are agreements not covered by that P.D. In such cases, the relevant articles of the Commercial Code (articles 90–94) and the relevant articles of the Civil Code (*i.e.* articles 713–729 regarding mandate) are applicable.

It would appear from the text of the P.D.s, there are no provisions as regards agents for services.

(2) What makes a distributor different?

The distributor acts in his own name and account, and assumes all the risks of an independent economic operator, whereas the commercial agent acts on the account of, and in the name of, the principal without assuming any risk and is usually paid on a commission basis for his services. Distributorship agreements are not governed by special legislative provisions and up to now the legislative provisions on agents of the Commercial Code and other provisions of the Civil Code (such as the relevant provisions on mandate) are applicable by analogy. The above has been confirmed by caselaw according to which distribution agreements constitute: "a particular form of a commercial co-operation agreement, in principle similar to the commercial agency agreement, which, in the absence of specific provisions is governed by the provisions of the Civil Code on mandate".

(3) What are the advantages of appointing a distributor?

Beside the undertaking of risk by the distributor, the appointment of a distributor may be considered to be advantageous in the light of the ability of the parties to draft their contract in a more flexible manner without complying with all requirements of the P.D.s.

(4) What are the rights and duties of distributors?

In the absence of specific legislation the parties are free to determine the rights and obligations of the distributor as they wish. However, it is possible to follow the provisions applicable for the agency agreement but it is advisable to mention, specifically, in the relevant contract the fact that it is a distributorship agreement and to include in detail the rights and duties of both the supplier and distributor as contracting parties.

(5) What are the general rights and duties of principals with distributors?

In the absence of specific legislative provisions, the parties are free to determine the rights and duties of the principal as they think fit, taking into consideration their particular needs and intentions. Nonetheless, it is usual in practice to follow the same pattern as in the case of a principal in a commercial agency agreement.

(6) Having decided to appoint a commercial agent, what should you do?

In Greece all commercial agents are obliged to register. Therefore the various Chambers of Commerce where all commercial agents are registered are valuable sources of information, if a decision is reached to appoint a commercial agent and the interested party (principal) wishes to carry out research. In spite of the harmonisation of the legislation relating to commercial agents throughout the EU, it is strongly urged that professional legal advice should be sought in order to draft the relevant agreement effectively.

Registration with the Chamber of Commerce is effected when the interested (future) agent submits the following:

- at least a high school certificate;
- a penal record certificate;
- a certificate that he is not under judicial restraint; and
- a non-insolvency certificate.

Only EU citizens as well as foreigners of Greek origin (for example Greek-Americans) may be registered as commercial agents.

(7) What should be included in a contract with a commercial agent?

A commercial agency agreement should include the following:

- The contracting parties.

- The type of agency created.
- The purpose of the agreement.
- Determination of the agent's territory.
- Duration of the agreement.
- A detailed list of the duties, rights and obligations of both contracting parties.
- Provisions to determine the remuneration of the agent and methods of payment.
- Confidentiality provisions and a non-competition clause.
- Provisions relating to the termination of the contract.
- Applicable law and jurisdiction (or arbitration) clause.

(8) What are the duties of the principal?

The principal is obliged to pay the agreed remuneration to the agent. In the absence of an agreed remuneration, the remuneration of the commercial agent, which usually amounts to a percentage of the value of the transaction for which he has intervened or which was concluded by the agent on behalf of the principal, shall be set out taking into account customary practices. In other words, the percentage may vary depending on the usual practice applicable in the place where the agent exercises his business activity and/or the goods or merchandise were sold. Where circumstances vary considerably, the agent is entitled to a reasonable remuneration, after considering all the data relating to the transaction.

(9) When is the commercial agent entitled to commission?

The commercial agent is entitled to commission for transactions concluded during the term of the commercial agency agreement:

- if the transaction has been concluded due to his intervention; or
- if the transaction has been entered into with a third party with whom the agent has concluded transactions of the same kind so as to be considered a customer; and

- if he is responsible for a specific geographical area or a group of persons and the transaction has been executed with a customer originating from that area or belonging to that group.

As regards agreements outside the ambit of the P.D.s, it is at the contracting parties' discretion to decide on the appropriate remuneration.

The remuneration of a commercial agent is considered to be "commission" and becomes due upon acceptance by the principal of the order placed by the agent.

(10) What other duties does the principal have?

The principal also has the following obligations:

- to provide his agent with all the necessary documentation regarding the goods concerned;
- to provide the agent with the necessary information for the performance of the agreement and in particular to notify the agent, within a reasonable time, once he anticipates that the volume of the transactions shall be significantly lower than that anticipated; and
- to inform the agent within a reasonable time of his acceptance or refusal, as well as of the non-conclusion, of a transaction which the agent has procured for him.

(11) Can any of these duties be avoided?

The principal's duties listed in (8), (9) and (10) above cannot be avoided.

(12) What are the duties of the commercial agent?

In general, the agent must serve the interests of the principal. More specifically he must:

- make proper efforts during the negotiation stage and during the conclusion of transactions assigned to him;
- comply with the instructions given by the principal and inform him about the conditions in the territory concerned.

(13) Can any of these duties of the agent be avoided?

The duties in (12) above are mandatory and cannot be avoided.

(14) Should you include performance quotas for a commercial agent?

Including performance quotas for a commercial agent is not expressly prohibited. However, such performance requirements should not be laid down in a manner which could support a claim for abuse of right (for example consist of excessive or minimal limits or thresholds).

(15) Are there any other ways in which you can monitor the agent's performance?

The monitoring of the performance of a commercial agent could be achieved by requesting reports on the agent's activities *(i.e.* sales realised, increase of clientele, turnover figures, market penetration etc).

(16) To what extent is a principal responsible for the acts of his agent?

Caselaw has held that article 334 of the Civil Code is applicable as regards the liability of a principal. On the basis of this article, the principal may be held liable for the acts of his agent when such acts constitute performance of the principal's contractual obligations.

(17) Does the principle whereby if the agent is "held out" as having authority to act on behalf of the principal, even if he does not have that authority, the principal is liable for his actions, apply in Greece?

There are two tendencies in jurisprudence as regards the liability of the principal in case of abuse of authority. The prevailing opinion holds that the principal is not liable, if the person suffering the damage was aware (or should have been aware) of the fact that the agent was acting in abuse of his authority.

(18) Is there any way of minimising that risk?

One way of minimising the principal's risk in respect of liability for the agent's actions is to include in the agency agreement an indemnity clause to cover cases of bad performance by the agent, due to his fault or negligence.

(19) How can you get rid of an agent for: a) bad performance; b) misrepresentation?

The principal may terminate the relevant agreement without the observance of a period of notice in cases where the agent does not perform any or all of his contractual obligations, as well as in cases of unforeseen events (*force majeure*).

In all other cases there is a requirement for a termination notice. The period of notice is one month for the first year of the contract, two months as from the beginning of the second year, three months as from the beginning of the third year, four months as from the beginning of the fourth year, five months as from the beginning of the fifth year and six months as from the beginning of the sixth and subsequent years.

(20) Do you have any remedy if the agent suddenly stops working for you or represents someone else or himself?

In these cases the principal can exercise his rights to seek compensation for damages, loss of profits and the like.

(21) What do you have to remember when drafting a clause which restricts the activities of an agent: a) during the period of the agency; b) after termination of the agency

The parties may include in their agreement the obligation of the agent not to compete during the period of agency as well as thereafter. However, a non-competition clause is only valid for a period of up to one year following the termination of the relevant contract.

Under article 10 of the P.D. 219/91, the non-competition clause is only valid if:

- it has been concluded in writing; and
- it concerns a geographical area corresponding to the agent's territory as well as the kind of goods which were the object of the contract.

Furthermore, the non-competition clause must not be contrary to good practice. In this regard, Greek caselaw even before the P.D.s already held that such clauses are valid provided that they are of short duration and concern a specific territory.

(22) Should the agency be for long or short fixed terms, renewable or indefinite?

Preferably, agency agreements should be for a fixed duration, renewable only after further agreement in writing. Indefinite agency agreements should be avoided.

However, the special characteristics of each agreement may be made applicable for its duration. The relevant specifications may concern the specific market, the goods promoted, the intention of the parties, etc. It should also be mentioned that if the parties are still acting under an agreement which has expired, that agreement may be converted into a contract of indefinite duration. Commercial agency agreements of an indefinite duration may be terminated by any of the contracting parties by observing the proper notice periods (see (19) above).

(23) What is the effect of termination, *i.e.* what are the liabilities and responsibilities of: a) the principal; b) the agent

According to article 9 of the P.D. 219/91, and provided that the commercial agent is not in default of his obligations under the relevant contract, the commercial agent is entitled to an indemnity in the case of termination, if he has brought the principal new customers or has significantly increased the volume of business with existing customers and the principal continues to derive substantial benefits from the business with such customers.

Furthermore, the amount of such an indemnity may not exceed an amount equivalent to the commercial agent's average annual remuneration over the preceding five years, and if the contract goes back less than five years the indemnity shall be calculated on the average for the period in question.

The agent may still be subject to the non-competition clause contained in the agreement.

It should perhaps be noted that in Greek law there is no distinction between the terms "indemnity" and "compensation". Greek law contains the following distinctions of damage giving rise to the right of the person who has suffered such damage to be compensated (or indemnified):

- Compensation for *positive damage* means the compensation owed for the reduction of the existing property of the person who has suffered the damage.
- Compensation for *loss of profit*. In this case there is no reduction of property but a prevention of property increase.
- Compensation arising from *contractual liability* (for example compensation for misrepresentation).
- Compensation in *tort*, namely, the right to receive compensation from an act or omission of another person not deriving from a contractual relationship (for example liability from negotiations).

Both compensation from contractual liability and in tort may under Greek law cover positive damage as well as loss of profit.

(24) What about the death or incapacity of the agent through, for example illness or assignment of the agency, or retirement of the agent? What are the respective duties then?

The right to an indemnity also exists in favour of the heirs of the agent whose commercial agency agreement is terminated due to his death.

The commercial agent is also entitled to an indemnity, if the termination of the relevant agreement is justified on the grounds of age, incapacity, illness or for other similar reasons.

However, the indemnity is not payable when, following an agreement between the agent and the principal, the former assigns to a third party the rights and obligations deriving from the commercial agency agreement with the consent of the principal (unless the agent can proceed to such an assignment without the principal's consent) and when termination is by the principal on grounds of the agent's default.

The commercial agent may not give up his right to indemnity described above before the expiry of the agreement.

(25) What about the choice of law if the agent is in: a) another EU country; b) an EFTA country; c) a third country?

According to article 25 of the Civil Code, the parties may choose the law which shall govern their commercial agency agreement. Thus, the origin of the agent does not affect in any way the determination of the applicable law since the contractual relationship of the parties may be regulated by the law of their choice.

Additionally, the same article of the Civil Code provides that in the absence of a clause specifying the applicable law, that shall be determined by the special circumstances governing the specific contract, *i.e.* the place of conclusion of the contract, the place of business activity of the agent, the place of performance, etc.

(26) Can part of a law be chosen? For example, English law except for the provisions relating to commercial agency?

According to article 3 of Law 1792/1988, which in Greece ratified the Rome Convention of 19 June 1980 on the law applicable to Contractual Obligations, the agreement is governed by the law chosen by the contracting parties. Such choice must be express or deriving from the provisions of the agreement. By such choice, the contracting parties may determine the applicable law for the whole or part of their agreement. Hence, it is possible for the parties to choose the applicable law for a part of their agreement even if they choose a foreign law. However, such a choice should not affect the applicability of national provisions of a compulsory character.

(27) If a dispute arises between a principal and an agent in different countries, for example in another EU country, in an EFTA country or a third country, is it possible to provide for litigation to be in the country of the principal and will national law ever be applicable?

As the parties are free to indicate the particular jurisdiction to which they wish to be submitted, it is possible that the country of the principal will be chosen, although professional advice should always be taken into consideration, since legal consultants can point out the complexities that may derive from the indicated forum. Reference should also be made to the EEC Convention of 27 September 1968 on Jurisdiction and the Enforcement of Judgments in Civil and Commercial Matters ("the Brussels Convention") applicable between the EU countries, which includes provisions concerning the regulation of the international jurisdiction of the courts and of contracting parties and which may determine the establishment of a particular forum or fora. As far as the EFTA countries are concerned, the Lugano Convention, applicable not only between the EFTA countries but also between EFTA and EU countries, reflects the provisions of the above-mentioned Convention with minor amendments.

In conclusion, as Greek legislation does not provide for specific jurisdiction as regards agency agreements, these agreements are subject to the general rule pursuant to which the territorial jurisdiction of a court is determined by the domicile of the defendant. However, choice of forum clauses are valid provided that they are in writing and are compatible with the legal relationship of the parties to such forum. Besides, provided that the aforementioned Conventions apply, executable judgments will be enforceable in any contracting State without complex formalities.

(28) Is it advisable to put an arbitration or conciliation and alternative dispute resolution clause in the agreement?

Arbitration or conciliation clauses are broadly used nowadays instead of addressing a dispute to the courts. However, arbitration clauses must be drafted with the utmost diligence to ensure that the parties benefit from their binding nature.

(29) Is there any small claims procedure which could apply to the settlement of disputes between principals and agents?

There are small claims procedures but the monetary thresholds are very low, and they are therefore not widely used.

(30) What about product liability? Does the agent carry any responsibility, and should he be insured?

The Law 2251/94 regarding consumer protection implemented EC Directives 85/374, 93/13 and 92/59 on product safety and liability. Under article 6 of that Law any person who imports a product for sale, hire, leasing or any form of distribution in the course of his business shall be responsible as a producer.

This means that, in the light of the above provision, a commercial agent within the ambit of that provision may be held to be liable for defective products as the producer, although he will enjoy a right of redress against the ultimate producer/manufacturer.

(31) What about the liability of the principal? Does having an agent in a country constitute carrying on a business in that country?

The existence of an agent acting in the name and on behalf of the principal does not constitute *per se* an establishment in Greece. A number of additional factors should be considered before deciding whether a principal can be considered to be carrying on business in a country where he has appointed an agent. Whether or not a foreign entity has an establishment in Greece depends on the actual facts of the case in conjunction with the provisions of the relevant bilateral convention for the avoidance of double taxation, provided that Greece has implemented the relevant convention with the State where the specific foreign entity has its registered seat. In these bilateral conventions the term "registered seat" means the seat of the real address and administration and not the seat provided for in the articles of association.

(32) What about bad debts? Must a principal pay the agent his commission even when he has not himself been paid?

The parties are free to determine how, and when, the commission payment to the agent will arise. It is strongly advisable that such agreements are evidenced in writing.

Greek law does not contain any specific provisions on *del credere* clauses and therefore the inclusion of such clauses in the agency contracts depends on the agreement of the contracting parties.

(33) What are the pitfalls which the principal should watch for when appointing an agent and how can he avoid them?

The principal should analyse the market from three perspectives: (i) the relevant product market (in this context the principal must check out parameters concerning the likely demand in that market for a specific product and the interchangeability of the product he wishes to promote with existing products); (ii) the geographical market (the principal should have a clear picture of the geographical area in which his products are going to be marketed, as well as of the conditions prevailing in that area); and (iii) the temporal (seasonal) market as the competitive conditions may vary and there are situations where two seasonal markets exist. Of course, the ability and the experience of the agent appointed is crucial, as he is the person who shall promote the relevant product in the market.

In addition, the national regulations concerning various issues such as licensing required by the pertinent authorities in the case, for example of medicines, foodstuffs, chemicals etc, should also be taken into consideration. Guidance to the agent as regards the company's policies developed through its international experience over time on various matters could be valuable. Furthermore, it is urged that it is most important to seek the assistance of legal advisors so that the relevant agreements are drafted as adequately and clearly as possible.

(34) How do competition provisions affect agency agreements?

When an agent is appointed, whose function will be to negotiate and enter into contracts on the producer's (principal's) behalf, the tendency is for the relevant agreement to be treated as forming a relationship which is a part of the business organisation of the principal and, hence, constitutes an internal matter. The result is that competition law is not applied, since such agreements do not fall within the ambit of its provisions.

In contrast to this, distribution agreements, whereby the principal sells the goods to an independent entity (the distributor) who further resells them on his own behalf, are examined within the context of the national competition rules. The relevant Law is 703/77, as subsequently amended by Laws 1934/91, 2000/91 and 2296/95. Articles 1 and 2 of that Law reflect almost identically articles 85 and 86 of the Treaty of Rome.

In all cases, however, knowledgeable legal advice should be sought in order to avoid difficulties.

CONTENTS OF CHAPTER 10

Ireland

10. IRELAND

Tony Burke and Wendy Hederman, Mason Hayes
& Curran, Dublin

(1) Introduction

The role of agency agreements in commercial life is of great importance. In particular, companies in businesses engaged in trade in the European Union often consider adopting agency as a means of entering the Irish market. The geographical isolation and the peculiarities of the local Irish market will make it commercially advisable for foreign manufacturers and companies to appoint a local agent or agents in Ireland.

(2) What is the legislative background?

Before 1 January 1994, the due date for implementation of the EEC Council Directive of 18 December 1986 on the co-ordination of the laws of the Member States relating to Self-employed Commercial Agents (86/653/EEC) ("the Directive"), there was little statutory intervention in the common law principles which had been established in relation to agency arrangements. The Factors Act of 1889 sets out the law relating to mercantile agents, while the agency aspects of partnership law are found in the Partnership Act 1890 and the Limited Partnerships Act 1907. Agency arrangements also exist in the areas of real estate (estate agents), insurance (insurance agents) and other professional relationships, such as that between a solicitor and client. Similarly to the rest of this book, this chapter concentrates on commercial agents, a term now given statutory recognition by the regulations implementing the 1986 Directive.

(3) What is the definition of "commercial agent" in Ireland?

The term "commercial agent" is defined in article 2(1) of the European Communities (Commercial Agents) Regulations 1994 ("the Agents' Regulations") as:

A self-employed intermediary who has continuing authority to negotiate the sale or purchase of goods on behalf of another person ("the principal"), or to negotiate and to conclude such transactions on behalf of and in the name of the principal.

It can be seen that this definition is almost identical to that contained in the 1986 Directive.

Queries have arisen as to whether the expression "self-employed intermediary" means that a commercial agent can only include natural persons and excludes other forms of legal entities such as limited liability companies. While this question has not yet been determined by the courts in Ireland, the prevailing opinion is that limited liability companies, and even partnerships of individuals, are included within the definition of commercial agent. It is also considered that the term commercial agent covers intermediaries regardless of whether the principal is disclosed to third parties or not. The Agents' Regulations seek to regulate the relationship between the principal and the agent, and are not concerned with whether the third party is aware that the intermediary is acting as an agent.

(4) What kinds of agent are excluded from the definition of "commercial agent"?

There are certain agents who are excluded by virtue of the wording of the definition, and there are six specific exclusions from the term of commercial agent contained in regulation 2(1) of the Agents' Regulations.

A careful analysis of the definition contained in regulation 2(1) gives rise to the following:

- A commercial agent must be self-employed, therefore agents who are employees are outside the scope of the Directive.
- A commercial agent must have the authority to negotiate on behalf of the principal or to negotiate and conclude transactions on behalf of, and in the name of, the principal. This requirement excludes intermediaries which, while acting on behalf of a principal, conclude the transactions in their own names. Therefore independent resellers (otherwise referred to as "distributors") are outside the scope of the 1986 Directive. Agents who do not disclose either the existence or the name of the principal

will nevertheless be within the scope of the 1986 Directive if they have continuing authority to negotiate on behalf of the principal.

- A commercial agent must have continuing authority to act, thereby excluding agents given authority to act only in a particular matter, such as an estate agent negotiating a one-off purchase of a house or land.
- The commercial agent must be involved *in the sale or the purchase of goods* thereby excluding intermediaries who are concerned with the provision of services, the conclusion of rental or leasing agreements or the sale or leasing of real property. If the intermediary as an agent acts in the negotiation of the sale or purchase of goods and services, that element of his agency arrangement which relates to goods should nevertheless be deemed to come within the scope of the Agents' Regulations. It is possible that if the service element of the agency arrangement is a relatively minor or insignificant part of the overall agency arrangement, then the entire agency arrangement will come within the Agents' Regulations.

Of the specific exclusions set out in the Agents' Regulations, the first two are identical to those set out at the first and second indents of article 1(3) of the 1986 Directive. The third exclusion, extended to cover examiners (a position similar to that of administrator in England and Wales), is similar to that in the third indent of article 1(3).

The other exclusions are:

- Commercial agents whose activities are unpaid (referred to in article 2(1) of the 1986 Directive);
- Commercial agents when they operate on commodity exchanges or in the commodity markets (referred to in article 2(1) of the 1986 Directive);
- There is an additional exclusion which is permitted by article 2(2) of the 1986 Directive. The Irish implementing Agents' Regulations have taken advantage of this to provide at regulation 2(1)(f) that a commercial agent does not include:

> A consumer credit agent or a mail order catalogue agent for consumer goods, whose activities, pursuant to paragraph (2) of this Regulation, are considered secondary.

Regulation (2) of the Agents' Regulations states that the activities of an agent of the category described in paragraph (1)(f) above shall be presumed to be secondary for the purposes of these Regulations unless established to the contrary. This explanation is not particularly helpful, but it must be assumed that a consumer credit agent and a mail order catalogue agent whose primary activity is something other than acting as agent are presumed to be excluded from the scope of the Agents' Regulations unless it is established that such activities are not secondary.

(5) How are agents distinguished from distributors?

Distributors often carry out similar functions to agents from the point of view of the manufacturer or supplier, both providing a means of selling goods within a particular territory. In legal terms, the distinction between being a distributor and an agent is dependent on the amount of financial risk accepted by the intermediary. In its classical sense, a distributor will acquire the goods from the supplier and will sell them on to customers on the distributor's account and at prices which the distributor has determined. If the distributor fails to sell all the goods which he acquired from the supplier, the distributor bears the loss; although in certain circumstances, the contract between the supplier and the distributor might entitle the distributor to sell some of the stock back to the supplier. On the other hand, an agent seeks out customers and obtains orders for goods, which orders are then passed back to the supplier. The supplier sells the goods directly to the customer, with the agent being remunerated by way of a commission or a percentage of the sale price to the customer.

The slight blurring of the lines regarding the bearing of financial risk arises in relation to *del credere* agents. A *del credere* agent, in addition to seeking customers and orders for the goods, undertakes to indemnify the principal for any loss incurred owing to the customer's failure to pay for the goods under the contract. The guarantee given by the *del credere* agent in respect of payment of the purchase price will usually mean that a high rate of commission is payable to the agent. In addition to any legislation considered here, a *del credere* agent is considered as a mercantile agent for the purposes of the Factors Act 1889. In most other respects, including in relation to competition law implications, *del credere* agents are in the same position as the standard commercial agent.

The issue of what financial risk is borne by the intermediary is highlighted in the EC Commission's Notice Concerning Exclusive Agency Agreements, issued in 1962. The Commission has taken the view that if an intermediary does not bear the main financial risk for the transaction (other than the guarantee which may be given by a *del credere* agent), then the agent will be considered to be acting only on behalf of the principal and not on his own account in the market. The agent is therefore not a separate "undertaking" within the meaning of article 85(1) of the Treaty of Rome. The consequence of coming within the term "agent" in the context of the EC Commission's Notice of 1962 is that the competition provisions of the Treaty of Rome, and by analogy of the Competition Act 1991, will not apply to the contractual arrangements between principal and agent. This question is discussed further in (20) below.

(6) What are the advantages of appointing a distributor?

Since the introduction of the Agents' Regulations, many companies are now considering appointing distributors instead of agents. Some of the advantages to a company of appointing a distributor are that the distributor will not be entitled to the rights (and in particular the payments on termination of the agency arrangement) which are set out in the 1986 Directive and the Agents' Regulations. Further, the distributor bears a greater part of the financial risk and will possibly undertake a greater responsibility for the success of the sale of the product in a particular territory or market. The reverse side of this is that the supplier may find it more difficult to control the activities of the distributor as compared to those of an agent. It is common for both agency agreements and distribution agreements to seek to control the activities of the agent and distributor in a territory, but in the latter instance a supplier must abide by the various competition laws affecting the distribution relationship.

(7) What are the rights and duties of a distributor?

While there may be terms implied into the distributorship relationship by law, the rights and duties of the distributor *vis-à-vis* the supplier are primarily governed by the terms of the distribution agreement entered into by the distributor and the supplier. The matters most commonly governed by the distribution agreement are set out in Chapter 2 on the UK position, and they will not be repeated here.

Where there is no written distribution agreement between the distributor and the supplier, the duties of the distributor may be ascertained from:

- The letter (if any) appointing the distributor;
- The content of any discussions or negotiations between the supplier and distributor prior to, or at the time of, the appointment of the distributor;
- The relationship which has grown up in practice between the supplier and distributor, as evidenced by any correspondence between them or any notes or memoranda of meetings; and
- The normal commercial practices prevailing within that particular product market or sector.

(8) What are the main statutory provisions affecting distributorship relationships?

The main statutory provisions in Ireland which may affect the rights and duties of a distributor to the supplier are the Competition Act 1991 and the Sale of Goods Act 1893 as amended and extended by the Sale of Goods and Supply of Services Act 1980.

(i) Competition Act 1991

The Competition Act 1991, which is very similar to articles 85 and 86 of the Treaty of Rome, has the effect of limiting to a certain extent the duties or obligations which can be imposed on a distributor by the supplier. For example, a supplier cannot:

- Restrict the distributor as regards which customers he will sell the goods to;
- Fix the price at which the distributor sells the goods, nor specify maximum or minimum profit margins which the distributor can charge; or
- Restrict the distributor from exporting the product.

While the law governing the relationship between a supplier and distributor, whether exclusive or not, arising out of the Competition Act 1991 is very similar to EU competition law, the fact that the Competition Act has a national, as opposed to an international, application (not being concerned with the possible effect on trade between Member States) could lead to a different (though not contrary) interpretation being given to the provisions of the Irish Competition Act 1991 than one might expect from the application of the provisions of articles 85 and 86 of the Treaty of Rome. Specific legal advice on obligations or restrictions contained in agreements between a supplier and an Irish distributor should be sought from qualified legal practitioners. Note that the Irish Competition Act 1991 may be relevant and must be considered even where the law of another jurisdiction is chosen as the governing law of the contract.

(ii) Irish sale of goods legislation

Irish legislation concerning the sale of goods is also relevant. The Sale of Goods Act 1893 as amended and extended by the Sale of Goods and Supply of Services Act 1980 forms the basic law. This legislation applies to persons who deal as consumers or in the course of business. It provides that the product sold must comply with its description, be of merchantable quality, be fit for its purpose, and, if a sample has been supplied previously, then it must also correspond with the sample. These provisions cannot be excluded where the dealing is with the consumer. However, these terms can be excluded in business contracts but only to the extent that the exclusions are fair and reasonable.

It will be the seller of the goods who is liable under this legislation. In a distributor relationship, the distributor is the seller of the goods, whereas in an agency relationship, the principal is the party liable. The principal in such circumstances would be relying on the agent to bring any exclusion clauses to the attention of the customer in advance.

(iii) Unfair contract terms

Note should also be taken of the Unfair Contract Terms Directive (93/13/EEC) which has been implemented in Ireland. It regulates and applies to contracts made between a consumer and the seller of goods which have not been individually negotiated. Any terms of such a contract which are found to be unfair because they are found in the black list of terms contained in that Directive or under its terms are not binding against the consumer. Again, it will be the principal who will be liable here.

In addition, care should also be taken where there are clauses excluding or limiting liability. The distributor or the principal, whichever is the party selling the goods and entering into the contract with the customer, should ensure that such clauses are brought to the attention of the customer in advance of a contract being made. Further, if a product being provided is a specialised one, the Irish courts have stressed that such prior notice is all the more important. However, these clauses can be binding if they have been incorporated into the contracts over a prolonged course of dealing involving successive contracts. Notwithstanding this, if there is a fundamental breach of a contract, *i.e.* where the breach is such that it goes to the root of the agreement, then the exclusion and limitation of liability clauses cannot be relied upon by the party in breach.

(9) What are the rights and duties of suppliers towards distributors?

A supplier's obligation towards his distributor will derive and be governed primarily by the provisions of the written contract between the parties, or, in the absence of a contract, will be implied by the practice that has developed between them and the terms and customs prevailing in that trade. The relationship between a supplier and a distributor is essentially one of supply and purchase. The supplier agrees to sell goods to the distributor, who agrees to purchase them and to sell them on to retailers, wholesalers or end users. Other provisions such as whether the distributor is exclusive for a particular territory, whether his sales must be limited to a certain territory, whether the goods must be sold on in a particular form, or in certain packaging, and whether the parties will co-operate in relation to advertising, promotions, etc are all at the discretion of the parties. Therefore, the extent of the rights and duties of each party can be as limited or as extensive as the parties agree.

Note, however, that there are limits on the parties' freedom to agree on certain terms in the contract arising from the Irish Competition Act 1991 as outlined in (8) above.

(10) What are the practical steps in appointing a commercial agent?

This matter is addressed in (28) below. A list of useful addresses is also included in Appendix D.

(11) What terms should be included in a contract with a commercial agent?

The Agents' Regulations implementing the 1986 Directive in Ireland are very brief. They do not select between the various options outlined in the Directive nor indicate how the 1986 Directive is to be applied to any particular Irish circumstances. There is therefore scope for confusion and ambiguity to arise in the relationship between a principal and an agent unless certain matters are clearly set out in a contract.

Previously, many agency arrangements with Irish agents were oral without any terms in writing, or consisted solely of a one sentence letter stating that X company hereby appoints Mr Y to be its agent for all X's products in Ireland. Since the introduction of the Agents' Regulations, there is a requirement that all agency contracts be evidenced in writing. Any agency contract which is not evidenced in writing shall not be valid for the purposes of the Agents' Regulations. This does not, however, require that all terms of the agency arrangement be in writing, nor that a formal contract be entered into. It is probably sufficient that one or other party makes a note in writing of what it considers to be the main terms of the agency contract. Further, arising from Article 13 of the 1986 Directive each party is entitled to receive from the other, on request, a signed written document setting out the terms of the agency contract including any terms subsequently agreed. It is therefore likely that from now on the majority of agency contracts will be set out in writing.

From the principal's point of view, and given the brevity of the Agents' Regulations, the following matters should be dealt with in a written agency contract:

- The identity and addresses of *the parties*.
- A *grant/appointment* clause, specifying what type of agent is being appointed, *i.e.* whether sole, exclusive, non-exclusive, *del credere* or otherwise. The appointment of a sole agent would mean that the principal could supply or sell himself to customers in the territory. Where the agent's appointment is exclusive, the principal cannot appoint any further agents for the same territory. As regards a *del credere* agent, see further (5) above.
- The *goods or products* covered by the agency contract (and whether this may be extended in future to cover new lines of goods or product ranges).
- The extent of the *territory*.

- The *date of commencement* of the agency relationship.
- The *duration or term* of the contract, making reference to the entitlement of either party to terminate on giving minimum notice and termination by one party by reason of the breach of contract by the other (see further (18) below).
- Setting of *sales targets* (if any) and provision for review of the same.
- *Duties of the agent.* These will vary from contract to contract in the light of the nature of the goods being sold. Other than the duties imposed on the agent by law (as regards which see (14) below) a principal may wish to insert some or all of the following in the agency contract:
    - specific tasks or activities which must be carried out by the agent, for example, a minimum number of visits to customers' premises during the year, attendance at certain trade shows or exhibitions, an obligation to carry a sufficient number of sample products;
    - an obligation to keep the principal advised of any legislative changes or any changes in commercial practice in the territory which might adversely affect the level of sales of the product;
    - an obligation to seek trade references from new customers and to endeavour as far as possible to seek only customers who are creditworthy and unlikely to result in bad debts accruing;
    - an obligation to be adequately trained in relation to, and knowledgeable about, the product, and, if relevant, to employ a sufficient number of suitably qualified staff to assist in performing the task of agent;
    - an obligation to maintain suitable premises for the purposes of the agency and to permanently display the name of the principal and the principal's products;
    - an obligation to attend promptly to any customer complaints in relation to the products and to liaise immediately with the principal in dealing with such complaints without admitting any liability in respect of the product or admitting that it is defective;
    - restrictions on the agent in relation to handling competing goods or engaging in any other activity which could undermine or detract from the efficiency of the agent acting on behalf of his principal (such non-competing provisions may, subject to compliance with the Irish Competition Act 1991, be extended for a certain period after the termination of the agency arrangement, in any event, not being longer than two years);

- obligations of maintaining the confidentiality of information made available to the agent by the principal, and in particular that such information will not be used other than for the purposes of carrying out his duties as agent;
- financial limitations on the agent, designed primarily to ensure that the agent does not pledge the credit of the principal or incur any debts on behalf of the principal other than as specifically agreed in advance; and
- duties of the agent in relation to queries or potential orders received from customers situated outside the territory.

- *Payment terms* — while specific provision should be made in the agency contract, the principal's obligation to pay the agent, and the timing of such payments is closely regulated by the 1986 Directive.
- *Duties of the principal* — other than the primary duty which is to pay the agent his commission — the duties of the principal again fall into the following main categories:
  - The duties of the principal in respect of the first two categories *viz*, duties implied by Irish law and duties imposed by the provisions of the 1986 Directive are considered in more detail at (12) below.
  - The third category comprises whatever other duties might be imposed by the agency contract. These duties would directly relate to the nature of the goods or the particular market. Examples might be:
    - to supply promotional material to the agent (either free of charge or at a nominal or full cost);
    - to comply with the requirements of national laws in relation to safety requirements, packaging, trade marks, etc;
    - to fulfil orders obtained by the agent within a specified time;
    - to provide the agent with such advice, assistance and such after-sales service as are required by the goods the subject of the contract.
- A clause clarifying *liability and responsibility for defective products* under the Liability for Defective Products Act 1991, and insurance provisions.
- *Termination* — a clause setting out the notice periods which will be given by the principal and the agent on termination of the agreement, which can be no less than the minimum notice set out in the Directive,

and details of consequences of termination shall be included. There should also be a clear choice made by the principal and the agent as to whether the indemnity or the compensation provisions in the Directive will apply. This is particularly important in view of the manner of implementation of the Directive in Ireland, which is discussed at greater length at (12) and (18) below.

- *Optional clauses* which could be inserted include:
  - An entitlement on the part of the agent to use sub-agents or a prohibition on the same (which given the personal nature of agency is not strictly necessary).
  - Clarification of whether the principal and/or the agent may assign the benefit of the agreement (with or without the consent of the other party).
  - Restrictive covenants to the extent permitted by law, with particular note being taken of the Competition Act 1991 and the decisions of the Competition Authority thereunder. In general, restrictive covenants cannot be any longer in duration, wider in geographical scope or more extensive in respect of the range of products or the categories of customers than is strictly necessary to protect the legitimate commercial interests of the principal. Also the nature of the product or service, the level of technical know-how involved and the structure of the market will all be relevant to determining the maximum permitted duration and scope of the restrictive covenant.
- General legal provisions ("Boilerplate" clauses) such as:
  - A *force majeure* clause.
  - A clause specifying the governing law of the contract and which courts shall have jurisdiction to hear disputes.
  - Provision for amendment of the agreement in the future and whether this should be by agreement between the parties in writing with the possible exception of price lists or product range which may be amended unilaterally by the principal.
  - Arbitration, mediation or conciliation clause.
- Usually various schedules are attached to the agreement setting out in greater detail a description of the goods the subject of the contract, the price and payment terms for the goods and other technical or contractual details which may need to be amended from time to time.

It must be remembered that each agency contract will vary depending on the nature of the goods, the specific duties which are required of the agent and the results of any negotiation which occur between the principal and the agent. It is strongly advised that no agency contract be entered into without both parties seeking and obtaining legal advice.

(12) What are the duties of a principal?

As mentioned at (11) above, the duties of a principal fall generally into three main categories which are:

- duties implied by Irish law;
- duties imposed on the principal by the Directive; and
- duties specifically provided in the agency contract.

(i) Duties implied by Irish law

This is generally expressed as the principal's duty to act in good faith towards the agent. This may be set out in greater detail in the agency contract, to include such matters as providing such information as the agent may require for the effective execution of agency transactions, to accept all offers forwarded to the principal by the agent, or to do all acts necessary for the promotion of the agent's activities. Even if not specified in the agency contract, the general duty of the principal to act in good faith would result in the principal being under the following duties:

- A duty to remunerate the agent. An agent is generally entitled to receive remuneration in consideration of the activities he has undertaken on behalf of the principal. This remuneration should be specifically agreed, but, if not, it would be calculated on the basis of the value of the services rendered to the principal, generally on a percentage basis according to the level of commission which would be standard in the trade. It is interesting to note that prior to the implementation of the 1986 Directive, the duty of a principal to pay remuneration would not, in the absence of express provisions in the agency contract, have obliged the principal to pay the agent commission on repeat orders or on orders placed with the principal after termination of the agency, even if the customer was one which had been obtained for the principal by the agent prior to termination.

- Duty to indemnify the agent. The principal is under a general duty to indemnify his agent for all costs and expenses incurred by the agent for activities which are within the scope of the authority granted to the agent. This duty, and the extent to which expenses will be reimbursable, may be varied by the agency contract and will be limited by the extent of the authority given by the principal.
- The above two duties of the principal to remunerate the agent and to reimburse him for expenses give rise to an implied right on the part of the agent to a lien on the goods of his principal of which he is in lawful possession. The lien will endure until all outstanding debts owing to the agent by the principal are satisfied.

(ii) Duties imposed by the Directive

These equate to the new rights which the agent has acquired under the 1986 Directive, and are in addition to the principal's duty to act dutifully and in good faith. The specific duties on the principal are:

- To provide the agent with the necessary documentation relating to the goods;
- To notify the agent of a potential downturn in the business arising in the agent's territory;
- To inform the agent within a reasonable period of the acceptance, refusal, and/or the non-execution of any commercial transaction by a customer which the agent has procured for the principal;
- To pay the commission due to the agent within not more than four months of the date when it becomes due;
- To pay commission on repeat orders from third parties whom the agent has previously acquired as a customer in transactions of the same kind;
- To pay commission on transactions arising with a customer belonging to a specific geographical area or group of customers with whom the agent has an exclusive right to act;
- To pay the agent commission after termination of the agency contract where the circumstances in article 8(a) or (b) of the 1986 Directive occur;
- To provide the agent with a written document setting out the terms of the agency agreement;

- To give the agent minimum notice of termination of the agency; and
- To indemnify and/or pay the agent compensation on the termination of the agency contract.

As an ancillary obligation to the above, the agent is entitled to demand that he is provided with all the information and, in particular, an extract from the books which are available to the principal which the agent needs in order to check the amount of the commission due to him.

(iii) Duties specifically provided in the agency contract

It is open to the parties to provide that there will be further obligations or duties imposed on the principal (see (11) above).

(13) Can any of the duties of the principal be avoided?

The duties which arise by virtue of Irish law, *i.e.* the duty to remunerate the agent, would generally not be excluded by contract, although it is open to the parties to agree that the agent will act on a voluntary unpaid basis, or on the basis that expenses only would be paid. The duty to indemnify the agent is central to the nature of the relationship between principal and agent, and therefore would be difficult to avoid, although it would be open to the principal and agent to agree what specific costs or expenses would be reimbursed by the principal and/or the mechanism for vouching or approving expenses on the part of the agent.

The majority of duties imposed by the 1986 Directive may not however be avoided. There is an option provided to Member States in the implementation of the Directive as regards the extra entitlement to commission, and Ireland has provided that this arises only where the agent has the exclusive right to a specific geographical area or group of customers and where the transaction has been entered into with a customer belonging to that area or group. As regards the duty to pay compensation or an indemnity on termination, no selection between these options was made by the Irish implementing Regulations. It would therefore be advisable for Irish principals and agents to resolve this matter between them, though in the absence of any court decision on this point, one cannot guarantee that a solution worked out between a principal and an agent during the term of the agreement would be legally enforceable by one party against the other. This is because article 19 of the 1986 Directive does not permit the parties to derogate from the compensation and indemnity provisions to the detriment of the commercial agent before the agency contract expires.

(14) What are the duties of a commercial agent?

The duties of the agent derive from three sources. They may be:

- implied from common law;
- contained in the Directive; or
- specified in the agency contract.

(i) Duties implied from common law

Common law duties are implied into all agency arrangements governed by the laws of Ireland unless expressly varied or excluded by the terms of the agency contract. They are as follows:

- Duty to exercise care and skill. Under Irish law, an agent has a duty to exercise a reasonable degree of care and skill in the performance of his functions. An agent who has held himself out as having particular skill or competence will be expected to perform his duties at that level of skill and competence.
- An agent must comply with all the terms of the agency contract and, in particular, must obey all instructions given to him by his principal from time to time unless such instructions are unreasonable, unlawful, or fall outside the scope of the agency contract.
- Duty to act personally. The relationship between a principal and agent is deemed to be of a personal nature and the agent may not, except with the express or implied authority of the principal, delegate the authority which has been granted to him. An implied authority for the agent to delegate may arise where the principal has entrusted the agent with carrying out such functions as would not be possible for one individual to carry out on his own.

- Duty to act in good faith. The nature of the relationship between the principal and the agent requires that the agent act in good faith for the benefit of the principal, and in particular:
  - the agent may not make any secret profit from the agency relationship, whether directly or indirectly;
  - the agent should not put himself in a position where his own interests and his duties as agent conflict;
  - the agent is under a duty not to act for any other principal whose products compete with those of the first principal; and
  - the agent is under a duty not to disclose or to make any personal gain from confidential information supplied to him by the principal.

The latter two of these duties are somewhat vague and will vary according to circumstances in each case and so such matters should be specifically dealt with in the agency contract.

- Duty to account to the principal. An agent must keep accounts and records of all agency transactions entered into by him on behalf of the principal, and must render such accounts to the principal when requested. Further all moneys received by the agent on behalf of the principal must be kept separate from the agent's own moneys and must be handed over to the principal when required.

(ii) Duties contained in Directive

The duties of the agent arising from the Directive as applied in Ireland by the Agents' Regulations overlap somewhat with those implied by Irish common law. This second category of duties comprises those contained in article 3(1) and (2) of the 1986 Directive.

The duties contained in article 3(1) and (2) of the 1986 Directive apply in Ireland and technically do not need to be repeated in an agency contract, though to do so may act as a reminder to the agent of his statutory obligations. These are:

- when performing his activities a commercial agent must look after his principal's interests and act dutifully and in good faith;
- the commercial agent must make proper efforts to negotiate and, where appropriate, conclude the transactions he is instructed to take care of;

- the commercial agent must communicate to his principal all the necessary information available to him; and
- the commercial agent must comply with reasonable instructions given by the principal.

(iii) Duties specified in agency contract

These will be negotiated between the parties, and may include some of the same duties set out at (11) above.

(15) Can any of the duties of the agent be avoided?

The duties implied by Irish common law can be contracted out of, provided the parties express a clear intention to do so. However, article 5 of the 1986 Directive provides that the duties of the agent contained in article 3 cannot be avoided. Neither can the agent derogate from his obligation to provide the principal with a written signed document, if requested, setting out the terms of the agency contract pursuant to article 13 of the 1986 Directive.

(16) How can the performance of the agent be monitored?

It is open to the principal to specify in the agency contract that a certain level of sales must be obtained by the agent in each quarter/year/other time period and if the agent does not attain such a level of sales, the principal may terminate the agreement immediately. Inserting such a sales target will give the principal a method of terminating the appointment of an agent who is not contributing sufficiently to the principal's business. However, any sales targets included should be reasonable and take into account market circumstances as is required by the principal's general duty to act in good faith towards the agent.

It should also be recalled that the Agents' Regulations pose a specific obligation on the principal to notify the agent of a potential downturn in the business arising in the agent's territory. In drafting a contract from the point of view of an agent, it is not uncommon to include a provision that the principal will not be entitled to terminate the agent's appointment if the failure to meet sales targets is as a result of circumstances beyond the control of the agent; for example, because of a general downturn in the economy, due to specific problems with the product not caused by the agent, or because of the entry of strong competitors into the market. If the principal wishes to rely on the provision in the contract entitling him to terminate the appointment, such as a failure to reach sales targets, these factors should be borne in mind in determining whether the principal's action is reasonable or not.

As regards generally monitoring the agent's performance, there is no substitute for paying careful attention to the activities of the agent, insisting on prompt delivery of monthly or quarterly reports and accounts, and making enquiries occasionally of customers as to the service they are receiving. Close attention to detail by the principal will also keep the principal up-to-date with any financial difficulties that may arise with any of his customers. With a *del credere* agent, any failure by customers to pay can be the responsibility of the agent.

(17) What is the principal's responsibility for the acts of the agent?

The essence of an agency relationship is that the agent is acting not on his own behalf but on behalf of his principal. Any contracts concluded between the agent, on behalf of the principal, and third parties are deemed to be created between the principal and the third party. The agent himself does not derive any rights from, nor does he incur any liabilities under the agency contract as it is the principal who is a party to the contract.

Subject to the qualifications set out below, the principal will be responsible for contracts entered into by the agent on his behalf where the agent has actual authority to bind the principal, which authority may be expressly given in the agency contract or be implied from it. A principal should be aware that not only authority but also *apparent* or *ostensible* authority of the agent to bind the principal will result in the principal being contractually bound.

Apparent or ostensible authority will arise where the principal has represented to the third party, or the circumstances of the agent's activities are such that a third party would be entitled to assume that the agent had authority to carry out the acts which he has done. For example, if the agent acts in a situation where an agent of that character would usually have the authority to bind his principal, the third party would be entitled to assume, in the absence of notice to the contrary, that the agent can bind the principal. Any agreement which is reached between the agent and the principal restricting the agent's authority will not prejudice the rights of a third party unless the third party actually knew of the limitation on the agent's authority. It should also be noted that any claim which the principal may have against the agent for having acted fraudulently, or for his own personal benefit, or outside his actual authority will not usually affect the contractual liability of a principal to a third party who had no knowledge of the agent's lack of authority. A principal may be held liable in tort for the negligent or fraudulent misrepresentations of the agent, if the agent was acting within his actual or ostensible authority at the time.

That said, the liability of a principal towards a third party for contracts entered into by the agent will vary depending on whether the existence of the principal was disclosed by the agent to the third party and, further, if the identity or name of the principal was also disclosed to the third party prior to any contract coming into force. In the circumstances where an agent concludes a contract with a third party without disclosing the existence of the principal, or that the agent is acting on behalf of the principal, the agent will have rights and liabilities under that contract as a principal party to the contract. If the principal wishes, he may disclose his existence to the third party who may then elect whether to treat the agent or the principal as the party primarily responsible under the contract.

The risks associated with an agent acting in a manner so as to bind the principal will be minimised by:

- The principal and the agent clearly agreeing in advance what authority the agent has to enter contracts on behalf of the principal.
- The principal making it clear to third parties *(i.e.* customers and potential customers) what authority the agent has to take orders or to enter into contracts with the customers on behalf of the principal.
- The principal putting in place procedures and documentation which clearly set out for the benefit of customers when a contract for the supply of goods or services will come into force.

Over and above these precautions, a principal should ensure that satisfactory trade references are obtained from trade creditors, and if possible other principals before appointing the agent.

(18) How can a principal terminate an agency contract?

An agent who fails adequately to perform the duties of an agent, whether these are duties implied by common law, imposed by the Agents'

Regulations or set out in the agency contract (see (14) above), may find his appointment as agent terminated by the principal. To avoid protracted disputes and possible legal action, the principal should ensure in advance that the circumstances in which the principal may terminate the agreement and the breach of what duties will result in termination are clearly set out in the agency contract. In this regard, a principal should exercise some degree of reasonableness, possibly by giving the agent sufficient time to remedy a breach if it is capable of remedy.

If the principal wishes to be able to terminate the agent's appointment for misrepresentation, this again should be clearly stated in the agency contract. It should be noted that the 1986 Directive does not require that the minimum notice period (see (21) below) should apply where the termination of the agency contract is because of the failure of one party to carry out all, or part, of its obligations. It should also be noted that where the principal is entitled under national law to terminate the agency contract immediately because of default attributable to the agent, then the entitlement to indemnity or compensation does not arise. Under Irish law, a principal will be entitled to terminate an agency contract immediately if the agent commits a fundamental breach of the agreement, or commits a breach of a term of the contract which is specified in the contract as a breach resulting in immediate termination, provided that such provision is reasonable.

If the agent ceases to carry out his duties under the agency contract (whether because of general inactivity or because the agent is acquiring business on his own account or acting for a third party), the principal's remedy will depend on whether the agent's action or inaction constitutes a breach of an express duty contained in the agency contract or an implied duty. By virtue of the 1986 Directive, an agent is obliged to make proper efforts to negotiate and, where appropriate, conclude the transactions he is instructed to take care of. If the agent fails to make such efforts, without having terminated the agreement in the manner provided for, the principal may have an action in damages against the agent where the principal can show loss or damage (including lost business) resulting to him because of the agent's inactivity.

The agent is also under a general duty not to make any personal gain from his position as agent, other than the remuneration agreed with the principal, and as part of the duty to act in good faith for the benefit of the principal, not to act for any other principal whose products compete with those of his first principal. In many instances, it has been expressly agreed between the parties that the agent may act for other principals, sometimes restricted to products or services which are not in direct competition with the products of his main principal. In such circumstances, the remedies which a principal may have will be much more uncertain unless the duties and obligations of the agent, and the consequences of breach, are clearly set out in the agency contract.

Finally, if the agent stops working for the principal because of old age, ill health, death or other infirmity, the resulting termination of the agency contract will still give rise to an obligation on the principal to indemnify and/or pay compensation to the agent (see further (21) below).

(19) Is it possible to restrict the activities of an agent?

As part of the general duty on the agent to act in good faith and in the best interests of his principal, an agent may be restricted from acting for any other principal whose products compete with those of the principal, and will be under a duty not to disclose to third parties any confidential information supplied by the principal. From the point of view of competition law, the Competition Act 1991 will not generally apply to agents who act only on behalf of third parties and are not engaged in commercial activities in their own right. The Competition Act 1991 (which is very similar to articles 85 and 86 of the Treaty of Rome) will only apply to "undertakings", by analogy with EU law, so that the agent is not regarded as a separate undertaking for the purpose of competition law, the commercial agent should "neither undertake or engage in activities proper to an independent trader in the course of commercial operations" (EC Commission Notice concerning exclusive agency agreements made with commercial agents, 1962). Therefore, as long as the agent is an integrated part of the principal's business, and carries no real financial risk in his own right, the Competition Act 1991 will not apply to restrictive covenants between a principal and an agent during the period of the agency.

(20) What about restrictive trade clauses following termination of the agency agreement?

Once the agency has terminated, the agent is no longer an integrated part of the principal's business and may then be a separate undertaking within the meaning of the Competition Act 1991. The 1986 Directive would permit a restraint of trade clause for up to two years after termination of the agency contact, provided that the restraint of trade covenant is concluded in writing and relates to the group of customers and the geographical area entrusted to the commercial agent and to the kind of goods covered by the agency under the agency contract, and no more. While the question has not yet been considered by the Irish courts, it is probable, from decisions taken by the Irish Competition Authority that the duration of a restraint of trade covenant may not extend for more than six months after termination of the agency contract. A longer restraint of trade covenant may be deemed to be an unlawful restriction on the agent competing with his principal, thereby denying the agent of his right to earn a livelihood, and so void and unenforceable under the Competition Act 1991.

It is important to note that the provisions of the Competition Act 1991 will apply regardless of whether the agent agrees to the restraint of trade clause or not. In situations where the agent is an "undertaking" within the meaning of the Competition Act 1991, that is, he enters into business on his own account (as opposed to being an employee or simply an agent of another company), and the restraint of trade clause is more extensive or for a longer duration than is strictly necessary to protect the legitimate commercial interests of the principal, the restriction should be notified to the Competition Authority for clearance. If it is not so notified and approved by the Competition Authority, the principal may find that he cannot enforce the restraint of trade clause against the agent.

While the circumstances of each restriction will vary considerably, in determining whether a restraint of trade clause is enforceable or not, the authorities in Ireland will look at three things:

- the duration;
- the geographical scope; and
- the business to which it applies.

The clause will not be upheld if it unreasonably prevents an agent from earning a livelihood because the clause is excessively long in duration, or it operates on a nationwide basis when the agency only applies to a part of the country. In addition, if the agency contract is exclusive and the clause prevents the agent from engaging new agencies on termination in the same area, this may very well be deemed an unreasonable restriction on the agent's right to earn a living. However, it should be noted that the Irish authorities do also recognise the validity of these clauses where they are employed as a genuine attempt to protect a legitimate commercial interest which is capable of protection. Essentially, the validity of each of these clauses will depend on each case's own circumstances. However, such clauses should always be severable if necessary from the agency contract. Thus, it is recommended that a severance clause be included in agency contracts, where a principal proposes relying on a restraint of trade clause, and specific advice should be sought from legal advisers with knowledge of Irish law.

(21) What about the duration and termination of the agreement?

Whether the agency contract is concluded for a long or short fixed term or an indefinite term will depend on the nature of the goods, the structure of the market, and the circumstances of the principal and agent. In many cases, it is appropriate to provide for an initial term of, say, two years with the agency contract being renewable by notice of either party; or else automatically renewed for further periods of, for example, one year, unless notice to terminate is served by one or other party.

Where the term of an agreement is stated to be for a short fixed term, for example, six months, and further fixed terms are entered into subsequent to the end of the first fixed term, the 1986 Directive provides that where a contract for a fixed period continues to be performed by both parties after that period has expired, the contract will be deemed to be converted into a contract for an indefinite period.

Where the contract is for an indefinite period, the minimum notice provisions contained in the 1986 Directive *(i.e.* one month's notice in the first year of the contract, two months' notice for the second year and three months' for the third year or more years) apply.

It should be noted that even if the agency contract terminates at the end of the fixed period, this will not prevent the agent's entitlement to compensation/indemnity, or to continuing commission on repeat orders, from accruing.

The consequences of termination of the agency contract are the most revolutionary aspects of the 1986 Directive for principals in Ireland. Prior to the introduction of the Agents' Regulations, there was doubt as to whether an agent was entitled to receive any commission on any repeat sales made by the principal to customers whom the agent had acquired for the principal, after the agency contract had been terminated. In several cases in the Irish High Court it was held that, because of the absence of express provision in the agency contract, the agent was not entitled to commission on repeat orders. This is no longer the case.

(22) What other provisions concern the governing law and jurisdiction?

The majority of agents operating in Ireland act on behalf of foreign principals, many of them being United Kingdom companies or enterprises based in other countries of the EU. It is also common for the agency contract to specify that the governing law of the agency contract shall be that of the principal's residence/jurisdiction.

The 1986 Directive is stated to apply to the laws of Member States governing the relations between commercial agents and their principals. Where the parties have agreed that the relations will be governed by the law of a country which is not a Member State, the 1986 Directive may not necessarily apply. The Irish implementing Regulations do not assist in clarifying the matter, as they simply state, at regulation 3, that the 1986 Directive shall, subject to these Regulations, apply to the relations between commercial agents and their principals from 1 January 1994.

Generally, it is open to the parties to agree between them what law will apply to the agency contract. An argument could be made that regulation 3, quoted above, has the effect of applying the 1986 Directive to commercial agents and their principals where either of the parties operates in Ireland. This question is not clear, and commercial agents acting for a principal based outside the EU and EFTA should be aware that they may not have the protection of the 1986 Directive.

A further problem may arise for agents in Ireland acting for principals based in the UK, under an agency contract which is stated to be governed by English law, in that the UK implementing Regulations are stated only to apply "in relation to the activities of the agent in Great Britain". In such an instance, English law, without the benefit of the implementing Regulations, will govern the agency contract, and the agent may be relying solely on rights accruing under the agency contract or at common law.

However, given the attitude of the Irish courts to agents, and the position taken in related matters, such as employment protection, and the need for a universal application of EU legislation, it is likely that where an agent is operating in Ireland, whether for:

- a principal based outside the EU with an agency contract stated to be governed by the law of the principal's jurisdiction; or
- acting for a UK company with English law as the governing law of the agency contract,

an Irish Court would look favourably on any action taken by an Irish agent claiming rights which would accrue to him under the 1986 Directive.

It should be noted that this area is fraught with difficulties and there has as yet been no clarification of the point by any court decision.

In relation to jurisdiction, the principal should specify that the courts of his own jurisdiction will hear any and all claims relating to or arising from the agency contract. It is advisable in all events to avoid the situation arising where the courts of one jurisdiction hear a dispute, but apply the law of another jurisdiction. Such a situation entails having legal experts to advise the trial judge on what exactly is the law of the other jurisdiction. It should be noted that some countries give jurisdiction to the courts of the agent's domicile (for example Spain) irrespective of provisions in the agency contract.

(23) What about arbitration/conciliation/alternative dispute resolution to settle disputes?

Where an agency contract contains many technical matters which could give rise to disputes between parties, it may be appropriate to have an arbitration or other alternative dispute resolution clause inserted into the agency contract so that a third party who is familiar with the technical side and jargon of the industry will be the arbitrator or conciliator. This is better than having the matter heard by a trial judge who may not be familiar with the technical aspects of the particular industry. On other occasions, principals may prefer to leave matters to be litigated in the courts, as this may deter the agent from becoming involved in a legal dispute over minor matters. Whether arbitration or alternative dispute resolution clauses are included will depend entirely on the circumstances of the relationship between the parties and the particular preference which the parties may have *vis-à-vis* alternative dispute resolution.

(24) Is there a small claims procedure in Ireland?

In Ireland, a small claims procedure was recently introduced for disputes up to £500 only and applies to consumer disputes. The procedure is relatively informal, the cost is low and legal advisers are not involved.

Disputes between principals and agents up to the value of £5,000 may be brought in the District Court. Here, the procedures are relatively straightforward and the cost is reasonable. It is not always necessary to engage legal representation in claims before the District Court, although it is generally advisable to do so. For any claims above £5,000 up to £30,000, proceedings are within the jurisdiction of the Circuit Court. The High Court has jurisdiction where claims exceed £30,000.

(25) What about product liability and insurance?

Since the introduction of the Liability for Defective Products Act 1991, implementing the EEC Directive on Product Liability (85/374/EEC), principals and agents have become more aware of the need to carry insurance against actions arising from defects in products. In most instances, the agent would not have a primary responsibility for any action brought by a customer under the Liability for Defective Products Act 1991, as the contract for the supply and sale of the goods is made directly between the principal and the customer.

The two instances in which an agent may become liable for an action arising from a defective product are:

- Where the agent is the importer of the goods into the EU the principal being based outside the EU and the customer has had no direct contract with the principal; and
- Where the agent enters into a contract for the supply of goods with the customer without disclosing the existence or the identity of the principal. In this event, the customer may, once the existence of the principal comes to light, opt whether to proceed against the agent on the basis of the contract, or to acknowledge the existence of the principal and proceed against the principal.

Where a principal carries product liability insurance, it would be advisable for an agent to have his interest noted on the principal's insurance policy, particularly where one or other of the above situations arises. If the agent's activities are such that at no time does he become a party to any contract for the supply of goods to the customer, then insurance for product liability should not be necessary. The agent may, however, be advised to take out and maintain employer liability insurance, and motor vehicle insurance with the risks extended to cover the agent's activities.

The question also arises as to whether the principal is carrying on business in the country of the agent. Generally the basic test in Ireland for the purposes of taxation is where do the operations take place from which the profits arise? The answer to this question will be considered in conjunction with all the other circumstances in relation to the way in which the business of the principal operates.

(26) What are the consequences of bad debts and when does the agent's commission become due?

The 1986 Directive sets out in some detail the latest time at which an agent must be paid the commission on transactions between the principal and the customer. Effectively commission becomes due when:

- the principal executes the transaction (for example delivers the goods agreed to be sold to the customer);
- the principal should have executed the transaction with the customer; and
- the customer executes the transaction (for example pays the price of the goods sold).

Therefore, if no specific provision relating to the time of payment to the agent is made in the agency contract, then the commission is due on the happening of the first of the above events. If the principal and agent specifically agree a longer time for payment between them, the latest point at which the commission becomes due to the agent is when the customer executes his part of the transaction or should have done so if the principal had executed or performed his part of the contract (usually, this would be the delivery of the goods by the principal).

It is therefore possible to provide in the agency contract that commission is only payable to the agent when the principal is paid. This is done by specifying that the commission will become due when the customer has paid the principal for the goods. Principals should be aware that unless the payment provisions of the agency contract are carefully worded, the commission could become due as soon as the principal has delivered the goods to the customer, even if the customer is not due to pay for those goods until the end of a specified credit period.

In the event that commission has been paid to an agent, and the customer turns out to be a bad debt, then article 11 of the 1986 Directive provides that the right to the commission of the agent is extinguished, and any commission which the agent has already received shall be refunded to the principal. The extinction of the right to commission occurs if it is established that the contract between the third party and the principal will not be executed and the non-execution is due to a reason for which the principal is not to blame. To avoid any doubt in this area, it may be advisable for the principal to state in the agency contract that the contract between the customer and the principal will not be deemed to be executed if the customer has not paid for the goods, regardless of whether the principal has delivered the goods and cannot regain possession of them.

Once it is established when the commission becomes due, it shall be paid not later than the last day of the month following the quarter in which it became due. By that date, the principal is also obliged to supply the agent with a statement of the commission due and setting out the main components used in calculating the amount of the commission.

(27) What general advice should be given to principals?

Both the size and nature of the Irish market make agency arrangements an attractive option for foreign principals wishing to sell their goods in Ireland. The Irish marketplace is sufficiently different to any other territory in Europe to warrant local expertise and contacts. On the other hand, given the nature of some goods, the size of the territory is often not sufficient to warrant establishing a subsidiary, a place of business or even a distribution network. There are many experienced agents prepared to act for foreign companies who can generate considerable business in Ireland.

Principals should, however, be aware that businesses in Ireland tend to take extended credit periods, which may in turn result in a greater proportion of debts being written off. While a company needs to be competitive in the credit terms which it gives to Irish businesses, principals would be well advised to develop tight credit control procedures for collecting debts promptly at the expiration of the credit period.

Specific issues which arise in Ireland that may not be encountered elsewhere are the failure of the Agents' Regulations to select between compensation and indemnity provisions regarding the termination of the agency contract. While legal advice should assist in producing an agency contract which is as clear as possible in relation to post-termination payments, principals should note that until there have been a number of court decisions regarding these post-termination payments, the position in Ireland is far from clear. The potential costs of post-termination payments (including both continuing commission on repeat orders and compensation and/or indemnity) should be factored into the cost of appointing and maintaining agents in Ireland.

Principals should also bear in mind the provisions of the Competition Act 1991, which affect post-termination "non-compete" covenants. The Act may also possibly affect restrictive covenants intended to run during the term of the agency contract if the agent acts in such a way that he is not sufficiently integrated into the principal's business to be considered a part of its economic unit.

In order to give the agency a greater chance of success, the principal would be well advised to:

- Carefully consider the agent's proven experience, competence and familiarity with the marketplace and the principal's products before appointment.
- Obtain and check trade and bank references carefully before appointing the agent.
- Provide the agent with oral assistance, information, promotional material and training in relation to the product so that the agent will be an effective seller of the principal's product.
- Keep a close eye on the agent's progress, ensuring in particular that regular reports and accounts are obtained from the agent.
- Develop and implement a thorough credit control mechanism to minimise late payments by customers and bad debts.
- Ensure the agent has a compatible computer system which might be able to network with the principal's. This could give added information flow and supervision where by use of a modem the principal could access the agent's system and examine the state of play of the agent's business.
- Obtain expert legal advice prior to appointing any agent, paying particular attention to the matters raised in this chapter. This advice is more important than ever following the inadequate implementation in Ireland of the 1986 Directive.

(28) What concluding advice should be given to agents?

The agent should thoroughly check the standing and reputation of the company or enterprise that will be his principal. Among the specific issues to be addressed by the agent are:

- the financial stability of the company (by way of a review of its most recent published accounts and any other information that is available);
- the credit-rating of the company;
- the quality of the products to be sold;
- the price-competitive position of the products in the market;
- the level of after-sales service, technical assistance and general back up provided by the company; and
- the structure and probable development of the market into which the agent will be selling.

In particular, the agent should be wary of taking on duties or obligations which are beyond his control. For example, provisions relating to sales targets should be reasonable, and where a sales target is not reached because of circumstances not attributable to the agent, then the agent should not be penalised. Such circumstances would include where the principal's products were defective and/or had to be recalled from the market, or where there was a general decline in that product market.

Also the agent should check that the provisions relating to payment of commission are in accordance with his entitlements under the Agents' Regulations. Legal advice to ensure that the agency contract is not excessively onerous or unreasonable should be obtained.

CONTENTS OF CHAPTER 11

Italy

11. ITALY

Avv. Antonietta Marsaglia, Studio Legale Spreafico Marsaglia, Milan

(1) What is meant by "commercial agent" in Italy?

Under Italian law an independent agent (*agente commerciale*) is an agent who acts at his own risk, undertaking to promote, for a commission, the conclusion of contracts on behalf of the principal in a specific territory. The object of the contract can be products or services.

Agents working for one principal only, are called *monomandatari* and those working for more than one principal are called *plurimandatari*. *Rappresentanti di commercio* are agents who have the power to represent the principal and conclude contracts binding on the principal. An agent whose power is limited to the promotion of contracts on behalf of the principal is an *agente di commercio.*

(2) Are there other forms of representation?

Yes. Independent agents must be distinguished from:

- *a mediator* who is a person who puts two or more parties into contact for the conclusion of a transaction without being bound to either of them by a relationship of collaboration, employment or representation and who is not a party to the contract;
- *a dealer* who acts for a principal but on an irregular and discontinuous basis with no specific territory or right of exclusivity;
- *an employed agent* who has an activity similar to that of the independent commercial agent but is an employee of the principal, enjoys welfare and social security assistance as an employee and bears no risk in relation to his activity; although, in some instances, he might receive a salary and a commission on sales as an incentive to generate business.

(3) Is there a registration requirement for independent agents?

Yes. The Law of 3 May 1985 No. 204 instituted a Register for independent agents where all agents must be registered. A contract entered into with an agent who is not registered in the Register is void as an agency contract, although it might, of course, have the characteristics of a mediation or similar contract.

The agents' Register is kept at the Companies' Registry Office (*Registro delle Imprese*) situated in each county town (*capoluogo di provincia*), which gives all the necessary information.

These are the main prerequisites for registration as an agent:

- citizenship of one of the EU countries or stable domicile within Italian territory (no specific qualifying period is required);
- secondary school diploma;
- the intention to act as an agent within Italian territory.

All agents acting within Italian territory have to be registered. Therefore:

- Italian agents acting in Italy have to be registered;
- foreign agents acting in Italy have to be registered;
- Italian subjects acting as agents abroad need not be registered; and
- foreign subjects acting as agents abroad for an Italian principal need not be registered.

(4) What must be included in a contract with a commercial agent?

(i) Formal requirements

The agency agreement need not be in writing to be valid. However, each party has the right to obtain from the other side a written copy of the agreement (article 1742 of the Civil Code).

(ii) Applicable law

Since 1 April 1991 under Italian law the law applicable to international contractual relationships has been established pursuant to the Rome

Convention on the law governing contractual obligations of 19 June 1980, which was ratified by Italy on 18 December 1984. Consequently the law applicable to agency agreements stipulated after 1 April 1991 has been established according to the following criteria:

- The parties can choose the law which they wish to be applicable to their relationship. The choice can be specified in the agreement or subsequently and does not need to be in writing (but see (4)(i) above). The stipulated law can cover only a part or the whole of the agreement.
- Where the parties have not specified the law governing the agreement, the applicable law will be that which is closest to the agreement. This is usually considered to be the law of the state where the agent carries out his activity.
- The laws of a foreign country will not be applied in Italy if they contravene the rules of public order.

(iii) Jurisdiction

The general principles which govern Italian jurisdiction are set out in articles 1–5 of the Civil Procedure Code. In particular, article 4 specifies the instances where a foreign subject can be called before the Italian courts. Under these rules there is Italian jurisdiction over the foreign party of an agency agreement if: (i) he has accepted Italian jurisdiction; (ii) he is resident or domiciled in Italy; (iii) the claim concerns obligations arising, or to be executed, in Italy; and (iv) on a basis of reciprocity the judge of the State to which the foreign subject belongs can decide claims made against an Italian citizen.

Where the relationship is between parties belonging to countries that have ratified or adhered to the Brussels Convention on Jurisdiction and the Enforcement of Judgments in Civil and Commercial Matters, 27 September 1968 ("Brussels Convention"), articles 1–5 of the Civil Procedure Code are substituted by the dispositions of the Brussels Convention, which therefore applies.

Under the Brussels Convention a subject can always be called before the judge of his place of domicile. Alternatively, the defendant domiciled in the territory of a contracting State can be called before the judge of another contracting State if this is the place in which the obligations being discussed in the claim have been, or must be, carried out.

Article 17 of the Brussels Convention also enables the parties to agree in writing, or with a verbal agreement confirmed in writing, specifying the courts having jurisdiction over the contract in derogation of the disposition of the Brussels Convention itself. The Lugano Convention of 16 September 1988 has extended the provisions of the Brussels Convention to the EFTA States. The Lugano Convention on Jurisdiction and the Enforcement of Judgments in Civil and Commercial Matters was signed between the EC Member States and the EFTA States at Lugano on 16 September 1988. It reproduces the text of the Brussels Convention with certain amendments to article 5 (for example the place of execution of an employment obligation is that where the employee normally has his activity).

(iv) Arbitration

Italian law considers an agency relationship between a principal and an agent who is a small entrepreneur as a labour relationship for the purposes of jurisdiction. This means that where the agent is a small entrepreneur, the introduction of an arbitration clause in the agreement will not prevent the agent from taking civil action through the courts. The arbitration clause will, on the other hand, have full effect where the agent is a company, or if the agent acts through a network which prevents him from being considered as a small entrepreneur and so enables him to take advantage of the protective provisions. In this latter case the New York Convention on the recognition and enforcement of foreign arbitral awards of 10 June 1958 (in force in Italy since 1 May 1969) applies, and Italian judges will not, therefore, hear disputes where the agreement provides for a valid arbitration clause. Similarly a foreign arbitration decision will be recognised in Italy under that Convention.

(v) Definition of the position of the agent

It is important to specify whether it is intended that the agent should promote contracts to be concluded by the principal, or whether he has the power to conclude contracts directly in the name, and on behalf of, the principal. The choice will be dictated by the kind of product to be distributed: where there is a product that requires capillary distribution and a large volume of sales, and an agent is to keep a deposit, the agent will usually conclude the contracts on behalf of the principal, under the conditions of sale set out by the principal. Where the products are of a higher value and the volume of sales is lower with longer terms for delivery, it will usually be preferable for the principal to conclude the contracts, thus keeping a better control over the sales and the risks involved.

Another consideration which must be taken into account is whether the fact that the agent represents the principal might lead to the taxability of the principal in the country where the agent is acting. Whilst there seems to be no doubt that in the countries that have adopted the OCSE model of the Convention against double taxation, an independent agent does not constitute a stable organisation of the principal even if the agent has representation for tax purposes; for countries that do not follow the OCSE model of the Convention against double taxation there are some doubts as to whether an independent agent with representation can in fact constitute a stable organisation of the principal, thus making the principal subject to tax for the sales promoted by the agent in the country where the agent is acting.

(vi) Specification of the contractual products

It is not advisable to refer to the products to be covered by the contract generally with a phrase such as "all products of the principal" this can lead to difficulties if, for instance, in the future the principal widens the range of his products and wishes to have particular agents for new lines. It is better to list the products in an enclosure or annex, or make reference to particular product lines.

If the principal sells his products under different trade marks the contractual products can be limited to those bearing a certain trade mark.

(vii) Territory

It is essential that there should be a clear specification of the territory to be covered by the agent.

(viii) Exclusivity

Pursuant to article 1742 of the Italian Civil Code the agent acts in a specific territory, but under article 1743 of the Civil Code the principal cannot have more than one agent in the same territory for the same range of products and the agent cannot act in the same territory and for the same range of products for more than one principal. It should be noted that under Italian law therefore exclusivity is a natural element of a contract of agency. It is not, however, essential and the parties can derogate from these provisions by agreement.

If the agent does not have exclusivity over his territory, he will not have the right to commission on business concluded directly by the principal otherwise due under article 1748 of the Civil Code and on business concluded by other agents in his territory.

Exclusivity in favour of the principal bars the agent from acting in the same territory and for the same range of products for companies in competition, and from carrying on, on his own account, an activity in competition with that of the principal. Exclusivity does not, on the other hand, mean that the agent will not be able to act for different principals which are not in competition. In fact the possibility of doing this is always present where it is not specified that the agent will act exclusively for one principal, and it is the basis of the autonomy and independence of the agent. Exclusivity binds the principal and the agent, but does not bind third parties in any way. This means there is no obligation of exclusivity between agents of the same principal who are acting in different territories, or agents and third parties. Therefore third parties are free to sell in any territory products they have purchased from the principal or through agents acting in another territory. If agents sell outside their exclusive territory, they act in breach of their contract with the principal and do not have a right to the commission which will accrue to the agent for the territory. If on the other hand, the agency agreement allows the agent to sell outside the territory, then it will be the principal who is in breach if he has granted exclusivity to other agents. In any event, the right of action will always be between the principal and the agent and not between the agents themselves as there is no contractual relationship between them.

(5) What are the duties and obligations of the agent?

The agent must promote the sales of the products which are the object of the contract within the territory (article 1742 of the Civil Code).

- The agency agreement can provide that this must be done through a particular sales network or leave the agent free to organise himself as he thinks best. The agency agreement can provide for a minimum quantity of orders that must be transmitted by the agent over a certain period. In fixing the minimum, the principal should keep in mind that it must always be reasonable, otherwise the agent could avoid the contract for impossibility of execution. Failure to promote sales adequately and, in particular, failure to reach minimums fixed in the contract can lead to the termination of the contract, or a claim in damages, a review of the range of products to be sold by the agent, or a review of the extent of his territory. The contract can provide for whatever the parties think best according to the market being covered.

- The agent must promote the sales of the principal's products following the instructions given by the principal and therefore apply prices and conditions of sales fixed by the principal (article 1746 of the Civil Code).
- The agent must keep the principal informed about the market conditions within the territory and give him any other useful information to enable the principal to evaluate each sale proposed (article 1746 of the Civil Code).
- It should be noted that in Italy it is also usual to include among the obligations of the agent that of guaranteeing the principal against losses due to the customer's default in paying (*star del credere*). According to the Collective Bargaining Agreement of 1956 applicable to all agency agreements governed by Italian law, the agent's liability is limited to 20% of the loss suffered by the principal and, in any event, cannot exceed one half of the commissions due to the agent for that year. According to the more recent Collective Bargaining Agreements which, however, apply only to parties registered with the Contracting Trade Unions or Associations, the liability is limited to 15% of the loss suffered by the principal and, in any event, cannot be higher than three times the commission on the sale. Thus where the principal recovers all or a part of the price due from the customer the agent shall be entitled to a proportional refund of "the *star del credere*" paid to the principal and of the corresponding commission.
- The agent can also be bound by a non-competition clause operating after the termination of the contract. To be valid such a clause must be in writing. The non-competition obligation must be limited to the same area, clientele, products or services contemplated by the original agency agreement, and its duration cannot exceed two years following the termination of the agreement (article 1751 of the Civil Code).
- In certain cases, it can be of the utmost importance to provide in the agreement for assistance to be given by the agent, on behalf, and at the

expense, of the principal, to clients for repairs and up-keep. Such an obligation is not provided for by law and must be agreed between the parties.

(6) What are the duties and obligations of the principal?

- The principal must provide to the agent all information concerning the products or services dealt with, and give him all necessary information for the performance of his contractual obligations. This is usually done by specifically detailing the principal's duty to supply booklets, brochures, etc (article 1748 of the Civil Code).
- The principal is also obliged to inform the agent within a reasonable time whether he intends to accept or refuse an order submitted to him by the agent (article 1748 of the Civil Code).
- The principal has the duty to pay to the agent commission as agreed in the contract. Pursuant to article 1748 of the Civil Code, commission is due on sales for which the price has been paid. In cases where the price has been paid only in part, the right to the commission will be proportional to the payment.

  On the basis of exclusivity, commission is also due on sales made directly by the principal in the agent's territory, except where the contract expressly provides to the contrary. Commission is due to the agent on sales concluded after the termination of the agency agreement if it is the result of the agent's activity during the agency agreement.

  It should be noted that the agent has no right to expenses borne unless otherwise specified in the contract.

  Regarding the payment of the commission the principal is bound to submit to the agent no later than the last day of the month immediately subsequent to the end of each quarter a written statement of account of the commission due. The statement of account shall indicate all items used in the calculation of the commission.

  The commission due must be paid to the agent within the aforesaid term, *i.e.* the last day of the month following the quarter to which the commission refers.
- The principal must place at the agent's disposal all necessary information so that he can check the amount of the commission due. For this purpose the principal can be asked to provide the agent with extracts of his accounting records.

- Within three months of the effective date of the agency agreement the principal must register any agent working in Italy whether on behalf of an Italian principal or of a foreign principal, and any Italian agent working abroad on behalf of an Italian principal, with Enasarco, the national institution which provides assistance and welfare to agents and their families and holds the pension scheme for agents. Quarterly contributions amounting to 4% of the commissions due, to be borne by the agent, plus 4% of the commissions paid to the agent to be borne by the principal, must be paid to Enasarco by the principal.

  Enasarco is a public body controlled by the Ministry of Labour and Welfare that has as its purpose the welfare of commercial agents. It administers the three funds provided for by the above-mentioned contributions, namely the insurance fund, the retirement and contract termination fund and the assistance fund.

(7) Termination

The termination of the contract is governed by articles 1750 and 1751 of the Civil Code as amended by Law 303/91, and where applicable, because the parties belong to the Contracting Trade Unions and Associations, by the collective agreements.

An agency contract can be for a limited or an unlimited term. In cases where it is for a limited term it ceases at the fixed expiry date. If in fact it continues, it is thereafter treated as a contract for an unlimited term.

How can an agency agreement be terminated? A contract for an unlimited term can be terminated by giving notice of no less than a month for the first year of duration of the contract, two months for the second year, three months for the third year, four months for the fourth year, five months for the fifth year and six months for the sixth year and thereafter. Where the collective agreements are applicable, the longer terms provided by them will be enforceable.

It is possible to substitute the notice period with an indemnity originally fixed by Decree of the President of the Republic of 16 January 1961 No. 145 and Decree of the President of the Republic of 26 December 1960 No. 1842 to the extent to which they have not been repealed by Law 303/91, for an indemnity to be fixed on the basis of commissions received by the agent during the preceding year divided by 12 and multiplied by the number of months of the notice period substituted with the indemnity.

For example commissions paid to the agent over the preceding year amount to 120.

The notice period is three months.

If the contract is terminated with immediate effect for the notice period is substituted an indemnity which is calculated as follows:

120 ÷ 12 = 10 (indemnity for one month)

10 x 3 = 30 (indemnity for three months).

When there is termination of the contract where the termination is not determined by the agent, an indemnity is due in cases where the agent has brought new clients to the principal or has developed business with existing clients in such a way that the principal is left with substantial advantages deriving from business with such clients, or where the payment of such an indemnity must be considered equitable bearing in mind all the circumstances, in particular the commissions deriving from those clients which the agent loses on termination.

The amount of indemnity due should not be calculated on the basis of fixed parameters, and is only fixed as to its maximum amount. This means it cannot be more than a sum corresponding to the yearly average calculated on the basis of the sum of the average of commissions over 12 months for each year of contract for the preceding five years or the shorter period of the duration of the contract.

Any claim by the agent concerning the indemnity must be made to the principal within a year of the termination of the contract. The payment to him of an indemnity does not deprive the agent of the right of advancing a claim for compensation of damages.

In cases where the Collective Agreements of 1992 apply, because the parties belong to the Contracting Trade Unions and Associations, the indemnity due should be a fixed indemnity calculated as a percentage of commissions received plus an indemnity for clients acquired for the principal. There is, however, an interpretation whereby the 1992 Collective Agreements in as much as they are in contrast with the Law No. 303 of 1991 are not applicable and therefore there is no particular indemnity for contracts which fall under such collective agreements. These collective agreements are not usually applicable to contracts with foreign principals who generally do not belong to employers' associations. The solution of the problem is still uncertain.

(8) Termination for breach of contract

The breach of obligations provided for by the law or the terms of the contract can lead to (a) the termination of the agreement under articles 1453 *et seq* of the Civil Code and (b) to a consequent claim for compensation by way of damages to be calculated by taking into account loss of commission where the party in breach is the principal, and loss of profits where the party in breach is the agent.

The agreement can provide for automatic termination given certain circumstances (compulsory liquidation, change of ownership of the company, etc).

Where the termination is due to the default of the principal the agent will, apart from compensation by way of damages, have a right to an indemnity for termination of the contract as provided in (7) above.

(9) Trial period

What is the effect of having a trial period for an agency agreement? It is now generally accepted that an agency agreement can provide for a reasonable trial period which does not give rise to a right to indemnity on termination. According to the most recent decision of the Supreme Court, it would appear that during such a trial period either party can withdraw from the contract at any time, but there still is a strong presumption that a trial period should not terminate before its stated expiry date. It is therefore important that if the parties intend that either party should be able to withdraw within the trial period, this should be clearly stated in the agreement. The period of the trial period and expiry date should also be clearly set out.

(10) Does the agent have any liability with regard to insurance?

The agent is not a party to the contract of sale and is not involved with the insurance of the goods being sold which will be arranged between the principal/seller and the buyer.

There is no specific provision of law relating to the insurance of goods held by the agent in stock on behalf of the principal; as the goods remain the property of the principal, it would be usual for the principal to provide for the payment of insurance.

(11) What about product liability?

The agent does not incur any liability for defective products (see Directive 83/189 enacted in Italy with the Decree of the President of the Republic No. 224 of 24 May 1988). Product liability lies with the producer (as defined by the Directive) the assembler, the supplier of components, or the distributor if the products originate from a country outside the EU.

(12) What is the difference between an agency and a distributorship agreement?

Both an agent and a distributor have the same economic function, *i.e.* the organisation and the promotion of the sales of products of the principals. However, there is a basic difference in their position. The agent promotes sales on behalf of the principal and receives a commission on the sale as compensation. The distributor purchases the products from the principal and resells them, and makes a profit on the difference between the purchase price and the reselling price. He differs from all other clients of the principal by way of the special terms that bind him to the principal and regulate the sales.

Italian law does not have particular dispositions governing the position of a distributor. However, there is a tendency to consider distributorship agreements as falling under the dispositions regulating regular supply contracts (article 1559 of the Civil Code); that is contracts whereby a party undertakes in exchange for a consideration, to supply goods regularly or periodically to another. However, because of their particular characteristics, in fact distribution agreements can only be partially covered by rules governing supplies, and should be considered on a case-by-case basis taking into account the terms and conditions of each single agreement and the general rules covering contracts and obligations.

There is no doubt that the position of the distributor is characterised by a higher risk than that of the agent, as he suffers exclusively and directly from the client's default in paying. On the other hand, the distributor enjoys better control of the market, and greater independence.

The choice to be made between appointing an agent or a distributor will be dictated by a series of factors concerning, for example, the kind of product to be dealt with, whether a deposit is necessary, whether the principal thinks he has to have direct control over the market, and the need for a facility to provide direct assistance to clients.

The table on page 226 indicates the main differences.

(13) Checklist of matters to be considered when drafting an agency agreement in Italy

(i) Definition of products and territory

- Date of the agreement.
- Names and addresses of the parties, names of the people representing companies and offices.
- Products, *i.e.* all products/certain models or ranges/exclusion of new products/right of option for new products.
- Territory.
- Functions of the agents, *i.e.* with/without representation; and with/without deposit.
- Exclusivity.

(ii) Obligations of the agent

- Sales promotion.
- Minimum turnover of sales, *i.e.* criteria for calculation; period for which applicable; consequences of failure to fulfil.
- Organisation of sales network, *i.e.* general obligation/specific description of the network required; personnel; sub-agents.
- Publicity, *i.e.* general obligation; fixing particular action and campaigns; material; exhibitions: participation with the principal or autonomously.
- Conditions of sale, *i.e.* obligation to follow the principal's conditions of sale; obligation to ask for specific instructions in certain cases.

	OPERATION	REMUNERATION	EXPENSES	OTHER PAYMENTS	MARKET CONTROL	RISK
DISTRIBUTOR	purchases and sells on his own account	difference between purchase and sale price	borne by distributor, sometimes publicity expenses shared	None	weak although the contract can provide for reports on clients etc	borne by distributor
AGENT WITHOUT REPRESENTATION	submits orders to principal	commissions on sales once price paid to principal	borne by the agent except accounts and often publicity	indemnity for termination ENASARCO	the principal knows the market through the orders	borne by principal
AGENT WITH REPRESENTATION	concludes contracts in the name and on account of principal	As ageed in agency contract	borne by the agent except publicity	As ageed in agency contract	contract can provide for visits to clients etc	except for *star del credere*
AGENT EMPLOYEE	acts under the direct control of principal with or without representation	salary and, if agreed, commissions	borne by the principal	heavy on the principal as Collective Contracts and National Assistance applies	principal has control	borne by principal

- Sales outside the territory, *i.e.* prohibition or other solutions.
- Information to the principal, *i.e.* periodic reports on clients and market; information on local legislation.
- Clients' solvency, *star del credere.*
- Assistance to the principal, *i.e.* general obligations; assistance in the recovery of credits; assistance in the protection of trade marks and patents; assistance in cases of unfair competition; forwarding of claims by clients.
- Trade marks, *i.e.* obligation to use principal's trade marks; prohibition from depositing trade marks in the agent's name or third parties' names.
- Secrecy.
- Obligation not to act in competition, *i.e.* general obligation; limited obligation; duties and commission relating to *spare parts.*
- Assistance to clients, *i.e.* general obligations; how to organise assistance; costs; the provisions relating to clients; the supply of *spare parts*; deposits.

(iii) Obligations of the principal

- Exclusivity, *i.e.* general; limited; certain clients reserved to the principal or other solutions.
- Commission, *i.e.* amount; business to which applicable; how to be calculated; how to be paid; taxes due; expenses.
- Information to the agent, *i.e.* material to be supplied by the principal; samples; return of material and samples; translation of instructions, booklets and other advertising material; conditions of sale.
- Technical assistance, *i.e.* documents; training of agent and agent's personnel; costs.

(iv) Termination

- Duration of the agreement, *i.e.* starting date; trial period; termination; notice; circumstances that lead to immediate termination (compulsory liquidation, bankruptcy, change in the ownership of the company, etc).

- Consequences of termination, *i.e.* stock of products; orders in course; trade marks; return of material and samples; assistance; termination indemnity.

(v) *Final dispositions*

- Applicable law.
- Arbitration.
- Jurisdiction.
- Original text.
- Assignment of the agreement.
- Partial nullity of the agreement.
- Additions and amendments.

(14) **Applicable law**

- Articles 1742 and 1752 of the Civil Code as amended by the Law decree of 10 September 1991 No. 303 enacting the EEC Directive 86/653.
- Law of 3 May 1985, No. 204 (Discipline of the Activity of Commercial Agents and Representatives);
- Law of 2 February 1973 (Nature and Duties of National Institutions of Welfare and Assistance for Trade Representatives and Agents, ENASARCO).
- Collective Agreement of 20 June 1956 enacted with Presidential Decree of 16 January 1961, No. 145; Collective Agreement of 30 June 1938 as modified by Collective Agreement of 13 October 1958 enacted with Presidential Decree of 26 December 1960, No. 1842.

The following Collective Agreements at present in force for trade and industry do not have the force of law and only govern the relationship between parties belonging to the Trade Unions and Associations which have stipulated the same:

- Collective Agreement of 30 October 1992 for Industrial Companies; and
- Collective Agreement of 27 November 1992 for Commercial Companies.

It should be noted that in the UK it would be unlikely for *both* parties to belong to the same unions albeit, for example an employer may recognise a trade union. It would have to apply a collective agreement specifically. However, in Italy there are workers' trade unions and employers' organisations or associations. The collective agreements are stipulated between workers' trade unions and employers' organisations or associations and they apply to the workers and employers belonging to the stipulated trade unions, organisations and associations.

CONTENTS OF CHAPTER 12

Luxembourg

12. LUXEMBOURG

Jean Brucher and Mark Sunnen, Brucher & Tabery, Luxembourg

(1) What legislation covers commercial agency in Luxembourg?

Gone are the days when principals and agents were able to contract freely. Prior to the law of 3 June 1994 ("the 1994 Law"), which will be more fully discussed below, an agency contract was governed by the Civil Code as well as by caselaw.

In particular, the courts used to define the agency contract through the general provisions of the civil law regulating contracts as well as through the provisions regulating the mandate.

The 1994 Law which regulates the relationship between independent commercial agents and principals, implements EEC Directive of 18 December 1986 on the co-ordination of the laws of the Member States relating to Self-employed Commercial Agents (86/653/EEC) ("the 1986 Directive").

The 1994 Law has also benefited from the BENELUX Convention relating to agency contracts of 26 November 1973 ("BENELUX Convention"), regardless of the fact that this convention never came into force as both Belgium and Luxembourg failed to ratify it.

Luxembourg legislation has, however, adopted several provisions in respect of the solutions provided by the BENELUX Convention, in particular those provisions where the 1986 Directive gives Member States the option as to which final provisions should be included in their domestic implementing legislation.

There are, in fact, many shared provisions between the 1994 Law and the Belgian law of 13 April 1995.

(2) What is the definition of "commercial agent" in Luxembourg?

The 1994 Law defines a commercial agent as a "self-employed intermediary having continuing authority, principally or in addition to his main duties, and against payment, either to negotiate the purchase and the sale of goods on behalf of another person, the principal, or to negotiate and to conclude transactions on behalf and for the account of the principal".

It should be noted that the agent can conduct his agency business as a main or secondary activity. However, the 1994 Law does not apply to intermediaries acting on a "one-off" basis or for a limited number of transactions.

The 1994 Law also specifies that a commercial agent is considered to be a business person and thus subject to the law of 28 December 1988 which lays down the conditions for entry into, and exercise of, certain trades and occupations.

The definition in the 1994 Law highlights the need for the commercial agent to be self-employed; thus he cannot be subordinate to, and controlled by, the principal.

(3) Are any persons who act on behalf of others excluded from the scope of the agency legislation?

It must be noted that certain professions and occupations are not covered by the 1994 Law. These include:

- an agent operating in commercial stock markets or commodity markets;
- an agent operating in the financial or insurance sector;
- an officer empowered to bind a company or association;
- a partner authorised to bind his partners; and
- a person acting as a trustee or as a liquidator.

(4) Are there any requirements as to the registration of commercial agents?

Agents and other business representatives are business persons within the meaning of the law of 28 December 1988 and are consequently subject to a business licence requirement.

The licence is issued by the Ministry for Small Businesses, after having sought the opinion of a committee which considers the applicant's qualifications and professional good-standing.

Evidence of good-standing is usually provided in the form of a certificate of solvency but the committee may also require production of a certificate of good character, or of a clean record from the police.

The licence is strictly personal; it is normally valid indefinitely, but can be revoked and ceases to be valid if it is not used within two years of its date of issue.

A new licence must be sought if there is any change in the aims of a business for which a licence had previously been granted.

In the event of the Minister refusing or revoking a licence, an appeal may be made to the Conseil d'État within one month following notification of the decision.

No licence is, however, required in respect of non-resident nationals of other Member States of the European Community who visit Luxembourg occasionally and temporarily take orders.

(5) Is there any specific provision under Luxembourg law regulating distribution agreements?

No, contrary to the Belgian law of 7 July 1961, Luxembourg law does not provide any specific regulation relating to distribution agents.

(6) What is the scope of the 1994 law on agency?

The 1994 Law was published in the Memorial (the Official Gazette) of 6 July 1994 and applies to all contracts existing on 1 January 1994 and to all those concluded after this date. Thus from that date, agents appointed under existing or new contracts will automatically have much better protection for the duration of the contract as well as more favourable treatment on termination.

(7) Are there any provisions under Luxembourg law as to the form of the contract?

Unlike Belgian legislation, under Luxembourg provisions any agency contract must be in writing. A written contract is required regardless of whether the agency agreement is for a fixed term or is open-ended.

There must be two original contracts; one each for the agent and the principal. However, if there is no such written contract, the agent can establish the existence and the content of the contract by any legal means and regardless of the amount of the claim.

The 1994 Law does not, however, allow this liberty to the principal: the written word is his only means of proving the existence of an agency contract.

(8) Are there any provisions concerning the rights and obligations of the parties which cannot be avoided?

The provisions of this chapter on rights and obligations of the parties and corresponding to articles 3, 4 and 5 of the 1994 Law are mandatory and cannot be altered by the parties (see (9) and (11) below).

(9) What are the rights and obligations of the commercial agent?

The agent has to carry out his functions in good faith and loyalty and must, in particular, use his best efforts to negotiate and conclude sales, communicate all relevant information to the principal and comply with all sensible instructions given by the principal.

These duties are identical to those set out in the Belgian legislation (see Chapter 4).

(10) What about minimum order stipulations and *del credere* agents?

Contrary to Belgian law, Luxembourg law does not make provision for specific clauses like minimum orders, *del credere* clauses or for the appointment of sub-agents.

However, such clauses relating to sub-agents, for example, are nevertheless compatible with the provisions of the 1994 Law and could contractually be included in an agency contract, particularly as the original draft legislation included provisions relating this to the appointment of sub-agents which were then deemed superfluous. These specific clauses are not regulated under Luxembourg legislation but can be used in an agency contract.

(11) What are the duties of the principal?

The 1994 Law provides that the principal must also act in good faith and loyally towards the agent. He must, in particular:

- provide all necessary information to the agent relating to the goods or services concerned;
- obtain for the agent any information necessary for the performance of the agent's duties and notify the agent within a reasonable period of any unexpected downturn in business volume; and
- keep the agent informed of his acceptance, refusal or of the non-execution of orders which have been arranged by the agent.

(12) What are the provisions relating to the payment of the commercial agent?

The commercial agent may either be paid:

- a fixed amount; or
- a commission; or
- a combination of both.

The commission is defined by the 1994 Law as every element of payment which varies with the volume or value of the transactions.

The mode of the payment should be contractually determined by the parties; if this is not done, the commercial agent is entitled to remuneration in accordance with the custom and practice of the economic sector where the agent has his usual business.

If there is no such custom, the agent is entitled to a reasonable and equitable remuneration taking into account all relevant elements of the transaction to be remunerated.

Principals are therefore advised to include specific commission provisions in the agency contract, otherwise they may find themselves paying the agent more than expected.

(13) Are there specific provisions relating to commissions?

The law distinguishes two situations:

- commissions for contracts concluded during the period of the agency agreement; and

- commissions for contracts concluded after the termination of the agency agreement.

(14) What about commissions for contracts concluded during the period of the agency agreement?

The provisions of the 1994 Law are in these circumstances identical to those of Belgian legislation.

To summarise the position, the agent is entitled to a commission:

- when the contract is concluded upon his intervention. Thus, where an order is mainly attributable to the agent's action, he may be entitled to commission in respect of that transaction;
- when the contract is entered into with a third party, if the agent has previously concluded similar transactions with the customers of this third party, *i.e.* repeat orders where those orders were not placed through the agent; and
- when the transaction is concluded with a person within the specific geographical sector or group of people which has been defined as the exclusive sector or group of the agent, unless such an exclusivity has been expressly ruled out.

(15) What about commissions for contracts concluded after the termination of the agency agreement?

The agent is entitled to a commission notwithstanding the fact of the termination:

- when the transaction has been concluded due to his efforts and within a *reasonable* time since the termination, (contrary to Belgian law, which provides a commission if the contract has been concluded within six months of the termination); and
- if the customer's order has been agreed by the principal or the agent prior to termination of the agency agreement but not concluded until after termination.

The "new" agent has no right to a commission if a previous agent is entitled to it, according to the provisions relating to commissions due following termination, unless it appears to be equitable to share the remuneration between both agents concerned. Thus a new agent will only be entitled to a share of any commission due to a previous agent in respect of a transaction concluded after the termination of that previous agent's contract.

(16) What is the time at which commission becomes due?

The commission is due when the:

- principal has executed the order;
- principal should have executed the order in accordance with the contract concluded with the customer; or
- customer has performed his part of the contract, or should have done so if the principal had carried out his part.

The parties cannot provide otherwise to the detriment of the agent.

(17) When must the commission be paid?

The commission earned has to be paid at the latest on the last day of the month following the quarter when the commission became payable.

The 1994 Law provides that the principal is also obliged to hand over to the agent a detailed statement of commissions, at the latest on the last day of the month following the quarter when the commission became payable. The agent is entitled to request the supply to him of all necessary information and in particular the accounts of the principal in order to check the amount which is actually due to him.

(18) When is the right to commission lost?

The provisions of Luxembourg legislation relating to extinction of the right to commission are less precise than those of Belgian law.

The 1994 Law simply states that the right to a commission will be lost only if, and when, it is established that the contract between the third party and the principal will not be executed and if this failure is not due to the fault of the principal. In such a case, the commission already paid to the agent has to be refunded to the principal.

(19) What about the conclusion or termination of the agency contract?

Luxembourg law provides that if a contract concluded for a fixed term is not terminated in accordance with the fixed term, it is deemed to have been transformed into a contract for an indefinite period.

(20) Termination and notice: what periods of notice must be given by either party to terminate an agency contract?

Each party to the agency contract may terminate the contract by giving written notice, regardless of whether or not the agreement is for a fixed term and provides for the possibility of anticipatory termination, or is open-ended.

The required period of notice is one month during the first year of the agency agreement, after which the initial notice period is extended by one month per additional year started, not exceeding six months.

As these periods are mandatory and cannot be modified to the detriment of the agent, the parties cannot agree on shorter periods but may define longer periods of notice.

If such is the case, the period of notice required from the principal cannot be less than the period to be respected by the commercial agent.

The 1994 Law provides that unless the parties have agreed on something else, the end of the notice period has to coincide with the last day of the relevant month.

The same provisions are applied to the situation where a fixed period contract has been transformed into an open-ended contract. The duration of the fixed period contract has, of course, to be taken into account in order to determine the actual duration of the notice period.

(21) What about termination for exceptional circumstances or for serious grounds?

Either party — principal or agent — may terminate the contract without notice or before the fixed term in the event of exceptional circumstances making it impossible to continue the professional relationship between the parties or in the event of any serious misconduct by either party.

The party who terminates the contract has to state the reasons for termination; the onus to demonstrate that the alleged reasons are well-founded is on the party stating them. The appraisal of the reasons falls within the competence of the court.

It should be noted that damages and interest may be payable by the offending party.

(22) What are the provisions relating to compensation on termination?

The agent is entitled after the termination of a contract to compensation as follows:

- when the agent has supplied the principal with new customers or has considerably developed business with the existing customers, resulting in the principal deriving substantial advantage from the business with those customers;
- the payment of the compensation has to be equitable taking all relevant circumstances into account. In particular, the commissions lost by the agent through the termination as well as the restriction of the agent's forthcoming activity by a non-competition clause, should be considered;
- the amount of compensation cannot exceed an amount equivalent to an annual indemnity calculated on the average of the last five years of the agent's activity as regulated by the terminated agency contract;
- the agent can claim complementary damages regardless of the compensation obtained if the prejudice suffered is not entirely compensated; and
- the right to compensation also exists if the contract is terminated by the death of the agent.

(23) When is compensation upon termination not due or payable?

Compensation upon termination is not due or payable when:

- the principal has terminated the agreement due to a serious shortfall or misconduct of the agent;
- the agent has terminated the agency contract, except when the termination is justified by the behaviour of the principal; or
- the agency is terminated due to reasons relating to the age or the health of the agent which preclude the continuation of the contract; or
- both parties have agreed that the agent transfers his rights and obligations to a third party.

It should be noted that the agent loses his claim to compensation if he fails to notify the principal that he intends to exercise his right to compensation within one year of the termination.

The parties cannot provide for other arrangements to the detriment of the agent before the end of the contract.

(24) What about damages?

The 1994 Law provides that the party who terminates the agency contract, without respecting either the term of the contract or the notice period and without the agreement of the other party, must pay damages, unless the termination is justified by serious grounds notified to the other party.

If the termination is justified by serious misconduct on the part of one party, that party is bound to pay damages.

A clause seeking to enable a party, either the agent or the principal, to decide when a situation should be treated as gross misconduct is null and void.

The party bound to pay damages has to pay an amount equal to the remuneration which the other party would have earned had the contract been properly performed. This amount is calculated on the basis of previous commissions.

The court may in such a case and in its discretion grant less than the amount claimed.

Instead of the damages calculated as described, the wronged person is entitled to claim for the entire compensation of the damage suffered. The onus in such a case is on the wronged party to prove his damage.

These provisions are again mandatory and cannot be altered to the detriment of the agent.

(25) What are the provisions in Luxembourg relating to clauses seeking to restrict the activities of commercial agents — such as a non-competition clause?

(i) As to the definition of a "non-competition" clause

The 1994 Law defines a non-competition clause as being "any clause or contract which restricts the professional activities of the agent, either during the agency agreement or after its termination".

(ii) As to the form, scope and duration of a "non-competition" clause

The clause must:

- be in writing to be valid;
- concern a specific professional sector and similar activities to those the agent was in charge of;
- concern the specific geographical sector or the group of persons the agent has been charged with as well as the type of goods or services the agent was supposed to represent; and
- not provide for restrictions which exceed a maximum of 12 months after the termination of the contract (whereas Belgian law provides a limit of only six months).

(26) When is a non-competition clause ineffective?

A non-competition clause is ineffective if:

- the principal has terminated the contract without the approval of the agent, without any notice and without any serious reason notified to the agent;
- the agent has terminated the contract because of a serious shortfall by the principal; or
- the contract has been terminated by a court order given in circumstances which the agent may oppose.

The court may, at the agent's request, cancel the non-competition clause or lessen its effect, if the effect of the clause is contrary to equity, *i.e.* that it would be unfair in all the circumstances. Moreover, if the principal has stipulated a penalty to enforce the clause, the court can, at the agent's request, reduce the penalty if its amount is perceived as being excessive.

(27) What about the choice of governing law and jurisdiction provisions in Luxembourg?

The 1994 Law, even though not specified, applies to all agents who undertake activities in Luxembourg (unless the agreement specifies that it will be regulated by the law of another country, provided that the mandatory provisions of Luxembourg law are not intentionally avoided).

The contract is also likely to be governed by Luxembourg law if the agent has his principal place of business in Luxembourg but works outside Luxembourg. Such a case cannot be excluded in view of the traditionally export-oriented inclination of Luxembourg business (see Rome Convention of 19 June 1980 concerning the law applicable to Contractual Obligations).

On the other hand, and according to the general rule that parties to an agreement are free to choose the governing law of the agreement, parties to an agency contract, where the agent works outside Luxembourg, may choose to have the agreement regulated by Luxembourg law.

Regarding jurisdiction, the additional protocol of the Brussels Convention of 27 September 1968 on the Jurisdiction and Enforcement of Judgments in Civil and Commercial Matters has to be borne in mind as it enables any person domiciled or having his principal place of business in Luxembourg to refuse the competence of a foreign court, even if the agency agreement provides for the competence of that specific foreign court.

(28) What about the effect of product liability legislation on commercial agency agreements?

There is no special provision relating to product liability in the precise context of an agency agreement, so the common law is applicable (articles 1382, 1383, and 1384 paragraph 1 of the Civil Code, as well as the law of 12 April 1989 relating to product liability).

CONTENTS OF CHAPTER 13

Netherlands

13. NETHERLANDS

Jan Willem Bitter, Trenité Van Doorne, Rotterdam

(1) What is meant by an agent under Netherlands law?

The rules relating to agency contracts are mainly set out in the fourth section of Title 7 of Book 7 of the Dutch Civil Code (articles 7:428 *et seq*). It follows from article 7:428 that an agent:

- acts as an intermediary in the negotiation and conclusion of contracts between his principal and third parties (the customers);
- does so for a remuneration;
- acts under a permanent contract with the principal; and
- renders his services in the name and for the account of the principal.

The rules laid down in articles 7:428 *et seq* of the Civil Code apply not only to the agent's role in the negotiation and conclusion of contracts of sale and purchase, but also to his activities in contracts for services (carriage contracts, for instance). The services rendered by an insurance agent, however, are expressly excluded from the provisions of articles 7:428 *et seq* of the Civil Code (article 7:428.2) . The activities of insurance agents, which according to a 1993 amendment are outside the scope of this chapter, are governed by the "*Wet Assurantiebemiddeling*" (Act on Insurance Agency).

An agent may be a natural or a legal person.

An agent is only empowered to conclude contracts in the name of his principal if such has been expressly agreed upon.

(2) Dutch agency law since 1936

The first Dutch law relating to agency dates back to 1936[1] and was inserted into articles 75a *et seq* of the Commercial Code. The objective of

[1] Act of 5 November 1936 (*Staatsblad* (Statute Book) 1936, No 207).

this rather ineffective regulation[2], was to accord protection to the agent as the economically weaker party in a principal/agency relationship. The 1936 Regulation was drafted onto German agency law and in many ways ran parallel to Dutch labour law prevailing in 1936.

On 1 July 1977 the 1936 Regulation was replaced by an entirely new Act[3], introduced into articles 74 *et seq* of the Commercial Code. This new Act was based on the 1967 BENELUX Model Act on agency, more in particular on the amended version thereof, as laid down in the BENELUX Treaty of 26 November 1973.[4]

The 1977 Act (article 74o of the (old) Commercial Code) introduced the goodwill indemnity payment. This entitles an agent who, by creating or expanding the principals customer base, has significantly increased the value of the principal's business, to obtain a goodwill indemnity, the amount of which shall not exceed the amount of one year's commission earned by the agent, to be calculated by the average of the last five years of the contract.

Dutch agency law was amended to some extent (but not fundamentally) by an Act of 5 July 1989[5], so as to give effect to the council of the European Communities Directive of 18 December 1986 on the co-ordination of the laws of the Member States relating to Self-employed Commercial Agents (86/653/EEC).

Lastly, as of 1 September 1993[6] the provisions relating to agency contracts were transferred from the Commercial Code to the Civil Code. The main — but not all — provisions relating to agency contracts have been incorporated into section 4 of Title 7 of Book 7 of the Civil Code (articles 7:428 *et seq*). The other three sections of Title 7 (section 1: Assignment; section 2: Mandate; and section 3: Mediation Contract) also comprise provisions relevant to agency contracts.[7]

(3) What are the formalities of an agency contract?

An agency contract need not be set out in writing, but each party is obliged to co-operate in making a written contract upon request by the other party (article 7:428.3 of the Civil Code).

---

[2] This term was coined by Doorhout Mees; see his *Nederlands Handels-en Faillissementsrecht*, Vol I. Haarlem 1974, para 259.

[3] *Staatsblad* (Statute Book) 1977, No 153.

[4] *Tractatenblad* (Treaty Book) 1974, No 4; the Treaty, incidentally, never entered into force, as Belgium and Luxembourg have failed to ratify it.

[5] *Staatsblad* (Statute Book) 1989, No 312.

[6] Act of 27 May 1993, *Staatsblad* (Statute Book) No 309.

[7] See, for instance: articles 7:401, 402, 403, 405, 426 and (for agents with the power to conclude contracts) articles 414 to 424 inclusive.

(4) To what extent can the agent conclude contracts for his principal?

The agent is only empowered to conclude contracts for the account, and in the name of the principal if such is expressly agreed upon by the agent and the principal. If so, articles 7:414–428 of the Civil Code (mandate) apply.[8]

As a rule, an agent acting outside the scope of the express power agreed with his principal who concludes a contract with a third party binds himself and not his principal. The principal will be bound, however, in the case where he has given rise to the third party's justified assumption that the agent had authority to represent him (article 3:61 of the Civil Code). Thus if a principal has permitted his agent to act on his behalf on other occasions, he may be stopped from taking the view later that he cannot be held liable because his agent was not authorised to act on his behalf on a particular occasion. Whether or not in a given case the principal has given rise to a third party's justified assumption of the agent's capacity to represent the principal will depend on all relevant circumstances of the matter. Since the power to represent the principal is never assumed, a principal wishing to protect himself against the risk of his agent's apparent power or representation should not allow his agent to enter into a contract on his behalf in a specific case without at the same time advising the other contracting party that the agent's power to represent the principal was based on a one-off power granted to the agent for the purpose of executing one specific contract.

(5) What about commission?

The remuneration to which the agent is entitled for acting as an intermediary in the negotiation or conclusion of contracts is called "*provisie*" (commission). The agent is entitled to this commission, provided that the contract has been:

- concluded through his activities as an intermediary;
- entered into with a third party whom the agent had previously introduced as party to a contract; or

[8] The referenced articles regulate specific contracts whereby one person instructs another person to act in his name and for his account or for his account only. They contain rules on the rights and obligations of both parties to such contracts. It is *inter alia* forbidden for a representative to act on behalf of his principal's contracting party at the same time as for his principal, and in principle the representative is not allowed to contract directly with his principal, instead of seeking a third party wishing to contract with his principal.

- entered into with a party who belongs to the agent's customer base or who is established in the territory exclusively assigned to the agent (article 7:431.1 of the Civil Code).

If the principal does not notify the agent within a reasonable period of time that he accepts the contract procured through the intermediary activities of the agent, the principal may in some circumstances be liable to pay commission, even if no contract between the principal and the third party is entered into at all (articles 7:430.4 and 7:432.1 of the Civil Code (see also (11) below)).

The parties may deviate from this rule by agreement and they may, in particular, provide that the agent's entitlement to commission is subject to the actual performance by the third party of its part of the contract (usually payment). Such provision must be made in express terms (article 7:432.2 of the Civil Code). However, the principal may not rely on this exclusion if the non-performance by the third party is caused by the inadequate performance of the contract by the principal himself (for example: the machine supplied by the principal does not function; the transport to be provided by the principal is not so provided). In such cases the agent is entitled to commission in spite of the provision referred to in article 7:432.2 of the Civil Code.

(6) What about remuneration?

If the agent is prepared to fulfil his obligations under the agency contract or has already fulfilled his obligations, but the principal has not used the agent's services at all, or used them to a lesser extent than the agent could reasonably have expected, the agent is entitled to a remuneration to be calculated on the basis of the commission previously earned by the agent, less the expenses which the agent saved himself by not performing work (article 7:435 of the Civil Code).

Example:

A shipowner in northern Germany operated a liner service from Cuxhaven through Eemshaven (Groningen, Netherlands) to Immingham (United Kingdom). After engine failure on one of its ships, as a result of which the shipowner had to take that ship out of service, the liner service stopped calling at Eemshaven without the contract with the Dutch ship's agent being terminated.[9]

The agent claimed payment by the principal of a remuneration for the period during which the shipowner did not enable the agent to perform the services agreed on. The claim was awarded.[10]

If the principal goes into voluntary liquidation, the agent is still entitled to a remuneration under article 7:435 of the Civil Code.[11]

(7) What about commission in the event of successive agents?

The agent's entitlement to commission is extended to contracts concluded after the termination of the agency contract. If the conclusion of the contract takes place within a reasonable period of time after termination and is mainly due to the (former) agent's activities, that agent (and not his successor) is entitled to the commission to be paid in connection with that contract. The same applies if the third party's order is received prior to termination of the agency contract and the commission did not become due until after termination (for instance, because the customer paid only after termination of the agency contract) (article 7:431.2 of the Civil Code). If the succeeding agent also contributed to the conclusion of the contract, the commission will have to be divided between that agent and his predecessor (article 7:431.3 of the Civil Code).

(8) What about the amount of the commission?

The amount of the commission is usually provided for in the agency contract. Failing such provision, the principal must pay the agent a commission to be calculated in the habitual manner and, if this does not apply, a reasonable commission (article 7:405 of the Civil Code). The "habitual manner" may refer to previous dealings between the agent and the principal, but also to the custom of the trade prevailing in the line of

[9] See (12) below on termination of the agency contract.
[10] County Court in Groningen, judgment of 22 June 1994 in *Vinke* v *Elbe Humber Rolines* (not published).
[11] District Court in Amsterdam, judgment of 6 February 1980, NJ 1980, No 459.

business in which the agent and the principal are working. If the agent is a natural person, it should be taken into account that the "*Wet Minimumloon en Minimumvakantiebijslag*" (Minimum Wages and Minimum Holiday Allowance Act) may apply.

(9) What about due date of the commission?

Commission becomes due as from the moment at which the principal is obliged to allow the agent to inspect the documents supporting the calculation of the commission (article 7:433 of the Civil Code). See also (11) below.

(10) What are the duties of the agent?

Under articles 7:401–403 of the Civil Code the agent is obliged to show loyalty towards his principal. The agent must:

- exercise the care of a "*goede agent*" (good agent) (article 7:401 of the Civil Code);
- follow the reasonable instructions of the principal (article 7:402 of the Civil Code);
- keep the principal informed of his activities; and
- render account to the principal (article 7:403 of the Civil Code).

The obligation under article 74a.2 of the (former) Commercial Code, that the agent must provide the principal with all necessary information and notify him immediately of all contracts he has negotiated or concluded for the principal, has not technically been part of Dutch law since 1 September 1993. However, this does not justify the conclusion that such an obligation no longer exists. It should rather be assumed that this obligation is considered to be included in the agent's general obligation of loyalty.[12]

The obligation to be loyal should not simply be regarded as a non-competition clause. Non-competition clauses (whether they are intended to be effective during the life of, or after expiration of, the agency

[12] *Handelingen van de Tweede Kamer der Staten-Generaal* (Proceedings of the Lower Chamber of the Dutch Parliament), vol 17779, No 4, p 12, (1989–90).

contract) must be included in the agency contract in express terms (see (15) below).

The law does not provide for a general obligation of secrecy for the agent with respect to all information on the principal's business which has come to his knowledge in the pursuance of his contractual duties, but such an obligation may, in certain circumstances, be deduced from the agent's obligation of loyalty under articles 7:401–403 of the Civil Code. The same applies to the agent's obligation, which some believe to exist, to inquire into the solvency of the customer.[13]

(11) What are the duties of the principal?

- The principal is obliged to remunerate the agent for his services (see (5) to (8) above).

- The principal must do all that is necessary to enable the agent to discharge his duties (article 7:430.2 of the Civil Code), *inter alia* by providing the agent with the necessary information relating to the goods or services for which the agent is to act as intermediary and relating to the conditions on which the said goods or services are to be offered (time for delivery, guarantee obligations, etc).

- The principal is obliged to notify the agent if he foresees that the volume of contracts to be concluded will be significantly lower than the agent could have expected (article 7:430.3 of the Civil Code).

- The principal is obliged to inform the agent within a reasonable period of time of his acceptance, refusal or non-performance of any contract concluded by the intermediation of the agent (article 7:430.4 of the Civil Code).[14]

- After the end of each month the principal must supply the agent with a written account of the commission due for that month, specifying the data on which the calculation is based. The parties may agree in writing that such accounts will be supplied at intervals of two or three months. The account must be supplied before the end of the month following

[13] *Cf.* Asser/Coehorst/de Leede/Theunissen, p 159; Smit, F.M, *De Agentuurovereenkomst tussen handelsagent en principaal*, Zwolle 1990, p 20; see (13) below for the agent's duty to guarantee the solvency of the customer.

[14] Failing a specific period included in the agency contract, the applicable term is one month, pursuant to article 7:432.1 of the Civil Code. The agent who is entitled to commission from the moment a contract is concluded is therefore in principle entitled to such commission if the principal does not within a period of one month refuse a contract procured by the agent.

the reference period. The agent has the right to demand inspection of the principal's accounts, to the extent that such is conducive and necessary to verify his entitlement to commission. However, the agent neither has the right to unlimited inspection of his principal's accounts nor the right to demand that the principal surrender any documents considered relevant by the agent which have surfaced in the course of the inspection. The parties may agree that a third party (an accountant, for instance) should be allowed access to the principal's accounts. The agent and the third party engaged for this purpose are obliged to keep confidential the contents of the documents to which the principal has allowed them access. Obviously, the third party may inform the agent of any information that may be relevant to the calculation of the latter's commission (article 7:433 of the Civil Code).

- Just as the agent has a duty of loyalty towards his principal, so the principal has an obligation of loyalty *vis-à-vis* his agent (article 15 7:431 of the Civil Code).[15]

(12) Termination

The agency contract is terminated:

- by one of the parties giving notice of termination to the other (article 7:437 of the Civil Code);
- upon expiry of an agreed fixed period;
- by the death of the agent or of the principal (article 7:438 of the Civil Code); and
- by any other circumstance which, pursuant to the contract between the parties, should result in the termination of the contract.

(i) Notice of termination and contracts for an indefinite period of time

Contracts concluded for an indefinite period of time may be terminated at any time.

[15] Dutch Supreme Court, decision of 10 January 1992, *Rechtspraak van de Week* 1992, No 27 (*Jehro/Brinkhaus*).

Contracts concluded for a fixed period of time may be terminated only to the extent that the contract comprises provisions for its termination (article 7:437.1 of the Civil Code). If the contractual provisions permit early termination, each party is entitled to terminate the contract with due observance of the contractual period of notice.

In the first year of the contract the period of notice may not be shorter than one month, two months in the second year, and three months in the third year and subsequent years of the contract. In the absence of a contractual provision relating to the period of notice, a period of notice of four months must be observed in the first three years of the contract, such period to be increased by one month if notice of termination is given upon expiry of three years, and by two months if the contract has existed for six years or more (article 7:437.1 of the Civil Code). If the agent is a natural person, if he performs his duties for no more than two principals and if he does not employ more than two employees, the contract may only be terminated with the prior permission of the "*Regionaal Directeur voor de Arbeidsvoorziening*" (Regional Director for Employment Services).[16] This rule is mandatory and accordingly it cannot be opted out of contractually by the parties.

(ii) Termination upon expiry of an agreed fixed period

Agency contracts which have been concluded for a definite period of time, without the contract providing for anticipated termination, end by the expiry of the definite period for which they were concluded. A contract that was concluded for a definite period and is tacitly prolonged is transformed into a contract for an indefinite period of time (article 7:436 of the Civil Code).

(iii) Termination without notice

Based on a so-called "urgent cause", an agency contract can be terminated without notice by either party. Urgent causes are presumed to exist in the event of a change of circumstances, implying that the terminating party cannot be reasonably requested to continue the contract any longer. In order to qualify as an urgent cause, the referenced change of circumstances

[16] *Cf.* for instance: District Court in Groningen, judgment of 24 July 1981, NJ 1983, No 476, and County Court in Arnhem, judgment of 21 June 1993, KG 1993, No 271.

should be substantial. This is considered not to be the case if the terminating party does not invoke the change of circumstances as a reason for termination immediately after the change of circumstances arose, or after the change of circumstances should reasonably have become known to him.[17]

Urgent causes may or may not be attributable to the other party. An example of an urgent cause which is not attributable to the agent could be an event when the shareholders of the agent's company decide to sell that company to a competitor of the principal. An instance of an urgent cause which is attributable to the agent is an event when the agent wilfully breaches a non-competition clause agreed on by the parties. If the urgent cause is founded on circumstances attributable to the other party, the latter party is liable for damages (article 7:439.3 of the Civil Code).

If a contract is terminated for an urgent cause and a court of law subsequently establishes that there was no such cause, the contract is terminated irregularly. The consequences thereof will be discussed in (12)(iv) below.[18]

(iv) *Irregular termination*

Termination of the contract when the party terminating the contract does not have the right to do so (for example when a contract for a definite period of time does not include a provision for early termination), constitutes an event of irregular termination.

Termination of the agency contract without due observance of the applicable period of notice also constitutes an event of irregular termination. Irregular termination is not void or voidable and the party terminating the contract is not liable to the other party for specific performance but he is liable for damages (article 7:439 of the Civil Code). The compensation for damages is equal to the commission which would have been paid to the agent over the period of notice not observed, or over the period of time until the date of expiry of the definite period for which the contract was entered into. For the purpose of determining the amount of the compensation, the commission earned previously to the termination is taken into account (article 7:441.1 of the Civil Code).[19] The agent claiming compensation for his loss of commission need not prove the extent of

[17] See, for instance, the District Court in Amsterdam, judgment of 20 August 1960, NJ 1961, No 7.
[18] *Cf.* County Court in Amsterdam, judgment of 25 September 1991, *Praktijkgids* 1991, No 3619.
[19] See, for instance, County Court in Zwolle, judgment of 22 February 1991, *Praktijkgids* 1991, No 3425, and Supreme Court, decision of 13 November 1992, *Rechtspraak van de Week* 1992, No 253 (*Het Financieele Dagblad/Van Weezenbeek*).

that loss. He would be required to do so, however, if, not content with a compensation for his loss of commission and alleging that the actual loss was much higher, he claims full compensation for the loss he has actually sustained (article 7:441.3 of the Civil Code).[20] In the latter case, the burden of proof rests on the agent. Accordingly, only in exceptional cases, will an agent demand payment of his real damages instead of payment of his loss of commission.

(v) *Termination by the County Court*

Under article 7:440 of the Civil Code, either party is entitled to request the County Court to terminate the contract, either on account of changed circumstances or on account of circumstances which constitute an urgent cause as referred to in article 7:439 of the Civil Code (see (12)(iii) above). If such circumstances can be attributed to the defendant, he is liable for damages as if the contract had been terminated for an urgent cause and without observance of the agreed period of notice. If the contract is terminated on account of changed circumstances, the County Court may, to the extent this is held to be reasonable, award compensation to one of the parties. The courts have a discretionary freedom for the purpose of fixing the amount of compensation. So far only three judgments have been published in which article 7:440 of the Civil Code was applied. In each of these cases[21] compensation was awarded to the agent equal to his lost commission during the notice period that would have applied if the contract had been regularly terminated.

(vi) *What is the effect of the death of the agent or the principal?*

If the agent dies, the agency contract is automatically terminated (article 7:438.1 of the Civil Code). The death of the principal, however, only results in the principal's heirs on the one hand and the agent on the other hand being entitled to terminate the contract within nine months of the

---

[20] Supreme Court, decision of 10 January 1992, *Rechtspraak van de Week* 1992, No 27, and NJ 1992, No 576 (*Jehro/Brinkhaus*).

[21] County Court in Zwolle, 22 February 1991, *Praktijkgids* 1991, No 3425; County Court in Amsterdam, 25 September 1991, *Praktijkgids* 1992, No 3619; County Court in Arnhem, 21 June 1993, *Kort Geding* 1993, No 271.

principal's death, with due observance of a period of notice of four months (article 7:438.2 of the Civil Code), whatever the length of the contract until the principal's death.

(13) What about the liability of the agent for the solvency of the third party ("*del credere*")

The agent is, in principle, not liable if the third party fails to fulfil his payment obligation to the principal under a contract negotiated or concluded by the agent. However, the parties may agree that in such a case the agent will assume liability *vis-à-vis* the principal to the amount of the agreed commission (article 7:429.2 and 7:429.3 of the Civil Code) but such a clause must be in writing (article 7:429.1). In principle, the only event covered by the clause is the non-fulfilment by the third party of his payment obligation; non-fulfilment by the third party of any other obligations (such as the obligation to supply goods) are not covered. It follows from article 7:429 that, if an article 7:429.1 clause has been included (the so-called "*del credere* clause"), the agent who received commission by virtue of the fact that the principal concluded a contract with the third party through the agent's intermediation is obliged to refund that commission in the event of non-payment by the third party. If the parties agree that the agent receives commission only after the third party has fulfilled its payment obligation, no commission is due and accordingly no repayment is necessary. The term often applied to this construction is "*versluierd del credere*" (veiled *del credere*).

The parties may agree that the agent assumes liability to a higher amount for a specific contract or if the agent has the right to conclude contracts in the name of the principal (see (2) above).

Incidentally, the mere fact that a *del credere* clause is absent from an agency contract does not necessarily mean that the agent is not at any time liable *vis-à-vis* his principal in the event of the third party's default in payment.

For example

A ship's agent was charged with the collection of freight with respect to a carriage agreement concluded by him in the name of the shipowner. He allowed the debts of one shipper over a period of about six months to amount to about NLG 65,000, without notifying the principal. Eventually, the shipper went into compulsory liquidation. The County Court decided that the agent had not discharged his obligation to provide the principal (the shipowner) with all necessary information (article 74a.2 of the (former) Commercial Code (see also (5) above)). On that ground the Court ordered the agent to pay the entire amount of unpaid freight (*cf.* the unpublished judgment of the County Court in Groningen, referred to at (6) above).

(14) Indemnity (or "goodwill payment") upon termination

The indemnity upon termination (*cf.* Regulation 17.3 of the Commercial Agents (Council Directive) Regulations 1993 (SI 1993/3053) is not compensation for damages. The indemnity is to compensate for the benefits the principal continues to enjoy after the end of the agency contract, such benefits being new customers the agent has brought to the principal, or a significantly increased volume of business with existing customers in relation to the situation at the commencement of the agency contract. Prerequisites for awarding this payment are:

- the agent has, mainly due to his own activities, increased the number of customers and/or expanded the volume of business;
- the principal continues to derive substantial benefits from the increased number of customers and/or the expanded volume of business; or
- the payment of an indemnity is just and equitable with regard to all the circumstances and, in particular, the commission lost by the agent on account of the termination of the agency contract.

The amount of the goodwill payment is limited to the amount of one year's commission calculated by taking the average annual remuneration over the preceding five years of the contract or, if the contract has lasted for a shorter period, by the average of the entire duration of the contract (article 7:442.2 of the Civil Code). For the purpose of calculating the maximum amount of goodwill payment, not only the remuneration earned by the agent for procuring new customers is taken into account. Even the remuneration earned for performing accessory services may be taken into account, if that remuneration is expressed as a percentage of the price charged to the customer.[22] Once it is established that an indemnity is due, its amount is determined with due observance of equitability[23] (*cf.* Regulation 17.3.b of the Commercial Agents Regulations 1993). The scarcity of caselaw on article 7:442 shows that the Dutch courts have tended to deem it equitable that the agent is entitled to the maximum payment for goodwill.[24] The position may be different if the agent does not lose any commission as a consequence of the termination of the contract. The Supreme Court of the Netherlands appears to have taken the view that, in the absence of any loss of commission, there is no ground to award any indemnity payment for goodwill.[25]

For the purpose of answering the question as to whether the agent is entitled to an indemnity payment for goodwill or not, the manner in which the contract was terminated is — in principle — irrelevant. However, no indemnity for goodwill is due in the following three instances:

- if the principal has terminated the agency contract because of or in connection with an "urgent cause" as defined before (see (12)(iii) above);
- if the commercial agent has terminated the contract, unless such termination is justified by circumstances attributable to the principal, or by his own age, infirmity or illness; and
- if the agent terminated the contract after having assigned, with the permission of the principal, his rights and duties under the agency contract to a third party.

---

[22] See County Court in Rotterdam (*Kersten Hunik/Lloyd Brasileiro*), 15 June 1995, case number 24498/CV/94/EL (unpublished).

[23] Generally speaking, an important factor will be the period during which the principal will continue to derive benefits for the agent's activities (see, for instance: District Court in Amsterdam, judgment of 6 February 1980, NJ 1980, No 459 (*Hopf/Opex*); District Court in Amsterdam, judgment of 20 March 1991 as derived from the decision of the Supreme Court of 13 November 1992, *Rechtspraak van de Week* 1991, No 253 (*Het Financieele Dagblad/Van Weezenbeek*); and Supreme Court, decision of 6 December 1991, NJ 1992, No 176 (*Rosa Ronstedt/Fashion*).

[24] *Cf.* the judgment, referred to in n 23, of the District Court in Amsterdam, 20 March 1991 (*Het Financieele Dagblad/Van Weezenbeek*).

[25] *Cf.* Supreme Court, decision of 2 March 1990, NJ 199, No 50 (*NBC/Select*) and Supreme Court, decision of 10 January 1992, NJ 1992, No 576 (*Jehro/Brinkhaus*); this view is contested by the annotator in his note on the decision of 2 March 1990.

(15) Non-competition clauses

The law does not contain any provisions concerning non-competition clauses effective during the term of the agency contract. The agent's obligation to refrain from competing with his principal must be expressly agreed by the parties. In the absence of such a clause, the agent's loyalty obligation (see (10) above) may provide a solution in extreme circumstances, but it would be positively unwise to presume this at the commencement of the contract. Accordingly, it will be important for a principal to include such a clause in the agency contract wherever it is required. The parties may also agree upon a post-termination non-competition clause, limited to a period of two years after the termination of the agency contract (article 7:443 of the Civil Code). Such a clause must be stipulated in writing, and relate only to the kind of goods or services covered by the agency contract and to the geographical area or group of customers entrusted to the agent. The court has the power to overrule a non-competition clause if it is of the opinion that the clause is unfairly prejudicial to the agent's interests (article 7:443.4 of the Civil Code). If the non-competition clause provides for a penalty payable in the event of breach, the court may also mitigate such penalty (article 6.94 of the Civil Code).

If the non-competition clause is maintained, the manner in which the contract was terminated is still relevant. The principal cannot derive any rights from the clause in the following three cases:

- if the contract has been terminated prematurely by the principal;
- if the agent has terminated the contract for an urgent cause based on circumstances attributable to the principal; and
- if the contract is terminated by a decision of the court founded on circumstances attributable to the principal (article 7:443.3 of the Civil Code).

(16) Limitation

Actions for damages based on irregular termination (see (12)(iv) above) have a limitation period of one year (article 7:444 of the Civil Code). All other actions have a limitation period of five years (article 3:316 of the Civil Code). The agent loses his right to an indemnity payment for goodwill if he does not invoke his right thereto within one year as from the termination of the agency contract.

(17) Proceedings before the Dutch court

(i) Jurisdiction

Unless the parties have agreed that they will submit their disputes to arbitration[26], the County Courts have jurisdiction in disputes between the agent and the principal (article 39 of the Code of Judicial Organization). Actions where the parties request termination of the agency contract pursuant to article 7:440 (see (12) above) are initiated by a "*verzoekschrift*" (petition), in which case the County Court in the petitioner's residence or place of registered office has jurisdiction (article 429c of the Code of Civil Procedure). All other actions are initiated by a "*dagvaarding*" (writ of summons), in which case jurisdiction lies, at the discretion of the plaintiff, with the County Court in the plaintiff's residence or the County Court in the place where the agent habitually carries out his activities (article 98.2 of the Code of Civil Procedure). The result is that an agent who habitually performs his activities, in one place and who wishes to start an action against his principal will always find a court with jurisdiction in his own residence/place of registered office. Unless the agent wishes to have the Court terminate the contract, he may also address the County Court having jurisdiction in the principal's residence or place of registered office. The principal wishing to start an action against the agent will in most cases have to address the County Court in the agent's residence/place of registered office. If, on the other hand, the principal wishes to request the Court to terminate the contract, he can only address the County Court in his own residence/place of registered office.

The parties are not allowed to choose — by contract — any County Court other than the County Court that would have been awarded jurisdiction by the law (article 100 of the Code of Civil Procedure).

As a general rule, proceedings starting with a petition will be heard within four weeks as from the date of submission of the petition (articles 7:440.4 and 7A: 1639w. 6 of the Civil Code). Judgments will, as a rule, be rendered within two weeks thereafter. Generally speaking, proceedings initiated by a writ of summons will be conducted in writing only. The Court may — in its discretion — pursuant to a request for that purpose by either party, order that an oral hearing shall be held. As a matter of experience, the duration of the referenced proceedings can be assessed at one year for the least complex cases. Dependent on the complexity of the case, the proceedings may continue for several years.

---

[26] Articles 1020 *et seq* of the Code of Civil Procedure.

(ii) Applicable law

Contracts between a Dutch principal and a Dutch agent are obviously governed by Dutch law. Since Dutch law has been partly based on the 1986 Directive, the Dutch law (of agency) must be interpreted in accordance with the 1986 Directive, which implies that the Dutch Supreme Court, if involved in proceedings about a conflict relating to agency, may in some circumstances be obliged to refer a conflict of interpretation to the European Court of Justice by means of a petition for judicial review.[27]

(18) International contracts — which court?

Where there are contracts between a Dutch party and a party with a registered office on the territory of one of the contracting States to either the EEC Convention of 27 September 1968 on Jurisdiction and the Enforcement of Judgments in Civil and Commercial Matters ("the Brussels Convention") or the Convention of 16 September 1988 on Jurisdiction and the Enforcement of Judgments in Civil and Commercial Matters ("the Lugano Convention"), either of the aforesaid Conventions will apply, and accordingly, it is at the discretion of the plaintiff to choose as a forum either the court having jurisdiction in the defendant's place of residence/registered office, or the court having jurisdiction in the place where the agent habitually performs his activities.[28] In all other cases (Dutch agent/principal versus foreign agent/principal) and in the absence of a jurisdiction treaty, Dutch courts will assume jurisdiction even if the proceedings were initiated by the Dutch party.

If a Dutch party and a foreign party (whether or not it has a registered office within the territory of the contracting States to either of the above Conventions) agree that the courts in one of the contracting States to the Brussels Convention or to the Lugano Convention shall have jurisdiction, such a clause is in principle valid.[29] However, if the parties agree on a court outside the geographical area defined above (a United States court, for instance), it should not be taken for granted that the Dutch court will honour such an agreement. It should be taken into account that the Dutch court will judge that the agreement conflicts with article 100 of the Code of Civil Procedure (see also (17)(i) above) and, accordingly, that it is void.[30]

---

[27] Article 177 of the EEC Treaty; the lower courts may submit pre-judicial questions but cannot be obliged to do so.
[28] *Cf.* articles 2 and 5.1 of the Lugano Convention.
[29] *Cf.* article 17 of the Lugano Convention.

The parties enjoy full freedom to agree that they will refer any possible disputes to arbitration.

If the parties have not agreed on a choice of law, as a rule the law applicable in the place where the agent's residence or place of registered office will apply to the contract.[31] The parties may, however, agree that the contract is governed by another legal system.[32] Contrary to the situation of parties to an employment agreement[33], the parties to an agency contract are not restricted in their choice of law. It is, however, not allowed simply to contractually exclude any disagreeable provisions of foreign law. The Court of Appeal in *'s-Hertogenbosch* considered the principal's duty of calculation under article 7:433 of the Civil Code (see (11) above) of such essential importance that it gave prevalence to the mandatory rules of law, notwithstanding the fact that Greek law applied to the agency contract.[34]

---

[30] See Supreme Court, decision of 16 January 1981, NJ 1981, No 663.

[31] See article 4.2 of the Rome Convention on the Law Applicable to Contractual Obligations of 19 June 1980 ("EVO Convention") and article 6 of the 1978 Hague Representation Convention (Treaty book 1987, No 138). As early as 1973 the Dutch Supreme Court judged in accordance with paragraph 3.2: Supreme Court, decision of 6 April 1973, NJ 1973, No 371 (*Topsø/del Prado*); in its decision of 10 January 1992 *Rechtspraak van de Week* 1992, No 27 (*Jehro/Brinkhaus*) the Supreme Court decided that the law of the place where the agent habitually carries out his activities applies.

[32] See article 3 of the EVO Convention (see n 31 above).

[33] See article 6 of the EVO Convention (see n 31 above).

[34] Court of Appeal in *'s-Hertogenbosch*, judgment of 9 May 1985 as derived from the decision of the Supreme Court of 24 January 1986, NJ 1987, No 56 (*Eurobrid/Garabedian*). The District Court in Arnhem examined whether in a case in which the law of the state of Ohio was deemed applicable the (Dutch) agent was nevertheless entitled to an indemnity for goodwill under article 74o of the Commercial Code (now article 7.442 of the Civil Code), but judged negatively on account of the case having too little connection with the Dutch legal order (District Court in Arnhem, judgment of 19 January 1990; NIPR 1990, No 297). At one time the County Court in Amsterdam even terminated a contract on the basis of article 7:440 of the civil Code, although English law applied to that contract (County Court in Amsterdam, judgment of 25 September 1991, *Praktijkgids* 1992, No 3619). In an unpublished judgment of 2 November 1994 (*Poelenjee/Vee en Vlees Export BV*); the County Court in Groenlo considered that rules of Dutch agency law aimed at protecting the agent may be applicable only to an agency contract governed by Dutch law if the agent has a registered office in the Netherlands.

CONTENTS OF CHAPTER 14

Portugal

14. PORTUGAL

Jaime Medeiros, Coelho Ribeiro E Associados, Lisbon

(1) What is meant by the expression "commercial agent" in Portugal?

Until 1986, there were no specific rules concerning agency contracts and agency activity in Portugal. This means that the expression "commercial agent" has had a common sense rather than a legal meaning. It is taken to refer to someone or a trade mark who represents a company within a country or with regard to a certain group of clients.

The uncertainty regarding the status of an agent is evident in some of the cases, where even in the judgments the activities of an agent and distributor have been confused.

In 1986, a law (decree-law no 178/86, of 3 July) governing agency contracts, activities of the agent, rights and obligations of the agent and of the principal was published, which reflected the provisions of the then EC Directive on commercial agency.

Today, the term "commercial agent" is clearly defined in Portugal and is generally understood to be a person or a company who promotes business on behalf of a third person known as the principal, and who is entitled to a commission due from the principal for his activities.

Promoting business must be the main purpose of the agent's activity, although other linked activities are commonly carried on by an agent in Portugal, such as, in the case of the sale of goods, ensuring the delivery of such goods to the customers and providing the assistance given to them under the guarantee period.

(2) Is there a distinction in Portugal between the supply of goods and the supply of services in terms of commercial agency?

Portuguese law does not make a distinction between agents for the sale of goods and agents for services. This means that in Portugal, a principal is allowed to use agents to promote and negotiate contracts involving any type of services as well as for the sale of goods.

The question arises in the case of an agent for services as to whether the agent himself can render the services on behalf of the principal. In the opinion of the author, the agent himself can render the contracted services but he would be acting in this case as a sub-contractor of the principal in the performance of the contract. Nevertheless, in the promotion of business the agent for services is subject to the legislation relating to commercial agency.

(3) What are the differences between an agent and a distributor in Portugal?

Since the adoption of the EEC Council Directive of 18 December 1986 on the co-ordination of the laws of the Member States relating to Self-employed Agents (86/653/EEC) ("the 1986 Directive") in Portugal it is easy to distinguish an agent from a distributor.

An agent promotes business on behalf of a principal in return for a commission, meaning that the contract itself is made directly between the principal and the client. Even when the agent has powers to conclude contracts, he will act as "an attorney in fact" of the principal, it being the latter who is always responsible to the client for the performance of the contract. The commission represents the gross turnover of the agent, and is therefore subject to invoicing from the agent to the principal.

A distributor buys the goods from the principal and resells them to his own customers, adding on his own profit. This difference lies in the fact that the distributor acts under his own name and no relevant mention is made of the principal, who is not responsible towards the distributor's clients for the performance of the contract. It should be noted that the EEC Council Directive of 25 July 1985 (85/374/EEC) on the approximation of the laws, regulations and administrative provisions of the Member States concerning liability for defective products, the principal may be directly responsible for the supply of defective products towards the final consumer. The distributor is not entitled to a commission from the principal because his earnings are based on a resale margin or discount. This is normally shown in the invoice from the principal to the distributor.

(4) Are there any provisions in Portugal which relate specifically to distributors?

No, there are no special Portuguese provisions or laws governing distribution contracts or a distributor's activity. This means that distribution contracts are mainly subject to the provisions agreed by the parties, although it should be noted that some dispositions concerning agency contracts (in particular termination rules protecting the agent) are currently being applied by the courts to distribution contracts.

Notwithstanding the above, it is important that the principal chooses carefully between appointing an agent or a distributor. This choice will depend on the level of participation and control that he wishes to have over the territory and the customers. Thus if the principal wants to have considerable control over the business and the customers in a particular area, for example, then he should appoint an agent for that territory. If this is not the case, then he may prefer to establish a distribution relationship with the local distribution enterprise.

(5) What are the mandatory rules applicable to agency agreements in Portugal?

Portuguese law has various types of provisions which must be taken into consideration when drafting and executing agency contracts.

Some provisions are mandatory by law as they are applicable even if the contract attempts to exclude them. Others are "subsidiary" and only applicable if the contract does not otherwise deal with the detail concerned.

If a contract does contain clauses avoiding the application of mandatory rules, those clauses are considered null and void but do not make the contract as a whole void, unless it is proved that it would not have been concluded without the void clauses.

Mandatory rules can be reproduced in agreements in what is sometimes a good negotiation strategy for the principal. In fact, if the contract reproduces mandatory rules, which in most cases are protective rules in favour of the commercial agent, the inclusion of such clauses can be negotiated jointly with other clauses in favour of the principal (for example exclusive representation, performance quotas, termination clauses for bad performance).

(6) What are the main provisions which are mandatorily included in commercial agency agreements under Portuguese law?

A brief *résumé* of these are:

- The right of either party to ask for a written agreement or, if an oral agreement is already in force, for a document signed by the other party containing the provisions agreed.
- General mandatory duties and obligations of the agent, such as the obligation to look after the principal's interests, to act dutifully and in good faith, to communicate to the principal all the necessary and available information and to comply with reasonable instructions given.
- General duties and obligations of the principal such as the duty to act in good faith, to provide his commercial agent with the necessary documentation relating to the goods concerned and to the performance of the agency contract.
- The agent's entitlement to a commission for contracts promoted and, in the case of exclusivity, also for contracts concluded with customers of his territory or circle of customers. If the agreement does not fix the "commission", this will be determined according to what is customarily allowed, or according to equity.
- Commission becomes due by the principal to the agent at the latest when the client has executed his part of the transaction or should have done so if the principal had executed his part as he should have, though it should be noted that there is a right to extinguish commission in some circumstances.

  The commission has to be paid to the agent not later than the last day of the month following the quarter when it became due.
- The agent is required to inform his clients of the extent of the powers granted to him by the principal, in particular the powers to complete contracts and to receive payments on behalf of the principal.
- The mandatory rules concerning termination and compensation for termination. These are analysed more fully at (12) below, taking into consideration their importance for principals and agents.

(7) What is the situation where the agent exceeds his authority to conclude contracts on behalf of the principal?

Under Portuguese legislation concerning third party protection, the deals concluded by an agent with no powers to conclude contracts will not bind the principal until they are ratified by him. Nevertheless, the contract is considered to be ratified if the principal does not express his opposition to the third party within five days after acknowledgement of the contents of the contract. The principal shall also be bound by, and responsible for, a contract agreed with an agent with no powers, if there were objective reasons for the client to believe in the good faith and legitimacy of the agent and the principal contributed to the client's belief.

(8) What should be included in a contract with a commercial agent in Portugal?

It is important to summarise the matters that should be covered in a contract as in their absence the Portuguese subsidiary rules are applied. Some specific matters which could be usefully included in an agency contract are as follows:

(i) Powers to conclude contracts

An agent has no powers to sign contracts on behalf of a principal unless otherwise agreed in writing. Therefore, a clause concerning the extension and limits of the powers of the agent is commonly included in a contract.

(ii) Powers to collect payments

An agent has no powers to collect payments unless otherwise agreed in writing. A clause should be included to deal with this matter.

An agent with powers to collect payments has the right to an extra commission which should be defined in the contract.

(iii) Exclusivity

The exclusivity of the agent is subject to a written agreement of the parties, otherwise Portuguese law will not grant any exclusive rights to the agent.

The status of "exclusive agent" involves a real *pacto de non contrahendo* for the principal giving to the exclusive agent a right to a commission for the contracts negotiated directly by the principal or by a third party in breach of the exclusivity agreement.

The agency agreement can also grant exclusivity in favour of the principal. In fact, Portuguese law permits the exclusivity in favour of the agent, in favour of the principal or in favour of both parties.

(iv) Sub-agents

An agent is a self-employed intermediary and is not an employee of the principal. This means that the agent is free to exercise his activity using sub-contractors (sub-agents) at his sole discretion. If the principal wants to avoid the use of sub-agents, a clause must be drafted accordingly and included in the agency agreement.

(v) Can the principal limit the agent's activities following termination of the agency agreement?

If the principal wishes to avoid competition from the agent with regard to his existing customers following termination of the agency contract, he may include a non-competition clause restricting the agent's activities following termination, but this is only valid if (a) it is for no longer than two years; and (b) it only covers the geographical area, or group of customers or clients included in the agency agreement.

Should a non-competition clause be agreed, then the agent is entitled to compensation on termination, which can be defined in the contract.

(vi) Star del credere *— can an agent be made responsible to the principal for payment by the purchaser or client?*

The performance of a contract by a client (namely the payment of the price) can be personally assured by the agent. Under a *del credere* agreement the agent will be personally liable towards the principal for the good execution of the client's part of the transaction.

This can represent a very important safeguard for the principal in order to avoid non-genuine transactions proposed by the agent and also to enable the principal to make deals within a new geographic area or unfamiliar group of clients.

The contracts or the clients in respect of which the agent personally guarantees and is responsible for payment should be properly identified in the agency agreement. If these details are not included in the agency contract then a specific agreement for each client or contract should be made.

The *del credere* clause gives the agent the right to immediate payment of his commission upon conclusion of the contract and also the right to an extra commission.

(vii) Does the agent have a right to expenses?

If not otherwise agreed in the contract, the agent shall incur and be paid all the general expenses incurred, or to be incurred, in the performance of his agency activity. Extraordinary expenses incurred on behalf of the principal are in principle supported by the principal. It is good practice to provide for these details in the contract.

(9) What other clauses can be included in a contract with a commercial agent in Portugal?

It is advisable to include the following in agency contracts:

(i) Performance quotas

The agent can be lawfully bound to perform quotas during the agreement and this is one of the most important ways the principal can monitor the agent's performance.

If the agency is for an indefinite period, the clause dealing with performance quotas should be carefully drafted so as to provide for the revision or increase of such quotas.

(ii) Information to be regularly provided by one party to another

Although some information must be provided by the principal to the agent in accordance with the 1986 Directive, another way to enable the principal to monitor the agency is by providing in the agreement that regular and detailed information should be given to him by the agent. The details in the clause should depend on the type of activity to be developed by the agent and should include binding deadlines for the agent to provide relevant information.

(iii) Stocks

If under the contract the agent has the power to execute contracts promoted by him then for that purpose he probably has in his custody or possession necessary stocks of goods concerned.

Normally, these remain the property of the principal and therefore a clause dealing with responsibilities and insurance of the goods should be included in the agency agreement, as should a clause to provide for the disposition of the stocks on termination of the agreement.

(iv) Third party protection

As far as rules protecting third parties acting in good faith are concerned, it is advisable to include a clause referring to the way the agent should act towards his clients or potential clients; namely his duty to give them information about the following: the extent of his authority (for example powers to enter into agreements or to receive payments), the identity of the principal, his ability in respect of indemnifying the principal as well as his obligation to prevent the principal from incurring any loss or damage for non-performance caused by, or arising out of, the agent's conduct.

It should also be noted that some obligations of the principal (for example the obligation not to unreasonably refuse contracts promoted by the agent and to dutifully perform the contracts accepted) can be included in a specific clause.

(v) *Promotional and marketing activities*

Nowadays, marketing and promotional activities are essential for the launching of new products in the market, and generally represent a major part of the commercial budget. If it is intended that the agent will also benefit from those activities, and from the investment point of view it appears to be important to involve the agent in such projects, then a clause in the commercial agency agreement should deal with this matter.

(vi) *Technical assistance*

Sometimes, the agent is responsible for technical assistance to be rendered to his clients following the acquisition of goods from the principal. It is very important that the client is made clearly aware of who is responsible for such assistance; either the principal, if the agent is a representative or a sub-contractor, or the agent himself. In the latter situation the principal has no commitment or responsibility whatsoever for the assistance or maintenance of equipment required. A clause should deal with this as the rendering of technical assistance is not contemplated by Portuguese law as part of the core of the agency agreement.

(vii) *Insurance*

If the agency involves the custody of stocks which are the property of the principal, a clause defining who is responsible for insurance and who supports the related costs is required.

(10) **Applicable law and jurisdiction**

According to Portuguese international private law the parties can agree upon the law which will govern the agency agreement. They can choose between the law of the domicile of one of the parties, the law of the geographic area where the agent is going to develop his activity, the law of the country where the principal has his main business or any other business related to the goods or services to be promoted by the agent.

Nevertheless, the parties cannot choose (1) a governing law which has no connection with the contract; or (2) one that does not represent their "serious intention" — *i.e.* there is no serious intention when, for instance, the agency agreement is subject to an iniquitous and/or unreasonable law *vis-à-vis* general principles of law recognised in Portugal.

However, it is in accordance with Portuguese private law for the parties to agree that some particular aspects, for instance rights and duties emerging from the agreement will be covered by different laws. For example, a clause establishing that the agreement shall be governed by the laws of the principal's domicile except as regards termination provisions which shall be governed according to the laws of the agent's domicile, is legally binding.

It must be noted, however, that in respect of the termination of a contract which is mostly performed in Portugal, Portuguese law will be mandatorily applicable, unless foreign law is more favourable to the agent.

It is also most important to take account of the fact that if the parties do not choose a specific applicable law for the contract or for part of it, then the subsidiary applicable law will be that of the domicile of the parties, if the applicable domiciliary law is the same, otherwise it would be the law of the place where the contract was signed. Thus for example, for an agency agreement signed in Paris between a principal domiciled in Madrid and an agent domiciled in Lisbon, which does not include a clause dealing with the governing law, the applicable law would be French (except with regard to the termination of the contract provisions as mentioned above).

(11) What about jurisdiction for settlement of disputes?

For the settlement of disputes arising from an agency agreement, Portuguese law allows the parties to choose between the jurisdiction of the registered office or of a branch of one of the parties or even the jurisdiction of international courts as long as their choice is allowed by the law of the elected court and corresponds to a serious interest of both parties or one of them. The elected court must be designated in a written agreement between the parties and the clause concerned has to define clearly the matters that should be submitted to the jurisdiction agreed.

(12) Is there any restriction on the use of arbitration clauses?

For the settlement of disputes arising from the execution or interpretation of an agency agreement, Portuguese law allows the parties to choose the jurisdiction of an arbitration court. As some of the most important issues or disputes arising from the execution of an agency agreement (for example disputes over commission or indemnities to be fixed in equitable terms) involve significant sums of money but may not be covered pragmatically by legislation, it may be considered that the choice of an arbitration court could solve those disputes in a quicker and more efficient way.

(13) Can Portuguese courts apply foreign law?

Yes. The negotiators of an agency agreement must bear in mind that Portuguese courts can settle disputes according to a foreign law. For instance, a clause that elects the law of the domicile of the principal to govern the contract (Spanish law, for example) and submits the contract to the jurisdiction of the Portuguese courts is a valid one.

As regards matters concerning the choice of law or jurisdiction, Portuguese law does not distinguish agents or principals from EU, EFTA or third countries.

(14) What is the position in Portugal relating to product liability?

The EEC Directive of 25 July 1985 on the approximation of the laws, regulations and administrative provisions of the Member States concerning liability for defective products has been adopted by Portuguese law but does not expressly refer to agents. Under the product liability regulation a commercial entity can be considered a producer if it imports goods from outside the European Union for sale, leasing or any other form of distribution.

If the agency only involves the promotion of business and does not involve powers to sign and perform contracts, or to collect payments, or to import goods to be delivered to clients then the agent shall not be liable for defective products.

Usually, agreements made with principals outside the European Union are not pure agency agreements, as they will also have some characteristics of a distribution agreement since the agent may be acting as an importer of the goods relating to the contracts promoted by him. If this is the case, the agent should be insured when carrying on his activity.

(15) Does engaging a Portuguese agent constitute carrying on a business in Portugal?

With regard to tax responsibilities, a foreign commercial entity can be considered as carrying on a business in Portugal if it has employees or other personnel under its instructions and supervision to look after the business in Portugal.

However, although an agent is an autonomous entity that should only comply with reasonable instructions and is not submitted to any hierarchical supervision from the principal, the distinction between an individual acting as an agent or as an employee can be sometimes rather difficult to prove before the tax authorities. This issue can be solved by using a commercial company rather than an individual to act as an agent in Portugal or for Portuguese clients.

(16) What are the provisions relating to the conclusion and termination of agency agreements?

Under Portuguese law, an agency agreement can be for an indefinite or fixed term, and may, or may not, be renewable. Indefinite agency agreements can be terminated by notice by one party to another. Agency agreements for fixed terms can only be terminated at the end of the term or upon its renewal, automatically or by notice. It is suggested that it does not carry any substantial advantage for the principal to conclude renewable fixed term agreements, as for indefinite agency agreements in force for less than a year, between one and two years or for more than two years, respectively, a one month, two month or three month written notice is required for termination The parties must have in mind that non-renewable fixed term agency agreements which continue to be executed by the parties after their terms are deemed to be converted into indefinite agency agreements.

(17) What is the effect of the death of the agent?

Agency agreements automatically terminate on the death of the agent, if an individual, or by the dissolution or bankruptcy of any of the parties.

(18) What about termination without due notice?

Termination of the agreement by one party without the necessary prior notice gives to the other party the right to be indemnified for the losses suffered. As an option the agent can ask for an amount to be calculated on the basis of his average monthly remuneration over the last 12 months multiplied by the period of notice which was not given by the principal.

The agency agreement can also be terminated early in cases of serious and/or repeated default or if there are circumstances beyond the control of either party that make the maintenance of the agreement impossible, such as in the case of the incapacity or prolonged illness of the agent.

In the cases mentioned in the above paragraphs the termination shall become effective by written notice containing the reasons for such termination. The right of termination shall be exercised within one month counting from the date of acknowledgement of the facts, which are the reasons for early termination, by the party. If the termination is due to circumstances not imputable to any party, the party to whom the notice of termination is addressed has the right to compensation according to equity. Also the defaulting party who breaches the contract has to indemnify the other party according to the general principles of law.

(19) What are the provisions relating to the agent's rights in respect of termination?

The provisions concerning the right of the agent to ask for compensation or an indemnity in case of termination of contract in Portuguese law give the agent the right to be indemnified, under article 33(1) of decree law 178/86. This is important and is therefore quoted in full:

> Without prejudice to any other right of indemnity which may exist pursuant to previous Articles, after the termination of the contract the agent has the right to be indemnified in respect of customers, as long as all the following requirements are fulfilled:
>
> a) The agent has brought new customers to the other party or has substantially increased the amount of business with the existing customers;
>
> b) After termination of the contract the other party will substantially benefit from the activity developed by the agent;
>
> c) The agent will not receive any payments for contracts negotiated or concluded after the termination of the contract with customers referred to in a).

This indemnity which must be granted to the agent by the principal is not an indemnity for damages arising from a default position of the principal. The agent is entitled to the above indemnity taking into consideration the termination of the contract, the benefits resulting from his developed activity and subsequent unjust enrichment of the principal. This indemnity is determined by equity but should not exceed the equivalent of the average annual remuneration received by the agent during the last five years of the agency agreement; if the contract has run for less than five years, then the average remuneration for the period of the agency is used as a basis for calculation. The agent is not entitled to this indemnity if the termination was due to his own initiative by reason of his giving notice of termination to the principal or due to his breach of the agency contract, or in the case of his assignment of the agency, to another agent with the consent of the principal.

CONTENTS OF CHAPTER 15

Spain

15. SPAIN

Juan Santamariá, Laura Mora and Jesús Martrat, Bufete Pinto Ruiz, Barcelona

(1) What is the law applicable to commercial agents whose duties are performed in Spain?

The first question that should be asked by actual or potential parties to an agency contract is whether or not that agency contract will be governed by Spanish law.

The normal practice is probably to provide in the contract for the application of the law which is most convenient in all the circumstances, but can this be done with agency contracts which are to be enforced in Spain? In other words, can the contracting parties exclude the application of Spanish law and agree to be subject to the law of another country? Or will Spanish legal provisions be enforced even if this is not the intention of the parties?

The answer to these questions requires a brief introduction. The trend in international law is towards enabling the contracting parties to agree freely on the law to be applied to their contracting relationships. The clearest example of these rules is article 3.1 of the Rome Convention (Convention on the law applicable to Contractual Obligations, submitted for signature in Rome, 1980 ratified by Spain on 19 July 1993), which reads as follows:

> Contracts are to be governed by the law selected by the parties. This choice must be express or appear certain from the terms of the contract or the circumstances of the case. Making this choice, the parties may designate the law applicable to all, or part of, the contract.

This rule is fully applicable in Spain, where private international law provisions also set out a similar principle. Article 10.5. of the Spanish Civil Code states:

> The law applied to contractual obligations shall be the law to which the parties are expressly subject provided that it has some connection with the business in question; the domestic law common to both parties is to be applied; or else the place of common residence, and lastly, the law of the place where the contract is concluded.

Thus, the Civil Code gives importance to the connections between the contract and the law to which both parties submit. This principle has also been taken into account by article 7.1 of the Rome Convention which states:

> When enforcing the law of a country, mandatory provisions of another country with a closer connection with the situation may also be enforceable, provided that according to the law of this latter country, such provisions are applicable whatever law governs the contract. (. . .)

Therefore, according to these general principles, the parties can make the agreement subject to the law they consider most convenient. However, if the contract has a closer connection with the law of a different country, the mandatory provisions of that country may be applicable.

The Spanish provisions regulating agency contracts are Law 12/1992, 27 May, Agency Contracts ("Law 12/92"), which incorporated EEC Directive of 18 December 1986, on the co-ordination of the laws of the Member States concerning Self-employed Commercial Agents ("the 1986 Directive") into Spanish law. This Law states in article 3.1:

> . . . the diverse forms of agency contract . . . shall be governed by this law, whose provisions are mandatory unless it is expressly stated otherwise.

It is suggested that this breaches the principle of freedom of the parties to fix the contractual law and is based, in our opinion, on the open door left by the Rome Convention which allows countries to establish mandatory provisions.

The effect of Law 12/92 is to require the application of its provisions except where otherwise stated in preference to any other law or agreement between contracting parties. This means the parties may only include in the contract particular clauses or submission to provisions of another legislation as long as these clauses or references do not contravene Law 12/92 provisions.

It is important to realise that the criterion is different from the legislation of various other countries (for example the United Kingdom) where both parties are allowed to choose the law of another country in respect of commercial agency contracts.

When are the mandatory norms of Law 12/92 to be applied to an agency contract? When both parties are Spanish? When one of them is Spanish? When the agency activity is performed in Spain, even though the parties are not from Spain?

Law 12/92 does not specifically refer to any of these situations, but the natural answer is that Spanish legislation must be applied to the extent that the agent's activities are performed in Spain. The main reason for this is that the provisions of Law 12/92 are mainly concerned with acknowledging and protecting the rights of agents who perform their duties in that country.

However, Law 12/92 should have explained its scope of application, as have the regulations in the United Kingdom which implemented the 1986 Directive, which expressly state that the provisions apply in relation to the activities of commercial agents in Great Britain and so by implication do not extend to such activities outside the UK.

(2) What is the definition of a "commercial agent" in Spain?

Appointment of a commercial agent is one of the many methods that businessmen can use to sell, distribute, and market their products.

Every company will choose the most appropriate form for its particular business and products and/or services. Thus, some companies choose to appoint distributors, while others set up a franchise network, while others have got their own employees who are in charge of sales, and finally, others decide to have commercial agents.

The defining elements of a commercial agent are described below and in (4) below a distinction is made between commercial agents and similar entities.

A commercial agent, as defined in Law 12/92 is an independent self-employed commercial individual or company who undertakes, in a continuous or stable manner, to promote commercial acts or transactions on behalf of a third party, or to promote and conclude such acts or transactions on behalf of, and in the name of, a third party in return for a remuneration, without assuming, unless otherwise stated, the risk and venture of such transactions.

The definition thus has four main elements:

- The requirement for independence which means that a commercial agent cannot be the employee of a principal, as any labour relationship involves a degree of dependency to link the employee to the principal, which is not consistent with being a self-employed commercial agent. Thus to come within the definition, agents must be free to organise their professional activity and the time devoted to such activity must be at their discretion.
- A requirement that a commercial agent must work in a continuous and regular way for the promotion of commercial transactions in the principal's interest. If his performance is limited to a specific contract or sporadic transactions, then there is no agency relationship and, therefore, Law 12/92 is not applicable.
- An agent must carry out any necessary activities to conclude commercial transactions between clients and his principal. Can a commercial agent handle goods and services in Spain? The purpose of agency contracts is usually the sale of products or goods, but an agency contract can also include rendering services, trade-in, leasing and, in short, any commercial transaction in Spain. However, Law 12/92 is not applicable to some types of agencies which are regulated by special laws (stockbrokers, insurance companies, travel agencies, etc).

  It should be pointed out that an agent can conclude contracts with clients on behalf of the principal provided that the principal has expressly empowered the agent to do so. Otherwise, an agent is limited to putting the client and principal in contact and acting as an intermediary, it being the principal himself who concludes the contract with the client.
- A commercial agent does not assume the risk and venture of the transaction, unless otherwise agreed. Thus the agent is not liable for clients' failure to comply with their obligations towards the principal, (which normally means payment of the price of the goods that the principal, by means of the agent, has sold to them).

Nevertheless, Law 12/92 allows the parties to agree otherwise provided that the agent receives an additional remuneration in return for his extra liability (what is called "*del credere* commission") (see (6)(iii) below).

(3) What is the distinction between a commercial agent and other commercial relationships?

In order to provide a better understanding of the definition, it is useful to compare a commercial agent with others that may appear to be quite similar but are, in fact rather different. These include commission agents, commercial representatives and distributors.

(i) What is the difference between a commission agent and a commercial agent?

Basically the difference lies in the absence of stability or a continuous link.

The duties of a commission agent are very similar to those of a commercial agent.

Thus a commission agent must work on behalf of another trader, and as a self-employed intermediary, for the conclusion of commercial business transactions, and mediate so that such transactions are concluded, receiving a remuneration for this job.

A commission agent always acts in specific and sporadic activities with regard to one or two specific transactions; whereas a commercial agent always keeps a regular and continuous link with his principal.

An example of a commission agreement would be a contract by which a company individual or enterprise entrusts to a third party (the commission agent) the sale of the old machines from his production plant.

As a final point, although a commission agent is not normally liable for the transactions in which he participates, the parties can agree otherwise, in which case the commission agent is entitled to the "*del credere* commission" mentioned in (2) above.

The conclusion is that a commission contract is like an agency contract in that the agent is self-employed, promotes commercial transactions and does not assume the risk in the transactions, unless otherwise agreed. The difference lies in the lack of continuity in his link to the principal.

The essential nature of commission agency is regulated in articles 244–280 of the Commercial Code.

(ii) What is the difference between a commercial agent and a commercial representative?

The duties of a commercial representative are the same as the duties of a commercial agent, *i.e.* the continuous regular promotion of commercial transactions on behalf of the principal but there are two peculiarities.

Firstly, a commercial representative is always dependent on a principal, to whom he is linked by a labour relationship, unlike commercial agents who (like commission agents) are self-employed commercial enterprises or individuals.

In this sense, Law 12/92 stipulates that individuals linked by a labour relationship to their principal, whereby they cannot freely organise their professional activity or the time they devote to such activity at their own discretion, shall not be considered commercial agents.

It is important to notice that a commercial representative does not need to be a principal's employee. Evidence of a "dependence" link to his principal will be enough (for example whether his principal fixes his work schedule, route, distribution criteria, etc).

Second, a commercial representative is never liable for the successful conclusion of the transactions, whereas an agent can take on this liability.

In conclusion, a commercial representative and an agent are alike in so far as stability and promotion of transactions are concerned, and totally different as to dependency.

(iii) What is the difference between a commercial agent and a distributor?

A distributor purchases goods in his own name and on behalf of the principal in order to resell them later, whereas a commercial agent always works on behalf of the principal and never purchases for himself the goods produced or marketed by the principal.

It should be noted that a distributor uses his own capital to purchase the principal's goods, and resale is carried out at the distributor's exclusive risk, without prejudice to the manufacturers' liability (see the recent Law 22/1994, 6 July, on civil liability for damages for defective products, whose purpose is to adapt Spanish law to EEC Directive 85/374). In other words, when there is a distribution relationship, the contract is not between client or end consumer and manufacturer or principal, but between client and distributor; whereas in a commercial agency relationship the contract is between principal (not agent) and client.

The legal consequences of this are significant, not only in the economic-financial field (as a distributor must have the economic means available to purchase the goods), but also with regard to liability to the end purchaser of the products, who, in the case of defective products or inaccurate fulfilment of the distributor's obligations, will obviously address his complaints primarily to the distributor, without prejudice to the liability of the manufacturer or importer of the products.

(4) What are the duties of a principal towards his commercial agent?

The main obligation of the principal is to pay the agent the remuneration agreed upon for the services rendered by the agent in accordance with the conditions set out in the agency agreement.

It is expressly provided by Law 12/92 that a principal must:

- Make available to the agent, in advance and in sufficient quantities, all the samples, catalogues, tariffs and other documents necessary for the performance of his professional activity. This is an essential point that will allow the agent to perform his activities dutifully.
- Provide the agent with all the information required to enforce the agency contract.
- Particularly warn him, when he foresees that the volume of acts or transactions is going to be considerably lower than the volume expected by the agent.
- Provide the agent with the information necessary to verify that the commissions he is entitled to have been duly settled.
- Notify the agent of the acceptance or refusal of the transactions proposed by the agent within a term of 15 days (Law 12/92). Even though Law 12/92 does not explain it, logically it has to be presumed that the section refers to the cases when the agent is not entitled or he has not been empowered to conclude contracts with clients; otherwise, it

would seem to be unnecessary to get the principal's approval before concluding the transaction, unless otherwise agreed.

- Also keep the agent duly informed of the time when the transactions are concluded with clients, whether wholly or partially, so that the agent can know whether his commission is due or not.
- Like the agent, must act dutifully and in good faith.

(5) What are the duties of a commercial agent?

An agent, like the principal, must act dutifully and in good faith. In addition Law 12/92 imposes some specific obligations on the agent, who must:

- look after promotion, and where appropriate, conclusion of any commercial acts or transactions entrusted to him with the due diligence of a good trader;
- communicate to his principal all the information available to him and where necessary properly manage the commercial acts or transactions whose promotion or conclusion has been entrusted to him;

  This duty to communicate includes information relating to the solvency of third parties with whom there may be transactions awaiting conclusion or promotion. This is very important, since should there be non-payment from clients who are not solvent, and the agent knew of their insolvency beforehand and did not communicate it to his principal, the agent may be liable for the loss suffered by his principal;
- perform his duties following reasonable instructions received from the principal, provided that such instructions do not affect his independence, which is essential to maintain his status as a commercial agent. These "reasonable instructions" must not interfere with his self-organisation;
- receive, on behalf of the principal, any complaints from third parties about faults or defects of amount or quality of goods sold or services rendered which arise out of transactions he has promoted, even though he, as agent, may not have concluded them. The agent shall immediately inform his principal should any of the previous events occur; and
- keep separate accounts relating to the commercial acts or transactions of the principal on whose behalf he is acting.

(6) **Remuneration of an agent**

(i) When does the agent's right to remuneration arise?

Just as the main duty of the agent is to promote, negotiate and/or conclude contracts on behalf of the principal, so the principal has the equivalent duty to remunerate the agent according to the principle of correspondence between sales of services.

The basic points of the question of the agent's remuneration are governed by articles 11–19 of Law 12/92, which reflects the provisions of the 1986 Directive.

(ii) What kinds of remuneration are there?

There are three methods of remunerating the agent's activity:

- a fixed amount;
- a commission; or
- a combination of both systems.

With regard to the fixed remuneration system; this is very rare. The general rule is to pay a commission, because a fixed remuneration is not consistent with the true nature of the agency contract, since if the risk of remuneration is removed which is dependent on various transactions the agent's incentive to pursue transactions and nurture clients in the principal's interest is also minimised.

With regard to payment of commission, which is more common in an agency contract, this can be established by agreement between the parties or according to normal trade practice (as in the case of a fixed remuneration). It does not need to be fixed beforehand, as long as it can be determined.

(iii) How is commission defined?

Law 12/92 defines commission as any element of the remuneration that varies in accordance with the volume or value of acts or transactions promoted and, where appropriate, concluded by the agent.

There are two different types of commission: (1) a commission on acts or transactions concluded during the agency contract; and (2) a commission on acts or transactions concluded after termination of the agency contract.

With regard to the commission on acts or transactions concluded during the agency contract an agent shall be entitled to commission:

- where the commercial act or transaction has been concluded as a result of his action; or
- where the transaction has been concluded with a third party with whom the agent had previously promoted or concluded a commercial act or transaction of the same kind.

  Therefore, the agent shall not only be entitled to commission when the contract has been directly concluded by him, but also when the contract is concluded as a result of his promotional activity, and such activity has been essential for the eventual conclusion of the commercial transaction between the principal and the client; and
- where he has an exclusive right to a specific geographical area or to a specific group of customers and where the transaction has been entered into with a customer belonging to that area or group, even if such act or transaction has not been promoted or concluded by the agent. This commission, which is known as indirect commission, is based on the need to satisfy the legal expectations of the agent in the case of possible intrusions in his area by the principal or by another agent, without the principal having paid to the agent a commission on such transactions.

With regard to commissions on acts or transactions concluded after the agency contract has terminated, an agent shall be entitled to such commission if:

- The act or transaction is mainly attributable to his efforts during the period covered by the agency contract and if the transaction was entered into within three months following the termination of the relationship.
- The principal or agent receives the request or order before the agency contract has terminated and if the commercial act or transaction had been concluded within the period covered by the contract, the agent would have been entitled to demand a commission.

Lastly, it should be noted that Law 12/92 enables refusal to entitlement to commission on acts or transactions concluded during agency contract, where the commission is due to a previous agent, unless in view of the current circumstances, it is fair to distribute the commission between both agents (article 13.2).

It is emphasised that the parties may agree that the agent is liable for the good performance of transactions, *i.e.* if the customer does not pay the amount of the product supplied or the service rendered by the principal, the agent will be obliged to compensate to the principal for such non-payment. This type of agreement is only valid when made in writing, and the agent has a right to "*del credere* commission".

(iv) *What is* "del credere *commission*"?

Del credere commission is the extra commission which is due to an agent in addition to the commission he would be entitled to on account of his normal agency services, as consideration for assuming liability for non-payment by customers.

Law 12/92 does not provide any criteria to fix the amount of this commission, but the customary practice is that the commission is composed of a fixed percentage of the principal's invoices for the contract obtained thanks to the agent's work.

(7) **Must a commercial agent be limited to one principal in Spain?**

A commercial agent can render his services on behalf of one or several principals in Spain.

This does not mean that the contracting parties (commercial agent and principal) cannot agree on the exclusive right of one or both parties. Thus, it is possible that a commercial agent undertakes to act as an intermediary only and exclusively in relation to the principal's goods; or the other way round, that the principal gives the agent the exclusive right to distribute his products. Or, as stated above, the exclusive right or obligation can be provided to both parties.

The exclusive right or obligation can be further restricted by incorporating other elements: geographical area, products and/or specific customers. For example, it can be agreed that the commercial agent undertakes to act as an intermediary only for the principal within the city of Barcelona, as different agents are appointed to operate outside this city.

Although Law 12/92 states that a commercial agent can serve several principals at the same time, it forbids the agent, unless he has the principal's approval, to perform on his own account or on behalf of another principal a professional or related activity with similar goods or services that may be in competition with those he has undertaken to promote.

This prohibition is consistent with the agent's legal obligation to act dutifully and in good faith, in looking after the interests of his principal or principals. What Law 12/92 seeks to prevent is a conflict of interests which may hinder the agent's good performance.

(8) Can the parties agree to limit the professional activities of the agent after the contract has terminated?

Yes, although there are some conditions which must be observed, and the effects of an agreement of this nature need to be taken into account.

The "clause of competition limits" (this is the term used by Law 12/92) cannot be for a period longer than two years following termination. However, if the agency contract is for a shorter period, the restrictive clause cannot last longer than a year.

Further to the maximum duration limits set out above, Law 12/92 imposes other conditions for the clause to be effective:

- the agreement on competition limits must be formalised in writing in order to be valid and effective; and
- the agreement can only be extended to the geographical area or the area and the group of people entrusted to the agent, and it can only affect the type of goods or service which are, or were, the purpose of the acts or transactions promoted or concluded by the agent.

The agreements on competition limits referred to above give the principal an important advantage: he can be sure that following termination of the contract he will be able to continue developing his marketing activities within the area and/or the clients with whom he was dealing so far introduced by the agent, without having the agent set up in competition with him for the specified period.

However, these agreements involve a huge sacrifice for the commercial agent: he cannot perform activities in the area and with the people (customers) he knows best, and, perhaps, the only people he knows, for the period agreed, which makes him lose revenue.

Law 12/92 has been sensitive to the disadvantages caused to agents by this agreement on competition limits, and provides that the existence or non-existence of these agreements will be taken into account when: (1) determining whether it is reasonable or not that a the principal pays compensation to the agent for the customers lost; and (2) when calculating the amount of such compensation.

(9) When is the principal liable for the acts of his agent?

The question as to whether the principal is liable or not for his agent's acts when such acts have brought damage to third parties is complex. For example an agent undertakes to supply to a client, on a fixed date, a certain volume of goods, which are essential for his production process, even though he is aware that the principal cannot complete such an order in such a short time. As a consequence of not getting the order completed in time, the client's factory has to stop working and the client claims considerable damages for this reason.

(10) Can the client claim against the principal or only against the agent?

This depends on the terms and regulations governing the relationship between principal and agent.

If the agent is limited to promoting commercial transactions, namely to visit clients, offering to them the principal's products, taking note of their orders, etc, since the agent cannot conclude contracts with clients, the principal's liability for the agent's acts is out of the question. This is because the agent's duties (simply promoting commercial acts or transactions on behalf of the principal) are those of an intermediary; that is to say, his purpose is to mediate in the relations between principal and third parties, just putting them into contact with each other with a view to their negotiating an eventual contract. His performance is thus limited to approaching the parties, without being linked to them.

(11) What happens if the agent concludes a contract with the client, declaring that he is entitled to do so without being really entitled? Will such an act create an obligation on the principal? Will the principal be liable for the consequences of such act?

In principle, the answer in Spain is clearly no. It is the client's duty to check whether the agent is empowered to enter into contracts or not, otherwise he must be liable for his lack of diligence. Of course, it is essential that the principal never ratified or consented to his agent's acts, otherwise he will be as liable as if he the agent were acting for him.

If the principal has empowered his agent to enter into contracts with clients, *i.e.* he has duties of promotion and to conclude transactions, the acts performed within the ambit of his authority are as binding on the principal as if he had performed such acts himself. The principal shall then be liable to the client, as here the agent not only promotes commercial acts or transactions, or acquires clients for the principal and encourages them to enter into contracts in favour of the principal, but he also concludes the commercial acts or transactions he has promoted with the third parties, *i.e.* he enters into contracts with clients in the name, and on behalf, of the principal.

In both these cases, (*i.e.* when the agent is merely promoting an agreement with a third party, and when he is empowered to conclude the agreement with the third party) it has to be stressed that the relationship is always between the principal and the customers with whom the agent has promoted the conclusion of a contract or has himself concluded a contract. The principal is thus directly linked to those third parties and is therefore liable to them for the consequences of the agent's acts; this is without prejudice to the relevant rights of action between agent and principal concerning the fulfilment of each other's obligations.

However, it is important to note that if the principal is forced to indemnify a client for the agent's acts (for example if the agent causes the delay of a delivery), the principal may later claim from the agent the amount he had to pay to the client (in Spanish legal terms this is the "repetition right").

From the point of view of the principal, therefore, it is advisable to minimise his liability and not to empower the agent to enter into contracts with clients. It should be stated expressly in the agency contract that such powers are not granted to the agent and that clients' orders can only be accepted by the principal.

As a general rule, the agent will not object to this, as it releases him from having to conclude transactions and from the liability resulting from such a duty.

If for various reasons the principal wishes to allow the agent to enter into contracts with clients, then it is advisable to set out in the agency contract some monitoring procedures: and, for example, to grant the power for a specific period, even if it can be extended later; or put the agent under an obligation to report periodically.

(12) How can an agency contract be terminated?

The following distinctions need to be made:

(i) Agency contracts for a specified period

These expire at the end of the period agreed. However, if the contract continues to be executed by both parties after the expiry date, it will become a contract for an unlimited period.

(ii) Agency contracts for an unlimited period

When no specific duration has been fixed, the contract shall be understood to have been entered into for an unlimited period.

In this case the agency contract can be terminated unilaterally by either party, provided notice is given.

With regard to such a notice, Law 12/92 states:

- The period of notice shall be one month per year of the contract up to a limit of six months. If the contract has been in force for a period shorter than a year, the term is at least one month.
- Longer terms can be agreed, but the period of notice from principal to agent cannot be shorter than from agent to principal.

Irrespective of whether the contract is for a specified or unlimited period of time, either party can terminate the contract in the following situations:

- for serious non-compliance, whether total or partial, by one of the parties, of their legal or contractual obligations; or
- when there is a bankruptcy statement or insolvency situation or the arrangements for suspension of payments have been accepted.

A notice is not necessary in either case, although a communication stating the grounds for termination is required.

An agency contract, whether for a specified or unlimited period, is also terminated by death or the grant of a death certificate regarding the agent, but not by the principal's death.

(13) What is the entitlement of the agent to compensation on termination?

There are different types of payment to which the agent is entitled as a consequence of termination of his agency contract:

(i) Compensation for goodwill

A commercial agent is entitled to goodwill compensation in the case of termination of an agency contract whether for a specified period or for an unlimited period, provided that he has brought new clients to the principal or has considerably increased the amount of the transactions with pre-existing clients.

Since the requirement to have added to the client base or numbers of sales is a prerequisite and reason for the entitlement to a goodwill compensation payment, Law 12/92 subjects this entitlement to a set of additional conditions:

- The activity of the commercial agent during the agency contract must continue to produce considerable advantages to the principal after termination of the agency relationship.
- In addition, the compensation agreement must be fair in accordance with the circumstances. For example, Law 12/92 provides that payment of compensation is appropriate when there are competition restrictions, *i.e.* when the agent is not allowed to perform competing activities once the agency contract is terminated.

Notice that compensation is based on the agent's unfair loss of revenue by reason of unilateral action by the principal leading to his profiting unfairly, when he continues to enjoy the goodwill resulting from the agent's activity.

Any entitlement to compensation for goodwill which arises following termination and the death of the agent or the grant of a death certificate shall accrue to the agent's estate.

Finally, Law 12/92 sets out provisions relating to the calculation of compensation, fixing as a maximum limit the annual average remuneration received during the last five years, or during all the period of duration of the agency contract, should this have been shorter than five years.

(ii) Compensation for damages (only for unlimited period contracts)

This is not incompatible with the goodwill compensation and can thus be claimed in addition.

This compensation can only be considered in respect of a contract for an unlimited period, as its purpose is to compensate the agent for the damage caused by an unfair termination of his contract by the principal. However, the law sets out as a precondition to entitlement to this compensation that such anticipated termination of the contract by the principal does not allow the agent to amortise his expenses which were related to the execution of the contract, undertaken according to the principal's instructions.

For example, if the principal has asked the agent to hire more employees or to purchase more cars and, soon after that, he cancels the contract, it is obvious that the agent cannot amortise these investments and can file a claim against the principal for this reason. However, it is suggested that if when the relationship is terminated, the agent can employ such staff and cars for other tasks, he will not be entitled to any compensation.

Caselaw has established that such expenses or damage caused to the agent as a consequence of an unfair termination by the principal have to be certain and proved, and the burden of the proof is on the agent to show the damaging consequences of the anticipated termination of the contract, as well as the causal relationship between such damages and the contract termination.

(iii) When is the agent not entitled to compensation?

The agent shall not be entitled to compensation for goodwill or for damages when:

- the principal terminates the contract due to non-compliance by the agent of his obligations;
- the agent terminates the contract, unless this is due to circumstances attributable to the principal, or to the agent's age, disability or illness, and he could not reasonably be required to continue his activities (in such cases he can claim compensation); or
- without the principal's approval, the agent has granted to a third party the rights and obligations he was entitled to by virtue of the agency contract.

It should be noted that article 3.1 of Law 12/92 provides that it is not possible for an agent to waive his right to compensation.

The mandatory nature of this provision is inferred from the relevant clauses, *i.e.* articles 28 and 29 of Law 12/92, which use expressions such as "will be entitled to compensation" or "will be obliged to compensate", and so show the mandatory nature of the right to compensation.

(14) Are disputes concerning agency agreements for Spanish agents usually heard in Spain?

Law 12/92 "Additional Provision" states that "competence for the hearing of actions derived from an agency contract shall lie with a judge in the agent's domicile, any agreement to the contrary being void".

This then is clearly a protectionist rule in favour of the agent, as it ensures that any legal action will take place in his own domicile, eliminating any practical and economic difficulties, and other problems derived from having the legal action take place in a different forum.

When the principal is Spanish and resides in Spain, application of that Additional Provision is not a problem. However, in practice it is common to find a foreign country principal who decides to hire a commercial agent to promote and sell his products in Spain (as in other countries), as an alternative to setting up a permanent establishment or a branch performing the duties of a distributor. When this is the case, the question arises as to whether in the agency contract it is possible to stipulate as competent courts for the purpose of the agency contract, not those of the agent's domicile (namely, Spain), but those of a foreign country.

Article 17 of the EEC Convention of 27 September 1968 on Jurisdiction and the Enforcement of Judgments in Civil and Commercial Matters ("the Brussels Convention") has been ratified by Spain. This establishes the freedom of the parties to subject settlement of disputes under their contracts to the courts of a contracting State.

Nevertheless, the Brussels Convention also sets out the principle of full recognition in article 27 of Member States of judgments produced in another contracting State, unless they are contrary to the "public order" in the State in question.

It should be noted that this principle of public order could be used to avoid execution in Spain of the judgment produced by a foreign court, on the grounds that the legal action relating to an Agent domiciled in Spain has been handled abroad, and not at the agent's domicile, as required by Law 12/92.

Even if on the other hand the parties subject disputes under their contracts to the jurisdiction of a foreign court that court would have to solve the conflict by applying the unavoidable mandatory rules of Law 12/92 (and will probably refer the case back to a Spanish court).

The conclusion to be drawn from this is that it is advisable, following the guidelines of Law 12/92, to provide in Spain that competent courts should be those of the agent's domicile, and should the agent have various domiciles, the Spanish domicile.

(15) What about arbitration?

The principal and agent can subject any litigious questions that may arise between them to arbitration, as Law 12/92 does not forbid it, and agency contracts are not prevented from using an arbitration procedure under Law 36/1988 of 5 December.

Please note, however:

- It is advisable that the arbitration be held in the agent's domicile, as in this way the protectionist spirit of Law 12/92 is not affected and objections on these grounds can be avoided.
- For hearings of any legal actions that may arise in relation to such arbitration, such as a legal application to formalise the arbitration or an appeal to cancel the award, only the courts of the agent's domicile shall be competent.

(16) What about product liability? Does the agent have any responsibility, and should he be insured?

The new product liability Law 22/94 of 6 July ("Law 22/94") has implemented the EEC Directive of 25 July 1985 on the approximation of the laws, regulations and administrative provisions of the Member States concerning liability for defective products in part ("the Directive").

Manufacturers and importers of products will be liable as a consequence of faults in the products. The liability is objective. In other words, the manufacturer and importer will be also liable if it was not their fault. However, they would not be liable, or their liability would be reduced, if the person injured was guilty.

The scope of application of Law 22/94 refers to the following cases: death, personal injuries or damages caused to objects.

If the damages have been caused by identical items with the same defect the liability is limited to 10,500 million pesetas (which exceeds the limit provided in the Directive).

The claim must be brought within three years, but in any case the liability of the manufacturer or of the importer will expire ten years after the product was introduced in the market.

If the commercial agent or distributor knew of the fault before selling the product he will also be liable. Therefore it would be wise to arrange for appropriate insurance cover.

CONTENTS OF CHAPTER 16

Sweden

16. SWEDEN

Thomas Pousette, Gunnar Lindhs Advokatbyrå HB, Stockholm

(1) Introduction

The purpose of this chapter is to describe the status of the commercial agent under Swedish law. For reasons of space the chapter will not, and cannot, be all-comprehensive but will hopefully give some useful advice for those seeking to enter into an agency contract.

In 1992 the "*lag* (1991:351) *om handelsagentur*" ("the Agency Act") entered into force, which brought about certain changes with regard to commercial agency. The Agency Act is based on Council Directive of 18 December 1986 on the co-ordination of the laws of the Member States relating to Self-employed Commercial Agents (86/653/EEC), and was intended to harmonise Swedish law with European law. Amongst other changes, it introduced in Sweden a somewhat wider definition of the term commercial agent and a stronger protection of the agent *vis-à-vis* his principal.

The main features of the Agency Act are set out below. It should be noted, however, that aspects of an agency contract which are not governed by the Agency Act are likely to fall under other legislation, and in particular under the Act generally covering contracts ("*lag* (1915:218) *om avtal och andra rättshandlingar på förmögenhetsrättens område*" (the "Act on Contracts")). Thus, the fact that the Agency Act does not regulate a specific matter, does not mean that one party to an agency contract can impose on the other, in a legally binding way, any provision deemed suitable.

The Agency Act is based on the principle of freedom of contract. There are nevertheless a number of provisions in the Agency Act which are mandatory. The mandatory provisions are of two different kinds; provisions from which no derogation at all may be made, and provisions from which derogation may not be made to the detriment of the agent. If the parties to an agency contract agree on a clause which is incompatible with a mandatory provision, the parties or the agent alone as the case may be, will not be bound by the clause, *i.e.* the mandatory provision will override the clause. It is expressly stated where a provision is mandatory in the way just described, and also to which of the two kinds it belongs.

At the end of this chapter the reader will find a summary of the mandatory provisions.

(2) What is the definition of a "commercial agent" in Sweden?

The Agency Act defines the term "commercial agent" as a self-employed, independent, intermediary who has continuing authority to negotiate or conclude the sale or the purchase of goods on behalf of another person, the principal.

Under earlier Swedish law the term commercial agent referred only to sales agents, and thus did not include agents for purchase. With the Agency Act this distinction has been dropped.

As can be seen, the definition only includes the sale or the purchase of goods. This means that agents for services have been left out. When it comes to agents for goods and related services an analogy with the "*köplag*" (1990:931) ("the Act on Purchases") must be made. Thus, when a commercial transaction contains elements of both goods and services, the transaction is deemed a sale of goods, unless the service element dominates the transaction. In the latter case the Agency Act will not be applicable.

Travelling salesmen, in principle not included by the earlier definition due to their lack of a permanent establishment, are considered as commercial agents under the Agency Act provided, of course, that they meet the requirements of the definition. In the following chapter, the term "agent" will refer to a commercial agent within the meaning of the Agency Act.

(3) What are the obligations of an agent?

(i) General obligations

In performing his activities, an agent must look after his principal's interests and act loyally and irreproachably. The fact that the agent must be loyal to his principal entails that where there is a conflict of interests between the principal and a third party, the agent must protect the interests of the former. Consequently, the situation of an agent differs from that of a broker, who has to be loyal both to his principal and to the third party.

The agent's obligation of loyalty does not necessarily prohibit him from undertaking transactions for the principal's competitors. In some cases it will be apparent that such activities would be incompatible with the agent's obligation of loyalty to his principal. In other circumstances it could be in the principal's interest for the agent to be able to offer clients different options.

In particular, the obligation of loyalty means that a commercial agent must make reasonable efforts to obtain offers and, if included in the agency contract, to conclude contracts. The agent must communicate to his principal offers obtained and contracts concluded, as well as other information of importance to the transaction. Further, the agent must comply with reasonable instructions given by his principal.

The parties to the agency contract will not be bound by clauses in the contract altering these obligations, but since the obligation of loyalty is somewhat vague it is recommended that a principal who does not want the agent to enter into agency contracts with the principal's competitors, should include in the contract a clause to that end. The principal must not, however, give such a clause too wide a scope, since that could cause the agent to lose his status as self-employed, in which case he would not be regarded as an agent as defined by the Agency Act.

(ii) What other obligations does an agent have?

Apart from these general obligations an agent also has more specific ones. Thus, he must take good care of goods and other items belonging to the principal and which are in the agent's possession. These "other items" include samples, business documents, brochures, etc. The level of care must be that which a conscientious and competent professional would exercise.

The commercial agent must keep the necessary property insurance and it must cover all property in the agent's possession, owned by the principal. The meaning of "necessary insurance" will have to be determined from case to case and will depend on, *inter alia*, the line of business and the character of the transaction. The contracting parties are free to decide that the principal shall provide the necessary insurance, that he shall bear the costs or that there shall be no insurance obligation on any of the parties.

There is also an obligation for the agent to keep his principal's goods separate from other goods. This is to preserve the principal's right of repossession in the event of bankruptcy on the part of the agent. If the agent has the right to receive payment for goods sold, he must keep the received funds separate from others. In such a case he must also account for the transactions.

The exact extent of an agent's obligations will in each individual case be determined by the contract, custom, and the circumstances of the transaction.

(4) What are the obligations of a principal?

(i) General obligations

The obligation to act loyally and irreproachably, mentioned in (3) above, is a mutual one. Thus the principal, in turn, must observe this obligation towards the agent. This does not necessarily mean that the content of this obligation is the same for the principal as it is for the agent. A typical lack of loyalty on the principal's part would be for the principal himself to carry on business within an area to which the agent has been granted the exclusive right in the contract of agency.

(ii) What other obligations does the principal have?

In particular, the principal has an obligation to provide the agent with samples, descriptions, price lists, and other necessary material regarding the goods concerned with the transaction. The principal must also provide the agent with the information necessary to perform the transaction. Further, the principal must, without unreasonable delay, inform the agent that he has accepted or rejected an offer forwarded by the agent, or that a contract that the agent has procured has not been executed.

Provisions in the agency contract altering these obligations will not be binding on the parties.

As in the case of the obligations of the agent, the exact meaning of the principal's obligations must be determined in the light of all relevant circumstances. The parties cannot in a binding way alter these obligations.

(5) Commission

(i) Entitlement of agent to commission

In the absence of an agreement between the parties on the agent's remuneration, the agent is entitled to the remuneration customarily allowed to agents in the place where he carries on his activities. If there is no such customary practice, the agent will be entitled to reasonable remuneration taking into account all the aspects of the transaction.

To conclude an agency contract without agreeing on how to calculate the commission, leaves the door wide open for future disputes on the matter, and is therefore not advisable.

The agent is entitled to commission on transactions concluded during the period covered by the agency contract, where the transaction has been concluded as a result of his action or where the transaction is concluded with a third party whom the agent has previously acquired as a customer for transactions of the same kind.

The agent is also entitled to commission on transactions concluded during the period covered by the agency contract, where he is entrusted with a specific geographical area or group of customers and the transaction has been entered into with a customer belonging to that area or group.

It should, in this context, be noted that the fact that an agent has been assigned to a certain area or a certain group of clients does not mean that he has been granted exclusiveness. A specific agreement on the matter is required for that purpose.

After the agency contract has ceased or has been terminated, an agent is entitled to commission on commercial transactions concluded:

- if the order reached the principal or the agent while the contract prevailed and the aforementioned requirements for commission are met; or
- if the transaction is mainly attributable to the agent's efforts during the period covered by the agency contract and if the transaction was entered into within a reasonable period of time after the contract ceased or was terminated.

If an agent succeeds a previous agent he will not be entitled to commission payable to the latter unless it is equitable for the commission to be shared between the agents.

Since the parties are free to agree on other terms on the above aspects of commission, a principal might for instance include a clause giving him the right to conduct business with certain customers within a geographical area otherwise exclusively entrusted to the agent. The principal might also want to stipulate that no commission at all should be paid to the agent after the cessation or termination of the contract.

(ii) When must the commission be paid?

The principal has to pay the commission within one month of the last day of the quarter in which the commission has been earned. If the agency contract contains a clause less favourable to the agent than this, the agent will not be bound by that clause.

Commission is earned when the principal has performed a contract with a third party or when the principal should have done so. The commission will also have been earned when the third party has performed the contract. If the agency contract states that the commission shall be earned at a later time than when the third party has performed the contract or would have done so, had the principal performed the contract as he should have, the agent will not be bound by that clause.

(iii) When is the agent's right to remuneration extinguished?

The agent's right to commission will be extinguished if it is established that the contract between the third party and the principal will not be performed and this fact is not in any way attributable to the principal. If the third party has not performed the contract and this is because the principal has granted him a respite in this respect or has agreed with him to cancel the contract, this shall not affect the agent's right to commission. If the third party performs the contract in part only, the agent will have a proportionate right to commission corresponding to the part that has been performed. A clause in the agency contract setting aside these rights will not be binding on the agent.

Should the agent's right to commission be extinguished for any of the above reasons, he will have to refund what has been paid in excess. The parties may, however, agree differently on this matter.

(iv) What details must the principal supply to the agent?

The principal has to supply the agent with a statement of the commission earned, not later than one month after the last day of the quarter in which the commission was earned. The statement shall set out all information of importance to calculating the commission. A clause in the agency contract less favourable to the agent is not binding on him.

The agent also has the right to obtain from the principal all the information available to the latter and which the agent needs in order to check whether the statement really contains all commission earned. If the principal fails to produce this information within a reasonable time the agent has a right to inspect the books of the principal, to the extent needed. It will be up to the principal to decide whether the agent himself should be allowed to make the inspection or whether it should be left to an accountant of the agent's choice. Clauses in the agency contract which are less favourable to the agent in this respect will not be binding on him.

(v) What is the consequence of non-payment of commission?

Should the principal not pay the agent on time, the latter is allowed to retain goods, documents and other items belonging to the principal and which the agent has received to perform the contract. Certain kinds of documents, vital to the principal, are however excluded, for example powers of attorney. After three months the agent is allowed to sell retained goods in order to cover the claims in respect of which the retention was made. If necessary due to the character of the goods retained, as in the case of goods that deteriorate rapidly, the agent may sell the goods before the end of the said period. The agent will not be bound by clauses in the agency contract which impair these rights.

(6) Relationships with third parties

The agent may not without specific authorisation conclude transactions in the name of his principal. Should he nevertheless do so, the principal will be bound by the agreement unless he, without unreasonable delay as from the moment he learned of the agreement, notifies the third party that the agent was not entitled to conclude the transaction.

Whether the agent should be authorised to conclude transactions depends on the principal's trust in him. One way to proceed might be to start with a fixed term agency contract during which the agent is not authorised to conclude contracts on behalf of his principal. After that period the principal will be in a better position to assess the qualities of the agent.

Without specific authorisation the agent is not allowed to receive payment for goods sold or, after the conclusion of a transaction, grant an extension of time for payment or a reduction or make other changes to the contract. Again, should the agent do so without authorisation, the principal must notify the third party without unreasonable delay that he will not validate the agent's action. If the principal fails to notify the third party to this effect, he will be deemed to have validated the agent's action. The same applies to the situation where the third party, for instance, claims defective goods and the agent, without specific authorisation, takes a decision regarding that matter.

(7) Cessation and termination

An agency contract concluded for a fixed period of time ceases on the expiry of that period. If the parties continue the agency relationship after the expiry of the contract, the contract will subsequently be regarded as a contract without a fixed period. Any terms in the contract derogating from this principle are not binding on the parties.

An agency contract which has not been concluded for a fixed period may be terminated by either of the parties by notice. Within the first year, the period of notice is one month. After the first year, one month will be added to the period of notice for each partial or complete year until the period of notice has become six months. The parties will not be bound by an agreement that the period of notice shall be shorter than described, except where there is agreement to making the period of notice three months on the part of the agent even if the contract has lasted for more than three years. If the parties agree to make the period of notice longer than prescribed by the Agency Act, the period of notice of termination by the principal may not be shorter than that of termination by the agent.

The parties to an agency contract are free to agree on the form of the notice of termination. If no such agreement is made, the terminating party may choose any form. To be able to prove that notice of termination has been given, it is nevertheless suggested that notice be given in writing.

There are two situations in which a party to the agency contract may terminate the contract with immediate effect:

- where the other party is in breach of contract, the breach is important to the first party, and the other party realises or should realise this; or
- where there is another important reason for renouncing the contract prematurely.

The party wishing to terminate the contract prematurely must do so without unreasonable delay from the time that he knew, or should have known, of the circumstance giving rise to his claim. The agent will not be bound by less favourable terms in the contract.

The importance of the breach does not relate to the character of the breach itself, but to the consequences it has for the other party. The reference to "consequences" aims mainly at economic consequences, but a breach by one party may also have such a detrimental effect on the trust felt by the other party as to give the latter the right of immediate termination without having to show any specific negative economic consequences of the breach. This could be the case after a breach consisting of an act of disloyalty or gross negligence.

One ground for termination with immediate effect by the principal might be that the agent does not achieve the minimum performance level set out in the contract. The parties are free to agree on provisions of this kind. Such provisions can determine an absolute minimum, or can be more or less vague descriptions of desirable goals. If the latter kind is chosen, it will naturally be more difficult to prove a breach, as well as its importance to the principal.

If an agent has been appointed as an exclusive agent, he may have a ground for immediate termination if the principal conducts business within the area or with the clients in question.

The term "otherwise important reason" cannot be defined exactly but it refers to something that must have occurred after the agency contract was entered into by the parties, and which completely alters the prerequisites of the contract. It might be an Act of God, long-lasting or serious illness or something else.

In the event of bankruptcy of a party to the agency contract, the contract will automatically cease. The agent may however, after the principal's bankruptcy and under certain circumstances, extend the validity of the contract until the bankruptcy is officially announced according to Swedish bankruptcy legislation.

The agent is entitled to a severance payment after cessation or termination of the contract if, and to the extent that, he has brought the principal new customers or that he has significantly increased the volume of business with existing customers and the principal will continue to derive substantial benefits from this.

The severance payment must be reasonable in view of all circumstances, and in particular, in view of the commission lost by the agent on the business transacted with the new customers or with the existing customers with whom the volume of business had increased. It may not exceed a figure equivalent to one year's indemnity, and it will be calculated from the agent's average annual remuneration over the preceding five years or, if the agency contract goes back less than that, from the average of the period in question. The above will be correspondingly applicable in the event of cessation of the contract due to the agent's death. Payment should in that case be made to the estate of the deceased agent. Terms in the agency contract that are less favourable to the agent will not be binding on him.

If the principal terminates the agency contract due to the fact that the agent has, intentionally or through carelessness, neglected his obligations, and this neglect is of a kind that constitutes a ground to terminate the contract with immediate effect, the agent will not be entitled to a severance payment. The agent will also lose this right if the contract ceases due to his bankruptcy or if he, in agreement with the principal, assigns the agency to someone else. If the parties agree on less favourable terms than these, the agent will not be bound by those terms.

There are two circumstances under which the agent himself may terminate the contract without losing his right to severance payment. One is if the termination is based on such a circumstance, on the part of the principal, as constitutes ground for termination with immediate effect; the other is if it cannot, due to the agent's age or illness, or other similar circumstances, reasonably be demanded that he continue his business. Terms in the agency contract that are less favourable to the agent will not be binding on him.

As the reference to illness shows resemblance to the "otherwise important reason" mentioned above, it should be said that the latter has a narrower scope than the provision now discussed. This means that illness as a ground for termination might be enough for the agent to have a right to severance payment but still not be enough to allow him to terminate the agency contract with immediate effect.

If the agent does not, within one year of the cessation or termination of the agency contract, notify the principal of his demand for a severance payment, he will lose his right to such payment. Terms in the agency contract that are less favourable to the agent on this matter, are not binding on him.

The agent will still have certain obligations towards the principal, even though the agency contract has ceased or has been terminated. Thus, until the principal can look after his own interests, the agent must take the necessary precautions to protect him against loss, unless this involves a considerable cost, inconvenience or economic risk for the agent. For this, he is entitled to a reasonable remuneration.

Further, the agent must return to the principal goods, material, and documents which he has received for the purpose of the contract, although he may retain the principal's property as security for claims, and, in certain cases, sell it.

With regard to the obligations of the agent after cessation or termination, it should be noted that the parties are free to agree on other terms than those described above, or to give them a more specific content. As to restrictions on the agent after termination, see (9) below.

(8) Damages

Either of the parties to the agency contract will be liable for damages, if he fails to fulfil his obligations under the contract, and if he cannot show that the failure was not due to his negligence.

Examples of situations that might give rise to a right to damages on the part of the principal are where the agent fails to pass on an offer from a third party, or the agent does not follow given instructions to attend fairs, or does not take part in publicity campaigns etc.

The agent may be entitled to damages if the principal fails to provide him with the necessary material or information to perform his part of the contract, and the agent thereby incurs costs which he would not otherwise have had. Another situation might be where the agent, not having been informed properly by the principal regarding operational cut-backs, makes unnecessary investments.

If the agency contract ceases as a consequence of the bankruptcy of one of the parties to it, the other party has a right to damages regarding losses arising out of the bankruptcy.

Claims for damages must be made without unreasonable delay, except when the other party has acted with gross negligence or in an otherwise dishonourable way. There is no definition of the term "unreasonable delay". Whether a delay in claiming damages should be deemed "unreasonable" or not, will be decided in the light of all the circumstances of each particular case.

The exception made by reference to the other party's conduct, does not give a party an unlimited period of time in which to make the claim. Lengthy failure to take action will, according to general principles, lead to the loss of the right to claim damages. It might also fall under the rules of statutory limitation. Terms in the agency contract which are less favourable to the agent than the above described, are not binding on him.

It may, in this context, be mentioned that there are special procedural rules for litigation concerning smaller claims, in order to keep costs down. For 1995 these rules apply to litigation regarding claims of up to approximately SEK 18,000.

(9) Competition clauses

To be binding on the agent, a clause restricting the business activities of an agent after the agency contract has ceased or been terminated must fulfil three requirements:

- it must be concluded in writing;
- it must relate to the geographical area or the group of customers entrusted to the agent; and
- it must relate to the kind of goods covered by the agency under the contract.

The agent will not be bound by a competition clause to the extent that its intended validity exceeds two years from the cessation or termination of the agency contract.

The term "competition" covers, amongst other things, new agencies, employment with the principal's competitors and activities as a distributor.

Competition clauses are not only subject to the restrictions found in the Agency Act. In this respect there is a direct reference in the Agency Act to the Act on Contracts. Consequently a competition clause, although fulfilling the above-mentioned requirements, may be disregarded or modified by a Swedish court if, for instance, it is considered to be unreasonable.

The desirable content and scope of a competition clause will, naturally, be dependent on the circumstances, but a principal who wants to be certain that the agent will not enter into competition with him once the agency contract has ended, should insert into the contract a clause which covers all forms of competition. It must, however, be born in mind that the clause must not be unreasonable.

(10) Choice of law

The parties are free to choose whichever law they desire to govern the agency contract. However, if they choose Swedish law, the parties cannot, to the detriment of the agent and by reference to foreign law, set aside a provision of the Agency Act, if derogation from that provision to the detriment of the agent is not allowed under the Agency Act. In other words, the parties cannot, with a reference to foreign law, circumvent the provisions of the Agency Act which are intended to protect the agent.

According to Swedish private international law, the applicable law, if the parties have not made a choice of law, will be the law of the country in which the agent has his place of business.

(11) Jurisdiction and arbitration clauses

The parties to an agency contract may include a clause on jurisdiction or arbitration. If they have not done so, a Swedish court will, if the principal's place of business is not in Sweden and the agent imports the goods, find that it has jurisdiction if, in a typical situation, the agent has claims on the principal and the latter has assets, in the form of claims on customers or otherwise, in Sweden.

Sweden has ratified the Convention of 16 September 1988 on Jurisdiction and the Enforcement of Judgments in Civil and Commercial Matters ("the Lugano Convention"). Therefore, the above does not apply if the country where the principal conducts his business has ratified the Lugano Convention as well. In that case, Swedish courts have jurisdiction if the dispute concerns an obligation under the agency contract, the performance of which should be in Sweden.

Arbitration clauses have their advantages as regards speed and discretion, but before including such a clause it is important to consider the costs involved. Often, the disputed claims under agency contracts will be relatively small and the costs of arbitration higher than the costs of traditional litigation in court, in which case the latter procedure might be preferable.

(12) Should an agency contract be in writing?

Although a party has a statutory right to have an agency contract in writing, it need not be written down to be valid. It is nevertheless always advisable to use the written form to avoid future disputes. Standard forms for agency contracts are available, and they can be remodelled according to the wishes of the parties. The Nordic Federation of Agents and the International Chamber of Commerce (ICC) have each drawn up their own form to this purpose. The reader will find the addresses to the Federation of Commercial Agents in Sweden and the Swedish national committee of the ICC in Appendix D.

It must be stressed that in order to avoid costly mistakes, the parties should, even if using a form, consult their legal advisers when drawing up a contract.

(13) What about the responsibility of an agent for bad debts?

An agent does not, unless there is a specific agreement on the matter, have any responsibility for payment being made by a customer to the principal. Such an undertaking on the part of the agent is unusual and should, arguably, entitle the agent to a higher commission.

The above responsibility for bad debts has nothing to do with the fact that the agent may become liable for damages should he convey, knowingly or negligently, insolvent clients to his principal.

(14) What about product liability?

In general, liability for defective products, *i.e.* product liability, does not lie with the agent as such, but with the producer or, if it is not a Swedish producer, the importer. In the situation of imported goods, there is a question of who should be considered to be the importer. Whether this should be the agent will have to be determined in the light of all circumstances. If, for example, customs clearance is made in the name of the agent, this will be an indication that he should be considered as the importer, and he would be wise to ensure that he has the appropriate insurance. It is suggested that this is a matter which should be dealt with in the agency contract.

(15) Under-agents

It would seem that the agent is not allowed to appoint under-agents unless there is a specific agreement to the opposite. If such an agreement exists, and the agent appoints under-agents he will be considered as a principal in those relations. Should the agent, without an agreement, appoint under-agents this might constitute a ground for termination by the principal.

To prevent complications, the authority to appoint under-agents should be included in the agency contract. The principal might be willing to accept under-agents as such, but might want to have control of which are chosen. If so, the parties could agree that agent be obliged to obtain the principal's permission in each case where the agent intends to have an under-agent.

(16) Distributors

A distributor is a person who has agreed for a fixed period to buy a certain product from a supplier, for the purpose of reselling it in his own name and on his own account within a specified geographical area.

The legal status of distributors has not been defined by legislation in Sweden but there is in many respects room for an analogous interpretation of the Agency Act. That is, for instance, the case with the rules on compensation for losses on investments. The rules on commission after the cessation or termination of an agency contract would, however, at least according to caselaw from the time before the enactment of the Agency Act, not seem to be analogously applicable to distributors.

(17) Summary of mandatory provisions

Finally, and since it may be helpful for someone wanting to determine rapidly the limitations of the freedom of contract under the Agency Act, a brief resumé of the mandatory provisions is set out below.

As stated at the outset of this chapter, there are two kinds of mandatory provisions. Accordingly, the summary will be divided into two sections. If a provision is not mentioned below, the parties are free to agree the clauses they require, in respect of the matter covered by the provision.

(i) Provisions allowing no derogation

The provisions on:

- the agent's obligations, except those regarding the obligations to keep the principal's goods and funds separate, and to keep property insured. The excepted provisions are not mandatory;

- the principal's obligations;
- the length of the period of notice of termination; and
- cessation of an agency contract with a fixed term, and on the consequences of the contract being extended.

(ii) Provisions where no derogation to the detriment of the agent is permitted

The provisions on:

- the point in time when the commission has been earned, and when it must be paid;
- the extinction of the agent's right to commission;
- the commission statement and the agent's rights to information and inspection in connection therewith;
- the agent's right to retain and sell the principal's goods;
- termination with immediate effect;
- the agent's severance payment;
- damages; and
- competition clauses.

Appendix A
Council Directive

of 18 December 1986 on the coordination of the laws of the Member States relating to self-employed commercial agents (86/653/EEC) (OJ 1986 L382/17)

THE COUNCIL OF THE EUROPEAN COMMUNITIES,

Having regard to the Treaty establishing the European Economic Community, and in particular Articles 57(2) and 100 thereof,

Having regard to the proposal from the Commission (OJ 1977 C13/2; OJ 1979 C56/5),

Having regard to the opinion of the European Parliament (OJ 1978 C239/17),

Having regard to the opinion of the Economic and Social Committee (OJ 1978 C59/31),

Whereas the restrictions on the freedom of establishment and the freedom to provide services in respect of activities of intermediaries in commerce, industry and small craft industries were abolished by Directive 64/224/EEC (OJ 1964 L56/869);

Whereas the differences in national laws concerning commercial representation substantially affect the conditions of competition and the carrying-on of that activity within the Community and are detrimental both to the protection available to commercial agents *vis-à-vis* their principals and to the security of commercial transactions; whereas moreover those differences are such as to inhibit substantially the conclusion and operation of commercial representation contracts where principal and commercial agent are established in different Member States;

Whereas trade in goods between Member States should be carried on under conditions which are similar to those of a single market, and this necessitates approximation of the legal systems of the Member States to the extent required for the proper functioning of the common market; whereas in this regard the rules concerning conflict of laws do not, in the matter of commercial representation, remove the inconsistencies referred to above, nor would they even if they were made uniform, and accordingly the proposed harmonization is necessary notwithstanding the existence of those rules;

Whereas in this regard the legal relationship between commercial agent and principal must be given priority;

Whereas it is appropriate to be guided by the principles of Article 117 of the Treaty and to maintain improvements already made, when harmonizing the laws of the Member States relating to commercial agents;

Whereas additional transitional periods should be allowed for certain Member States which have to make a particular effort to adapt their regulations, especially those concerning indemnity for termination of contract between the principal and the commercial agent, to the requirements of this Directive,

HAS ADOPTED THIS DIRECTIVE:

Chapter 2
Scope

Article 1

1. The harmonization measures prescribed by this Directive shall apply to the laws, regulations and administrative provisions of the Member States governing the relations between commercial agents and their principals.
2. For the purposes of this Directive, 'commercial agent' shall mean a self-employed intermediary who has continuing authority to negotiate the sale or the purchase of goods on behalf of another person, hereinafter called the 'principal'; or to negotiate and conclude such transactions on behalf of and in the name of that principal.
3. A commercial agent shall be understood within the meaning of this Directive as not including in particular:

- a person who, in his capacity as an officer, is empowered to enter into commitments binding on a company or association,
- a partner who is lawfully authorized to enter into commitments binding on his partners,
- a receiver, a receiver and manager, a liquidator or a trustee in bankruptcy.

Article 2

1. This Directive shall not apply to:

- commercial agents whose activities are unpaid,
- commercial agents when they operate on commodity exchanges or in the commodity market, or
- the body known as the Crown Agents for Overseas Governments and Administrations, as set up under the Crown Agents Act 1979 in the United Kingdom, or its subsidiaries.

2. Each of the Member States shall have the right to provide that the Directive shall not apply to those persons whose activities as commercial agents are considered secondary by the law of that Member State.

Chapter II
Rights and obligations

Article 3

1. In performing his activities a commercial agent must look after his principal's interests and act dutifully and in good faith.
2. In particular, a commercial agent must:

(a) make proper efforts to negotiate and, where appropriate, conclude the transactions he is instructed to take care of;
(b) communicate to his principal all the necessary information available to him;
(c) comply with reasonable instructions given by his principal.

Article 4

1. In his relations with his commercial agent a principal must act dutifully and in good faith.

2. A principal must in particular:

(a) provide his commercial agent with the necessary documentation relating to the goods concerned;
(b) obtain for his commercial agent the information necessary for the performance of the agency contract, and in particular notify the commercial agent within a reasonable period once he anticipates that the volume of commercial transactions will be significantly lower than that which the commercial agent could normally have expected.

3. A principal must, in addition, inform the commercial agent within a reasonable period of his acceptance, refusal, and of any non-execution of a commercial transaction which the commercial agent has procured for the principal.

Article 5

The parties may not derogate from the provisions of Articles 3 and 4.

Chapter III
Remuneration

Article 6

1. In the absence of any agreement on this matter between the parties, and without prejudice to the application of the compulsory provisions of the Member States concerning the level of remuneration, a commercial agent shall be entitled to the remuneration that commercial agents appointed for the goods forming the subject of his agency contract are customarily allowed in the place where he carries on his activities. If there is no such customary practice a commercial agent shall be entitled to reasonable remuneration taking into account all the aspects of the transaction.
2. Any part of the remuneration which varies with the number or value of business transactions shall be deemed to be commission within the meaning of this Directive.
3. Articles 7 to 12 shall not apply if the commercial agent is not remunerated wholly or in part by commission.

Article 7

1. A commercial agent shall be entitled to commission on commercial transactions concluded during the period covered by the agency contract.

(a) where the transaction has been concluded as a result of his action; or
(b) where the transaction is concluded with a third party whom he has previously acquired as a customer for transactions of the same kind.

2. A commercial agent shall also be entitled to commission on transactions concluded during the period covered by the agency contract:

- either where he is entrusted with a specific geographical area or group of customers,
- or where he has an exclusive right to a specific geographical area or group of customers,

and where the transaction has been entered into with a customer belonging to that area or group.
Member States shall include in their legislation one of the possibilities referred to in the above two items.

Article 8

A commercial agent shall be entitled to commission on commercial transactions concluded after the agency contract has terminated:

(a) if the transaction is mainly attributable to the commercial agent's efforts during the period covered by the agency contract and if the transaction was entered into within a reasonable period after that contract terminated; or
(b) if, in accordance with the conditions mentioned in Article 7, the order of the third party reached the principal or the commercial agent before the agency contract terminated.

Article 9

A commercial agent shall not be entitled to the commission referred to in Article 7, if that commission is payable, pursuant to Article 8, to the previous commercial agent, unless it is equitable because of the circumstances for the commission to be shared between the commercial agents.

Article 10

1. The commission shall become due as soon as and to the extent that one of the following circumstances obtains:

(a) the principal has executed the transaction; or
(b) the principal should, according to his agreement with the third party, have executed the transaction; or
(c) the third party has executed the transaction.

2. The commission shall become due at the latest when the third party has executed his part of the transaction or should have done so if the principal had executed his part of the transaction, as he should have.
3. The commission shall be paid not later than on the last day of the month following the quarter in which it became due.
4. Agreements to derogate from paragraphs 2 and 3 to the detriment of the commercial agent shall not be permitted.

Article 11

1. The right to commission can be extinguished only if and to the extent that:

- it is established that the contract between the third party and the principal will not be executed, and
- that fact is due to a reason for which the principal is not to blame.

2. Any commission which the commercial agent has already received shall be refunded if the right to it is extinguished.
3. Agreements to derogate from paragraph 1 to the detriment of the commercial agent shall not be permitted.

Article 12

1. The principal shall supply his commercial agent with a statement of the commission due, not later than the last day of the month following the quarter in which the commission has become due. This statement shall set out the main components used in calculating the amount of commission.
2. A commercial agent shall be entitled to demand that he be provided with all the information, and in particular an extract from the books, which is available to his principal and which he needs in order to check the amount of the commission due to him.
3. Agreements to derogate from paragraphs 1 and 2 to the detriment of the commercial agent shall not be permitted.
4. This Directive shall not conflict with the internal provisions of

Member States which recognize the right of a commercial agent to inspect a principal's books.

Chapter IV
Conclusion and termination of the agency contract

Article 13

1. Each party shall be entitled to receive from the other on request a signed written document setting out the terms of the agency contract including any terms subsequently agreed. Waiver of this right shall not be permitted.
2. Notwithstanding paragraph 1 a Member State may provide that an agency contract shall not be valid unless evidenced in writing.

Article 14

An agency contract for a fixed period which continues to be performed by both parties after that period has expired shall be deemed to be converted into an agency contract for an indefinite period.

Article 15

1. Where an agency contract is concluded for an indefinite period either party may terminate it by notice.
2. The period of notice shall be one month for the first year of the contract, two months for the second year commenced, and three months for the third year commenced and subsequent years. The parties may not agree on shorter periods of notice.
3. Member States may fix the period of notice at four months for the fourth year of the contract, five months for the fifth year and six months for the sixth and subsequent years. They may decide that the parties may not agree to shorter periods.
4. If the parties agree on longer periods than those laid down in paragraphs 2 and 3, the period of notice to be observed by the principal must not be shorter than that to be observed by the commercial agent.
5. Unless otherwise agreed by the parties, the end of the period notice must coincide with the end of a calendar month.
6. The provisions of this Article shall apply to any agency contract for a fixed period where it is converted under Article 14 into an agency contract for an indefinite period, subject to the proviso that the earlier fixed period must be taken into account in the calculation of the period of notice.

Article 16

Nothing in this Directive shall affect the application of the law of the Member States where the latter provides for the immediate termination of the agency contract:

(a) because of the failure of one party to carry out all or part of his obligations;
(b) where exceptional circumstances arise.

Article 17

1. Member States shall take the measures necessary to ensure that the commercial agent is, after termination of the agency contract, indemnified in accordance with paragraph 2 or compensated for damage in accordance with paragraph 3.
2. (a) The commercial agent shall be entitled to an indemnity if and to the extent that:

- he has brought the principal new customers or has significantly increased the volume of business with existing customers and the principal continues to derive substantial benefits from the business with such customers; and
- the payment of this indemnity is equitable having regard to all the circumstances and, in particular, the commission lost by the commercial agent on the business transacted with such customers. Member States may provide for such circumstances also to include the application or otherwise of a restraint of trade clause, within the meaning of Article 20;

(b) The amount of the indemnity may not exceed a figure equivalent to an indemnity for one year calculated from the commercial agent's average annual remuneration over the preceding five years and if the contract goes back less than five years the indemnity shall be calculated on the average for the period in question;

(c) The grant of such an indemnity shall not prevent the commercial agent from seeking damages.

3. The commercial agent shall be entitled to compensation for the damage he suffers as a result of the termination of his relations with the principal.

Such damage shall be deemed to occur particularly when the termination takes place in circumstances:

- depriving the commercial agent of the commission which proper performance of the agency contract would have procured him whilst providing the principal with substantial benefits linked to the commercial agent's activities,
- and/or which have not enabled the commercial agent to amortize the costs and expenses that he had incurred for the performance of the agency contract on the principal's advice.

4. Entitlement to the indemnity as provided for in paragraph 2 or to compensation for damage as provided for under paragraph 3, shall also arise where the agency contract is terminated as a result of the commercial agent's death.

5. The commercial agent shall lose his entitlement to the indemnity in the instances provided for in paragraph 2 or to compensation for damage in the instances provided for in paragraph 3, if within one year following termination of the contract he has notified the principal that he intends pursuing his entitlement.

6. The Commission shall submit to the Council, within eight years following the date of notification of this Directive, a report on the implementation of this Article, and shall if necessary submit to it proposals for amendments.

Article 18

The indemnity or compensation referred to in Article 17 shall not be payable:

(a) where the principal has terminated the agency contract because of default attributable to the commercial agent which would justify immediate termination of the agency contract under national law;

(b) where the commercial agent has terminated the agency contract, unless such termination is justified by circumstances attributable to the principal or on grounds of age, infirmity or illness of the commercial agent in consequence of which he cannot reasonably be required to continue his activities;

(c) where, with the agreement of the principal, the commercial agent assigns his rights and duties under the agency contract to another person.

Article 19

The parties may not derogate from Articles 17 and 18 to the detriment of the commercial agent before the agency contract expires.

Article 20

1. For the purposes of this Directive, an agreement restricting the business activities of a commercial agent following termination of the agency contract is hereinafter referred to as a restraint of trade clause.

2. A restraint of trade clause shall be valid only if and to the extent that:

(a) it is concluded in writing; and

(b) it relates to the geographical area or the group of customers and the geographical area entrusted to the commercial agent and to the kind of goods covered by his agency under the contract.

3. A restraint of trade clause shall be valid for not more than two years after termination of the agency contract.

4. This Article shall not affect provisions of national law which impose other restrictions on the validity or enforceability of restraint of trade clauses or which enable the courts to reduce the obligations on the parties resulting from such an agreement.

Chapter V
General and final provisions

Article 21

Nothing in this Directive shall require a Member State to provide for the disclosure of information where such disclosure would be contrary to public policy.

Article 22

1. Member States shall bring into force the provisions necessary to comply with this Directive before 1 January 1990. They shall forthwith inform the Commission thereof. Such provisions shall apply at least to contracts concluded after their entry into force. They shall apply to contracts in operation by 1 January 1994 at the latest.

2. As from the notification of this Directive, Member States shall communicate to the Commission the main laws, regulations and administrative provisions which they adopt in the field governed by this Directive.

3. However, with regard to Ireland and the United Kingdom, 1 January 1990 referred to in paragraph 1 shall be replaced by 1 January 1994.

With regard to Italy, 1 January 1990 shall be replaced by 1 January 1993 in the case of the obligations deriving from Article 17.

Article 23

This Directive is addressed to the Member States.

Done at Brussels, 18 December 1986.

Appendix B

Equivalent organisations to the DTI/BOTB in Western Europe (Information provided by DTI January 1996)

Austria

Federal Chamber of Commerce
Trade Policy and Foreign Trade Dept
Wiedner Hauptstrasse 63
Postfach 150
1045 Wien
Tel: 0222 501 05–Durchwahl (DW)

Belgium

Office Belge Du Commerce Extérieur
World Trade Centre
Tour No 1
Boulevard Jacqmain
1210 Brussels
Tel: 010 322 219 4450

Denmark

Ministry of Foreign Affairs Trade Dept
Asiatisk Plads 2
DK–1448 Copenhagen K
Tel: 01 92 0000

France

Centre Francais du Commerce Extérieur
Service Des Reglementations
5 Rue Pierre de Serbie
75383 Paris Cedex 16

Finland

Kauppa-Jateollisuusministerio
P.O.B. 230 SF– 00171
Helsinki
Tel: 90–1601

Federal Republic of Germany

Der Bundesminister Fur Wirtschaft
5300 Bonn 1
Villemombler Str 76
Tel: 02 28 6 51
Contact: Martin Bangemann

Greece

Ministry of Industry Energy & Technology
80 Michalacopoulou Street
115 28 Athens
Tel: 770 8615/9
Contact: P Tsolopoulos

Iceland

Ministry of Commerce
Vidskiptaraduneytid
Arnarhvall
150 Reykjavik
Tel: 1–25000

Ireland

Department of Industry, Trade, Commerce and Tourism
Kildare Street
Dublin 2
Tel: 789411

Italy

Ministry of Industry
Ministero Dell'Industria Commercio E Artigianato
Via Veneto
33– 00187 Rome
Tel: 06/4705

Luxembourg

Ministere Des Affaires Estrangeres
Du Commerce Extérieur Et De La
Cooperation
5 Rue Notre Dame
2910 Luxembourg
Tel: 478–1

Netherlands

Netherlands Foreign Trade Agency
Ministry Of Economic Affairs
Bezuiddenhoutswed 151
2594 AG ' S– Gravenhage
Tel: 070 798811

Norway

Ministry of Industry
Industri og Handverksdepartementet
Akersgatan 42
PO Box 8014 wep
Oslo 1
Tel: 02 11 90 90

Portugal

Ministerio Da Industria Energia &
Exportacao
Secr Ger 15–CV Horta Seca
1294 Lisboa Codex

Spain

Ministerio De Economia Y Hacienda
Alcala 11
28014 Madrid

Sweden

Handelsdepartmentet
(Ministry of Trade)
Fredsgatan 8
S– 103 33
Tel: 010 46/ 8763 1000

Switzerland

Schweizerische Zentral Fur
Handelsforderung OSEC
Stampferbachstrosse 85
CH– 8035 Zurich
Tel: 0104113655151

Appendix C

Eurochambers — the Members

Full Members:

Belgium:

Fédération Nationale des Chambres de Commerce et d'Industrie de Belgique
Avenue des Arts, 1/2, bte 10
B–1000 Bruxelles
Tel: 32 (2) 217 36 71
Fax: 32 (2) 217 46 34

Denmark:

The Danish Chamber of Commerce
Borsen (Royal Exchange)
DK–1217 Copenhagen K
Tel: 45 (33) 95.05.00
Fax: 45 (33) 32.52.16

Germany:

Deutscher Industrie- und Handelstag (DIHT)
Adenaurallee 148
D–53113 Bonn (Postfach 1446, D–53004)
Tel: 49 (228) 1040
Fax: 49 (228) 104 158
Brussels Office: Boulevard Clovis, 49A, 1040 Bruxelles
Tel: 32 (2) 286 16 11
Fax: 32 (2) 286 16 05

Greece:

Union of Hellenic Chambers of Commerce
Akadimias 7–9
Gr–10671 Athens
Tel: 30 (1) 363.27.02
Fax: 30 (1) 362.23.20
Brussels Office: World Trade Centre, Bd E. Jacqmain 162, bte 3, 1210 Bruxelles
Tel: 32 (2) 203.00.90
Fax: 32 (2) 203.10.67

Spain:

Consejo Superior de las Camaras de Comercio, Industria y Navegacion
Claudio Coello 19, 1º
E–28001 Madrid
Tel: 34 (1) 575 34 00
Fax: 34 (1) 435 23 92 – 435 42 55
Brussels Office: Boulevard Général Wahis, 15, 1030 Bruxelles
Tel: 32 (2) 245 47 50
Fax: 32 (2) 245 45 40

France:

Assemblée des Chambres Françaises de Commerce et d'Industrie (AFCI)
Avenue d'Iéna, 45
F – 75769 Paris
Tel: 33 (1) 40 69.37.00
Fax: 33 (1) 47 20.61.28
Brussels Office: Avenue des Arts, 1–2, bte, 1040 Brussels
Tel: 32 (2) 221 04 11
Fax: 32 (2) 217 69 87

Ireland:

The Chambers of Commerce of Ireland
Merrior Square 22
IRL – Dublin 2
Tel: 353 (1) 661.28.88
Fax: 353 (1) 661.28.11
Brussels Office: Rue Montoyer, 17–19, bte 3, 1040 Brussels
Tel: 32 (2) 512.33.33
Fax: 32 (2) 512.13.53

Italy:

Unione Italiana delle Camere di Commercio, Industria, Artigianato e Agricoltura,
Piazza Sallustio 21
I – 00187 Rome
Tel: 39 (6) 47 041
Fax: 39 (6) 474.47.41
Brussels Office: Boulevard Clovis, 85/87 1040 Brussels
Tel: 32 (2) 231 12 75
Fax: 32 (2) 230 81 43

Luxembourg:

Chambre de Commerce du Grand Duché de Luxembourg
7, rue Alcide de Gasperi
Boîte Postale 1503
L – 1015 Luxembourg
Tel: (352) 43.58.53/54/55
Fax: (352) 43.83.26

Netherlands:

Vereniging van Kamers van Koophandel en Fabrieken in Nederland
Watermolenlaan 1
NL – 3447 GT Woerden
Tel: 31 (3480) 269 11
Fax: 31 (3480) 243 68

Austria:

Wirtschaftskammer Österreich
Wiedner Hauptstrasse 63,
Postfach 150
A – 1045 Vienna
Tel: 43 (1) 50105
Fax: 43 (1) 50206
Brussels Office: Avenue de Cortenberg, 118–128,
1040 Brussels
Tel: 32 (2) 735 40 31
Fax: 32 (2) 735 91 88

Portugal:

Associacao Comercial de Lisboa, Camara de Comercio e Industria Portuguesa
Rua Portas de Santo Antao, 89
P – 1194 Lisboa Codex
Tel: 351 (1) 342.32.77
Fax: 351 (1) 342.43.04
Brussels Office: Rue Joseph II, 40,
1040 Brussels
Tel: 32 (2) 230 92 70
Fax: 32 (2) 230 08 37

Finland:

The Central Chamber of Commerce
Aleksanterinkatu, 17
P.O. Box 1000
SF – 00101 Helsinki
Tel: 358 (0) 69.69.69
Fax: 358 (0) 65.03.03
Brussels Office: Rue de la Charité, 17,
1040 Brussels
Tel: 32 (2) 209 43 09
Fax: 32 (2) 223 08 05

Sweden:

The Association of Swedish Chambers of Commerce and Industry
Västra Trädgardsghatan 9
Box 16050
S – 10321 Stockholm
Tel: 46 (8) 613.18.00
Fax: 46 (8) 411.75.70
Brussels Office: Avenue des Arts 21,
1040 Brussels
Tel: 32 (2) 286 14 37
Fax: 32 (2) 286 14 41

United Kingdom:

The Association of British Chambers of Commerce
Tufton Street, 9
GB – London SWIP 3QB
Tel: 44 (171) 222.15.55
Fax: 44 (171) 799.22.02

Affiliated members:

Bulgaria:

Bulgarian Chamber of Commerce and Industry
Saborna Street 11A
BU – 1000 Sofia
Tel: 359 (2) 87.78.26
Fax: 359 (2) 87.32.09

Cyprus:

Cyprus Chamber of Commerce and Industry
P.O. Box 1455, Chamber Building
38, Grivas Dhigenis Ave
CY–Nicosia
Tel: 357 (2) 44.95.00
Fax: 357 (2) 44.90.48

Czech Republic:

The Economic Chamber of Commerce of the Czech Republic
Argentinskà, 38
CZ – 17005 Praha 7
Tel: 42 (2) 77 21 48
Fax: 42 (2) 77 21 98

Estonia:

Estonian Chamber of Commerce and Industry
Toom-Kooli 17
EE – 0001 Tallinn
Tel: 372 (2) 44.49.29
Fax: 372 (2) 44.36.56

Hungary:

Hungarian Chamber of Commerce
Kossuth lajos tér, 6–8
H – 1055 Budapest
Tel: 36 (1) 153 33 33
Fax: 36 (1) 269.46.28
Brussels Office: Dunaholding Belgium sa — Hungarian CCI Representation
Avenue de l'Espinette Centrale 1,
1640 Rhode St Genèse
Tel: 32 (2) 358 42 52
Fax: 32 (2) 358 12 67

Iceland:

Iceland Chamber of Commerce
Kringlan, 7
IS–103 Reykjavik
Tel: (354–1) 88.66.66
Fax: (354–1) 68.65.64

Latvia:

The Latvian Chamber of Commerce and Industry
21 Brivibas Blvd
Riga — Latvia LV 1849
Tel: 371 (2) 225595
Fax: 371 (2) 332276

Lithuania:

Association of Lithuanian Chambers of Commerce
V. Kudirkos Str. 19
LT – 2600 Vilnius
Lithuania
Tel: 370 (2) 22.26.17
Fax: 370 (2) 22.26.21

Malta:

The Malta Chamber of Commerce
Exchange Building
Republic Street
MW – Valletta VLT 05
Tel: (356) 24 72 33/23 38 73
Fax: (356) 24 52 23

Poland:

Polish Chamber of Commerce
Ul. Trebacka, 4
PL–00074 Warszawa
Tel: 48 (22) 260 221
Fax: 48 (22) 274 673
Brussels Office: Avenue des Arts, 1–2 bte 9, 1040 Bruxelles
Tel: 32 (2) 221 04 33
Fax: 32 (2) 217 69 87

Romania:

The Chamber of Commerce and Industry of Romania
22 N. Balescu Blvd
R – 79502 Bucharest
Romania
Tel: 40 (1) 613 52 71 – 615.47.03 – 614.04.48
Fax: 40 (1) 312 38 30

Slovakia:

Slovak Chamber of Commerce and Industry
Gorkeho str. 9
CS – 81603 Bratislava
Slovenska Republika
Tel: 42 (7) 33 32 72
Fax: 42 (7) 33.07.54

Slovenia:

Chamber of Economy of Slovenia
Solvenska cesta 41
SL – 61000 Ljubljana
Tel: 386 (61) 125.01.22
Fax: 386 (61) 21.95.36

Switzerland:

Chambre de Commerce de Zurich
Bleicherweg, 5
Case Postale 4031
CH – 8022 Zurich
Tel: 41 (1) 221 07 42
Fax: 41 (1) 211 76 15

Turkey:

Union of Chambers of Commerce, Industry, Maritime Commerce and Commodity Exchanges of Turkey
Ataturk Bulvari 149
TR – Bakanliklar, Ankara
Tel: (90–312) 417.77.00
Fax: (90–312) 418.32.68
Brussels Office: Franklin Roosevelt Avenue, 148A, 1050 Bruxelles
Tel: 32 (2) 646.40.40
Fax: 32 (2) 646.95.38

Correspondent members:

Israel:

Federation of Israeli Chambers of Commerce
P.O. Box 200–27
Habasmonnaim Street 84
IL – Tel-Aviv 67011
Tel: (972–3) 561.24.44
Fax: (972–3) 561.90.25

APPENDIX D

Useful Addresses

Austria

Austrian Trade Delegation
45 Princes Gate
London SW7 2QA
Telephone: +44 171 584 4411
Fax: +44 171 584 2565

Contact names: Paul Pfanner;
Karin Längle

Denmark

Association of Commercial Agents of Denmark
Børsen, Christiansgade
DK–1217 Kopenhagen K

Telephone: +45 114 4941

Finland

Finnish Foreign Trade Agents' Federation
Museokatu 9 B 21
SF–00100 Helsinki

Telephone: +358 90 44 6768

France

Fédération Nationale des Agents Commerciaux et Mandataires (FNAC)
23, rue de Rome
F–75008 Paris

Telephone: +33 14 293 6124
Fax: +33 1 4293 1127

Germany

Centralvereinigung Deutscher Handelsvertreter-und Handelsmakler-Verbände
(Central Office of the German Commercial Agent's Associations) (CDH)
Geleniusstraße 1 (CDH-Haus)
D-50931 Köln

Telephone: +49 221 51 4043
Fax: +49 221 525767

British-German Jurists' Association
14 New Street
London EC2M 4TR
Telephone +44 171 972 9727
Fax: +44 171 972 9723

Contact name: John Rhodes

German-British Chamber of Industry
and Commerce
Mecklenburgh House
16 Buckingham Gate
London SW1E 6LB

Telephone: +44 171 9 233 5656
Fax: +44 171 9 233 7835

Contact names: Angelika Baumgarte;
Bernd Atenstaedt

British Chamber of Commerce in Germany
Severinstrasse 60
D–50678 Cologne

Telephone: +49 221 31 4458
Fax: +49 221 31 5335

Contact name: David Pinder

British Consulate-General Düsseldorf
Commercial Section
Yorckstrasse 9
40476 Düsseldorf

Telephone: +49 211 94480
Fax: +49 211 486359

British Consulate-General Frankfurt
Commercial Section
Bockenheimer Landstrasse 42
60323 Frankfurt/Main

Telephone: +49 69 1700020
Fax: +49 69 729553

Greece

Association of Commercial Agents Athens
(Syndesmos Emborikon Antiprossopon
Athinon)
Voulis Str. 15
GR–105 63 Athens

Telephone: +30 13 26 22

Ireland

The Irish Small and Medium Enterprise
Business Association
32 Kildare Street
Dublin 2
Telephone: (01) 662 2755

The Irish Business and Employers
Confederation
Baggot Bridge House
84 Lower Baggot Street
Dublin 2
Telephone: (01) 660 1011

Spain

Commercial Agents Association of Barcelona
calle Aragon no 390, 2nd floor
P.O. Box 08013
Barcelona
Telephone: +2319412.

Official Chamber of Commerce, Industry and Navigation of Barcelona
Paseo Isabel 11, no 1
P.O. Box 08003
Barcelona
Telephone: + 3192412.

Avenida Diagonal no 454;
PO Box 08006
Barcelona
Telephone: + 4169300.

Chamber of Commerce for Spain
calle Corcega no 301–303, 302
PO Box 08008
Barcelona
Telephone: + 2373883.

Spanish-Swedish Chamber of Commerce in Barcelona
calle Mallorca 279
PO Box 08037
Barcelona
Telephone: + 4880503.

Italian Chamber of Commerce in Barcelona
Gran Via de les Corts Catalanes no 637
PO Box 08010
Barcelona
Telephone: + 3184999.

British Chamber of Commerce in Barcelona
Paseo de Gracia no 11, esc. A, 20 1 a
PO Box 08007
Barcelona
Telephone: + 3173220.

French Chamber of Commerce in Barcelona
Paseo de Gracia n'2, 3'
PO Box 08007
Barcelona
Telephone: + 3176738.

Sweden

The International Chamber of Commerce:
Internationella Handelskammaren
Box 16050
103 22 Stockholm
Sweden
Telephone: + 46 8 24 38 10
Fax: + 46 411 31 15

Federation of Commercial Agents in Sweden:
Sveriges Handelsagenters Förbund
Hantverkargatan 46
Box 12705
112 94 Stockholm
Sweden
Telephone: + 46 8 654 09 75
Fax: + 46 8 650 35 17

INDEX